Forest Focus

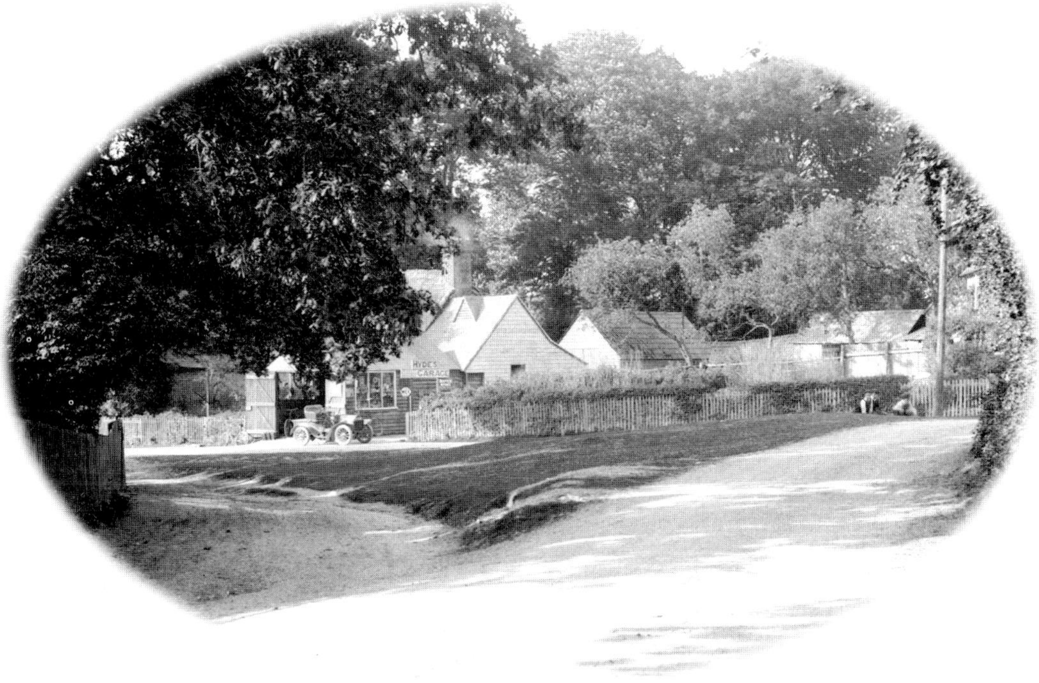

Introduced by **Brian P Martin**

Born in Hampshire, Brian Martin has been a full-time author since 1991. His 20 previous books include the best-selling Tales of the Old Gamekeepers, Tales From the Country Pub and the award-winning Sporting Birds of the British Isles. Previously he spent many years as commissioning Editor of Shooting Times & Country magazine. He has also contributed to many magazines and newspapers and is well-known for his Rusticus column in both The Countryman and Shooting Times.

Above & Cover Burley in quieter days.

Next page The lads at Sopley Bridge, Angels every one!

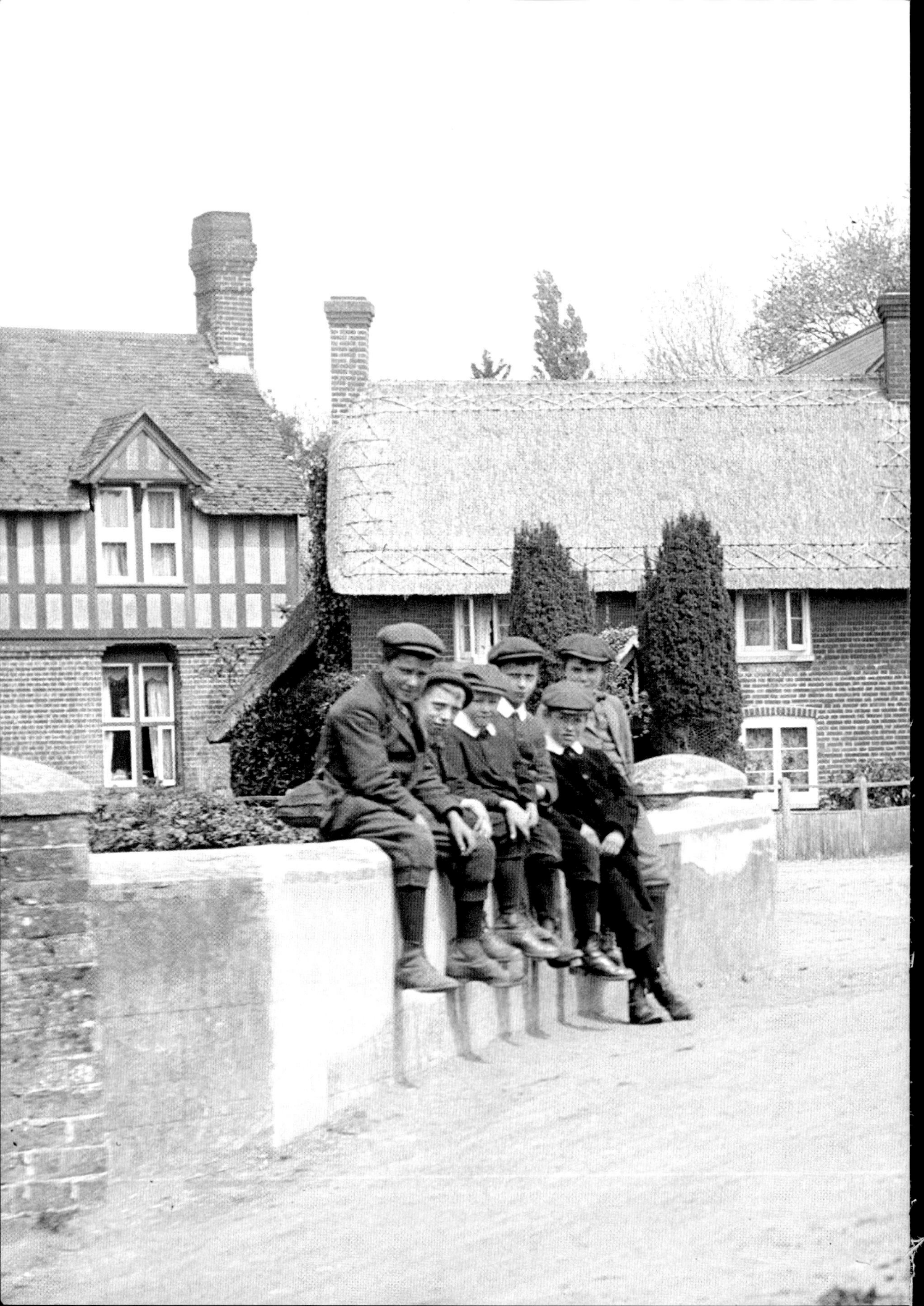

Forest Focus

old photographs from
in and around

The New Forest

Introduced by
Brian P Martin

focusing Ltd

First published November 2000
by Focusing Ltd

While every care has been taken with the accuracy of this book, including identification of locations, the publishers would welcome readers' useful observations for possible future amendments.

A catalogue record for this book is available from the British Library.

ISBN 0 9539 366 00

Printed and bound by:
Itchen Printers Limited, Itchen House, 184 Empress Road, Bevois Valley, Southampton SO14 0JY.

Available from all good bookshops or by direct order from:

Focusing Ltd, Station Road, New Milton, Hants BH25 6HL. Telephone 01425 617800
www.focusingltd.com

CONTENTS

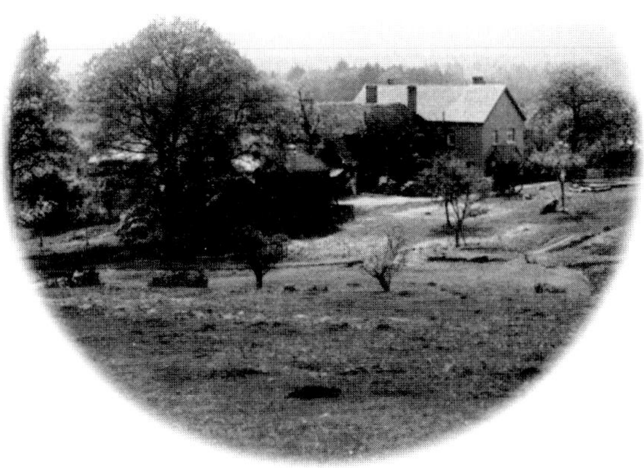

'The Forest has been known and loved by a limited number of persons always; the general public have only discovered it in recent years.'

WH Hudson, Hampshire Days, 1903

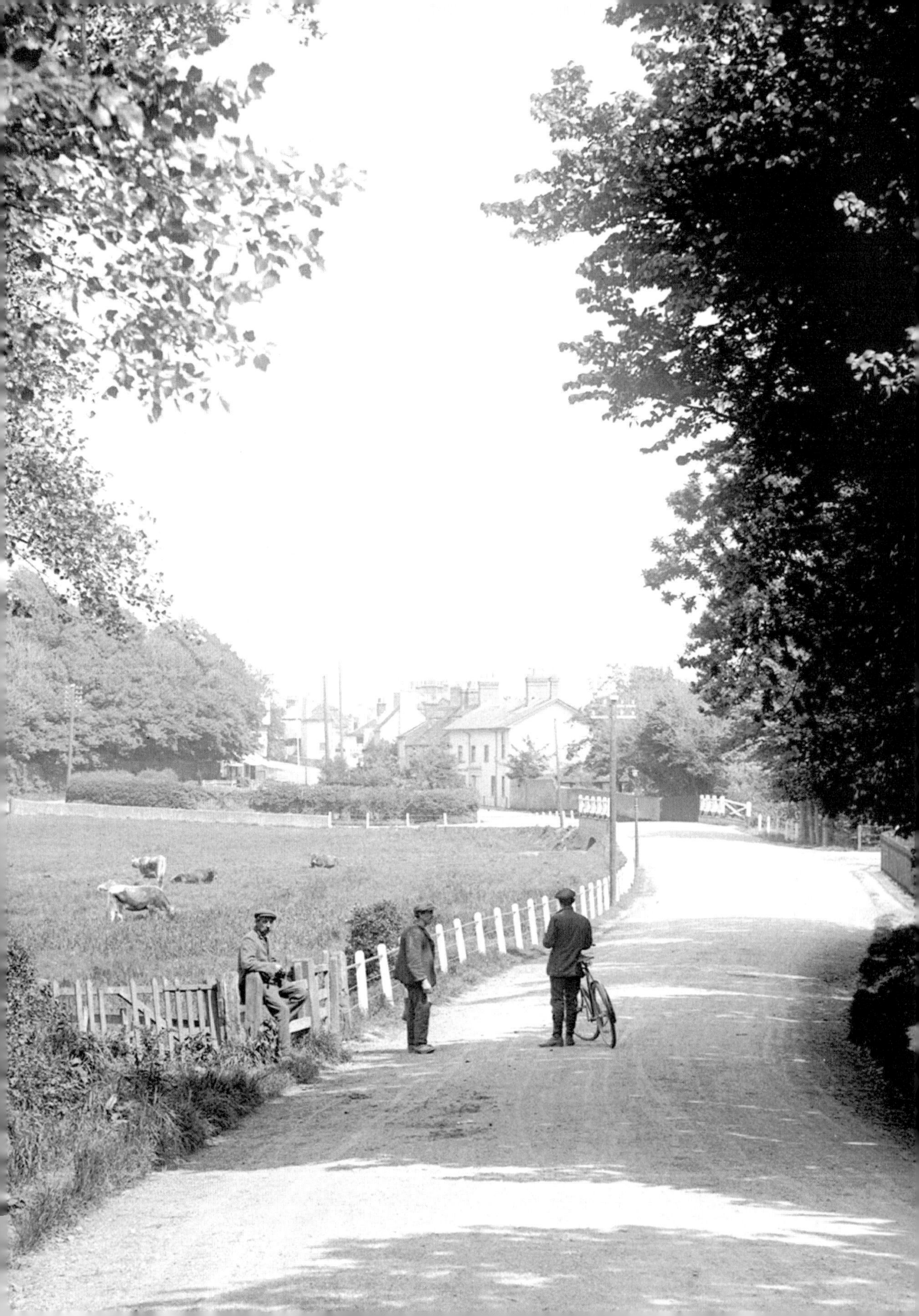

INTRODUCTION

The largest spread of old lowland woodland in north-west Europe, the 145-square-mile (37,560 ha) New Forest is a kind of 'living museum'. Here nature and natives struggle to coexist against alien forces, not least the huge pressure exerted by some 8.5 million visitors a year, us folk whom tongue-in-cheek Forest residents refer to as grockles but local businesses must regard as a goldmine!

As we go to Press it seems inevitable that before too long the Forest will become a National Park and the Government's Countryside Agency is already consulting widely to ensure that the National Parks Authority will work in sympathy with established Forest authorities, including the Court of Verderers and their acting officers - the agisters. Not surprisingly, many locals ('commoners') resent such change, suggesting that the system has worked well enough for a very long time. But they, in turn, are sometimes accused of having too much vested interest, contrary to the international importance of the area.

The argument has been going on for decades, some two-thirds of the Forest's 92,810 acres already being open to the public. One of the stumbling blocks has been that since 1923 control of the Crown lands - some 67,000 acres - has been in the hands of the Forestry Commission, whose constitution precludes it from pursuing the primary duties of conservation and recreation incumbent upon National Park authorities. However, in 1971, a Government instruction to the Forestry Commission stated: 'The New Forest is to be regarded as a national heritage and priority given to the conservation of its traditional character.' Since then the Forestry Commission has been closely involved with the Countryside Commission, the Nature Conservancy Council, local and other authorities in discussions about the Forest's future.

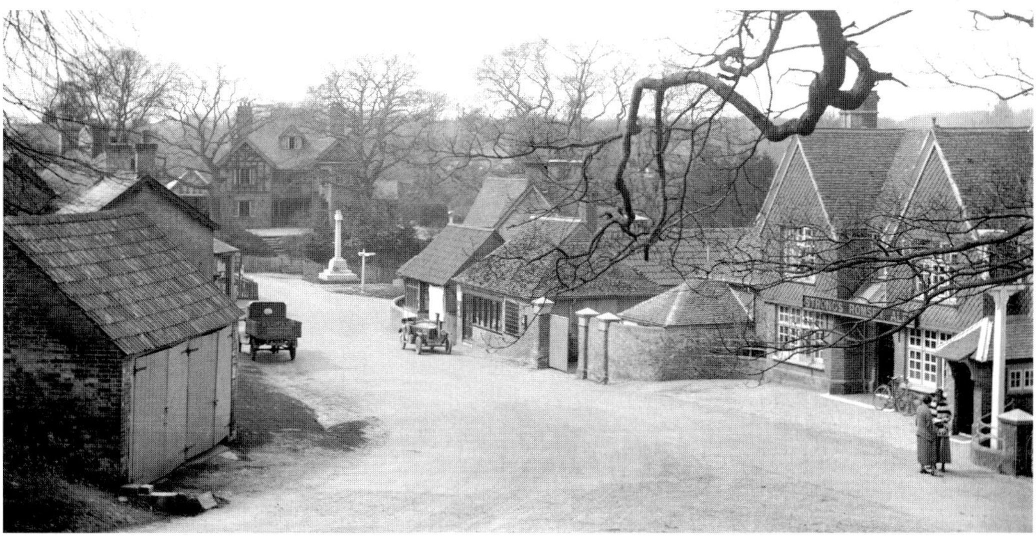

Above Burley's fine, sheltered position, well off the main road from Southampton to Bournemouth, became the destruction of its charm, attracting considerable settlement after World War I.

Left Resting weary legs, at Milford-on-Sea.

Also the largest area of open land in southern England, two-thirds of it not being covered by woodland, this is the oldest of the great forests of England, but for William the Conqueror it was literally a new forest. How much - if any - truth there is in the legend that the Conqueror laid waste to two or three dozen villages in establishing the New Forest as a royal hunting preserve, we do not know. However, what we can be certain of is that since the Conqueror's time the Forest has undergone sustained change, resulting in today's hotchpotch of dense, coniferous, commercial woods; more open and attractive, largely indigenous deciduous woods; great heaths golden with gorse or purple with heather in season, close-cropped grazing lands; bogs, ponds and streams; cattle and semi-wild ponies wandering at will across any and every road; chocolate-box churches and thatched cottages; now permanent camping sites, cafés and cream teas; hotels, car parks, golf courses and sports grounds; and towns and villages struggling to retain their identities in the face of economic development. Changing climate, warfare, fashion and population drift have played their parts too, but it is the ever-accelerating rate of change which is causing increasing concern, the number of visitors having doubled in the last 20 years!

When Victoria ascended the throne the Forest remained much as it had done for centuries, but halfway through her reign the alarm bells were already ringing. For example, in 1862, in his classic book 'The New Forest: Its History and Scenery', John Wise noted: 'Instead of the archer's bow, the sunset gun at Portsmouth sounds every evening. Government should spare some of the finest trees for the sake of their beauty and for the delight they will give to future generations.' Sadly, such conservation-consciousness was rare in those days, and remained so when world war gave timber production precedence over forest scenery.

By Edward VII's reign much improved transport and communications had already established tourism to wild backwaters. In 'Hampshire Days' (1903), WH Hudson wrote: 'The flow of visitors to the Forest will go on at an ever-increasing rate... With the modern means of locomotion there is no more attractive spot than this... in England. As it grows in favour in all the country as a place of recreation and refreshment, the subject of its condition and management, and the ways of its inhabitants, will receive an increased attention. The desire will grow that it shall not be spoilt.'

Unfortunately, it has been spoilt, not least through timber production, settlement of increasingly mobile commuters and commercial greed in the face of overwhelming tourism; and in some ways it is unfortunate that even books such as this might add to the weight of numbers. At weekends and during the main holiday season, simply getting into the heart of the Forest, through traffic bottlenecks such as Lyndhurst, is already a nightmare with tail-backs often miles long. Such problems need to be addressed urgently and with far more regard for the long-term, wider picture.

That said, this wonderful jewel in Hampshire's crown is still studded with gems both natural and man-made. Make an effort to leave the car and honeypot picnic sites way behind you and venture by foot to find the real Forest, where uncommon plants such as narrow-leaved lungwort, coral-necklace and beech fern and scarce birds such as hawfinch, honey buzzard and Dartford warbler may still be found in inspirational settings. The deer are a main attraction, too, with a small number of red, an ever-increasing number of

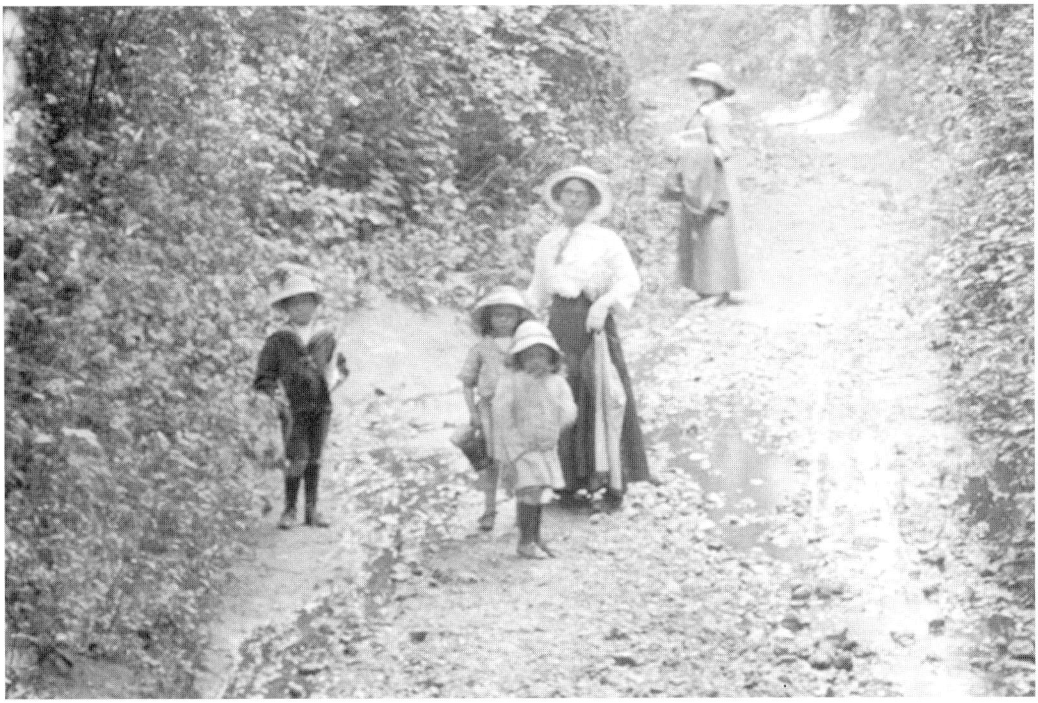

For many decades the Forest has been a great adventure ground for families on day trips.

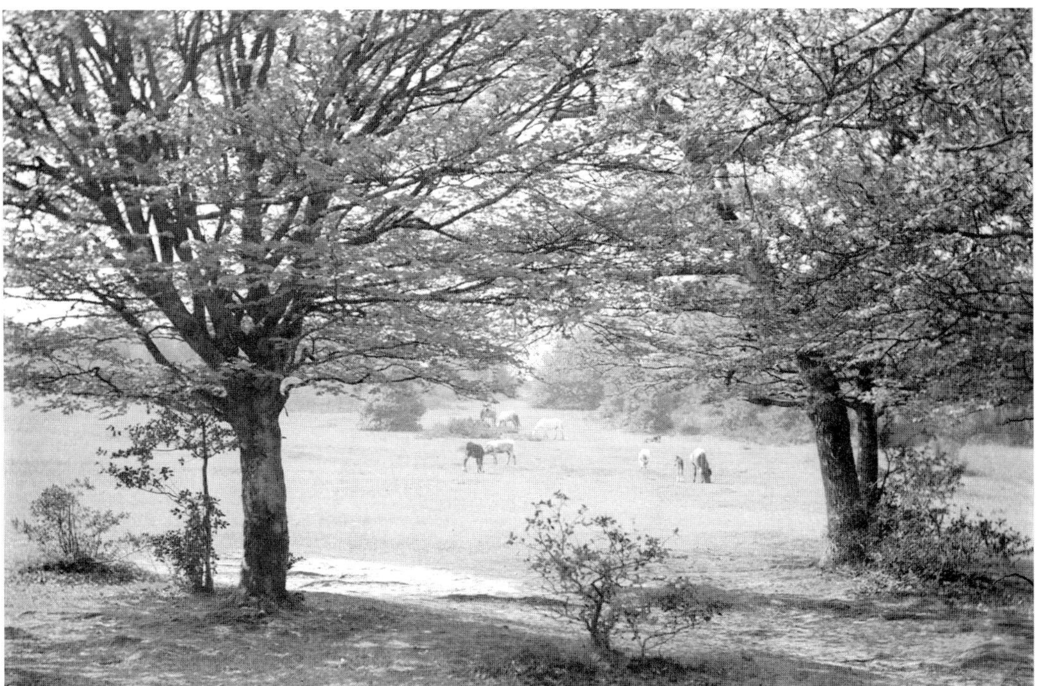

Forest ponies pick up a livelihood from herbage, such as furze, that would starve an ordinary stable-bred animal.

roe and some 600 fallow which remain to remind us of the original purpose of the Forest. In recent years the number of deer species has increased, with colonisation by sika and muntjac, but modern grazing could never sustain the earliest 17th Century count of almost 400 red deer and over 7,500 fallow.

SANCTUARY FOR MEN AND WILDLIFE

'One could imagine the time come when this one small piece of England which lies between the Avon and Southampton Water will be a sanctuary for all rare and beautiful wildlife and a place of refreshment to body and soul for all men.'

WH Hudson, Hampshire Days, 1903

Go at all times of day and in all seasons, too. Spring and summer certainly have their attractions, when the lush canopy is bursting with birds, while woods and heaths abound with an outstandingly rich insect life, ranging from beautiful and scarce butterflies to Britain's only cicada. And who can deny the pleasures of autumn, especially the more elderly, many of whom find the multi-coloured trees, moderate temperatures and reduced crowds much more in keeping with the autumn of their own lives. But winter is my favourite time, when few folk brave the tempest and I can be alone with my thoughts and the grand architecture of ancient trees is laid bare before me.

Rambling has long been a main Forest activity, whether pottering randomly a few hundred yards from the car or purposefully striking out for miles in organised groups clutching OS maps. But there are many other activities to suit all tastes. Hunting with hawk, hound and longbow may no longer be possible - for the visitor at least, but there is excellent game and coarse fishing on the Avon and many small lakes and streams; and widespread stables provide mounts for riding and pony-trekking. There is also plenty of golf and cricket, and inevitably nearby a quaint old pub where the energetic may immerse themselves in history as well as flagons of best Hampshire bitter.

On the walls of the Forest pubs and hotels the observant visitor will see many old photographs of how the buildings and their surroundings used to be, before transport and tourism took over. He may even spot one or two of the photographs in this book, some of which were used on postcards, for which demand was enormous in the days before widespread use of telephones. However, he will not see most of the photographs in this book, many of which have never been published before.

This superb set of photographs were all taken by one man - the late PW Hobbs, who ran JJ Hobbs & Sons - wholesale and retail stationers - from a shop based in Blandford Forum, Dorset. Between 1890 and 1930, Hobbs photographed many of the villages and much of the countryside in southern counties and prints of these were sold to the public in the Blandford shop as well as to other shops as images on postcards in both sepia and black and white.

Unfortunately, Hobbs appears to have been a shy man and no photographs of him appear to have survived. However, we do have a picture of his faithful old car, which is reproduced here and shows how it was specially adapted at the rear to carry all the heavy, cumbersome equipment then necessary to take photographs.

By modern standards, Hobbs' camera would have been huge and extremely heavy and would have taken a long time to set up. The photographs were taken on a format called half plate, the images fixed on large glass slides. The camera must have been mounted on a large wooden tripod to avoid spoiling the picture, because in those pre hand-held days exposure times averaging 2-3 seconds were normal. However, while exposure times were very long in the early shots, they became progressively shorter as film sensitivity increased. Even so, in some of the photographs you will see blurring caused by movement of people, which in some way can add to a picture's charm.

Black and white postcards based on some of the photographs remained on sale as late as the 1960s, when colour became much more affordable and postcards were produced much more commercially by specialist companies with national networks. The thousands of plates so lovingly produced by Hobbs and his contemporaries throughout the land became redundant and were stored for posterity. Unfortunately, because of their fragile nature, many were accidentally broken.

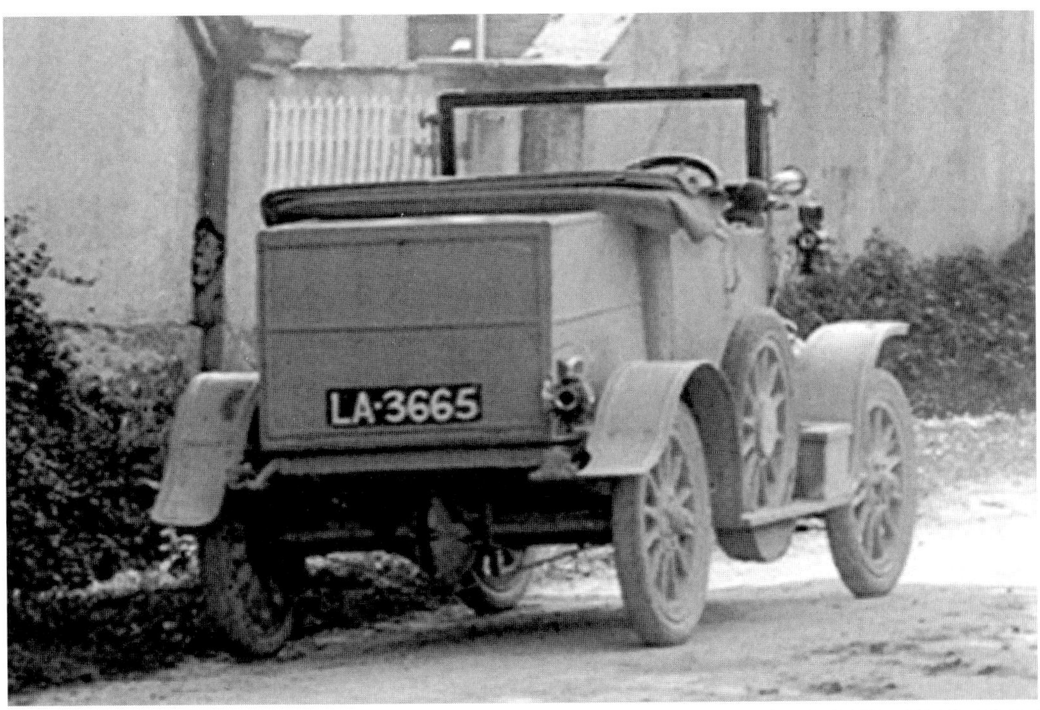

The photographer's car was modified at the rear to carry all his heavy, cumbersome equipment.

After the death of Hobbs, in 1979, a director of the business rediscovered the plates in a void under a staircase, during alterations to the shop. In due course the plates were given to the director's son, another professional photographer, and subsequently he gave them to Focusing Ltd - the publishers of this book - on joining them as a director. How lucky we are that such a fortuitous discovery has enabled us to glimpse again so many wonderful images of the old New Forest, hitherto existing only in the memories of a few elderly commoners.

Brian P Martin

September 2000

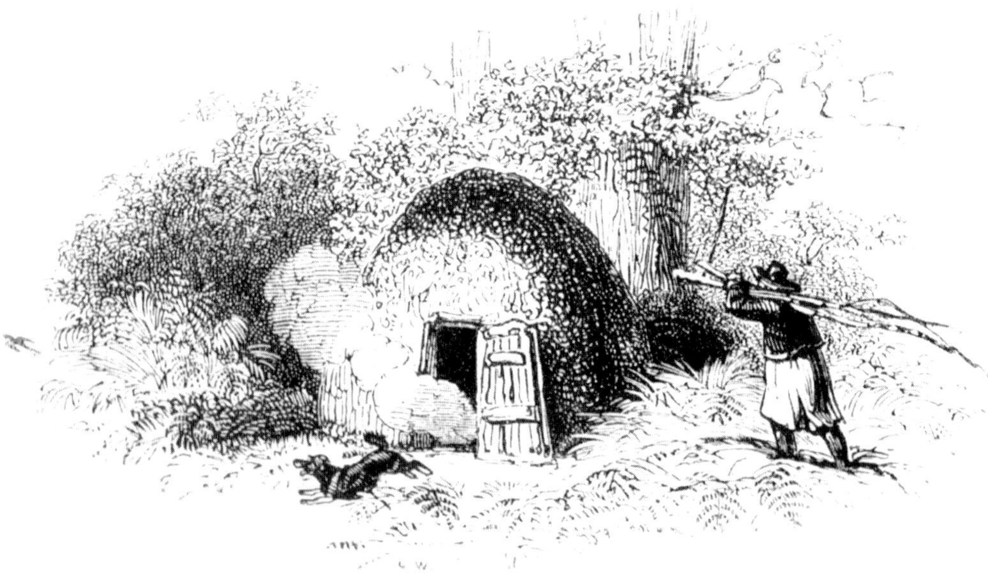

FOREST CROPS

'The peasants, too, still value the woods as they did in the Conqueror's time, for the crop of mast and acorns - still peel off the forest turf, and cure their bacon by its smoke. The charcoal burner still builds the same round ovens as in the days of William the Red.'

John Wise, The New Forest: Its History and Scenery, 1862

IN TOWN & VILLAGE

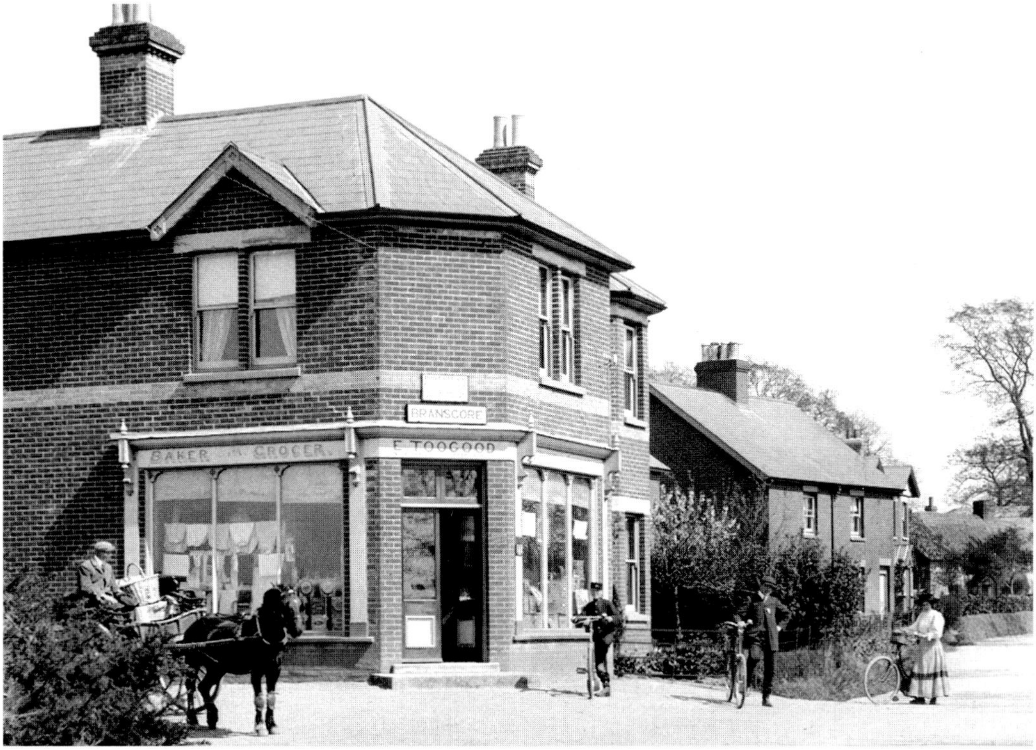

In the days of pony and pedal power, Bransgore's tradesmen served a whole cluster of villages in the south-west corner of the Forest.

When these photographs were taken most communities were much more self-sufficient than those of today. Even the smallest village could boast a church or chapel, school, farrier, blacksmith, grocer, butcher and baker; while most folk could make their own clothes, had a good kitchen garden and generally did a great deal of home cooking. Furthermore, even before the widespread use of motor cars and vans, deliveries were usually excellent and reliable with daily milk and post rounds and bread, groceries and even fish being brought by horse and cart at least once a week. But in any rural community there was always a need to get together regularly at markets in towns such as Ringwood, to buy and sell livestock, cereals, hardware and so on. Furthermore, such markets acted as great social occasions, places to exchange smalltalk in an age when many folk did not have regular newspaper deliveries, let alone a telephone or wireless. And while the men paid their bills over a few pints the women would parade that new hat or shop for that long-promised dress. But inevitably, as motor cars and trains made travelling much easier, rural towns and villages were invaded by commuters wishing to escape the almost unchecked pressure and pollution of early industry. With no thought of conservation and only an eye on the bank, new buildings sprang up at random, destroying the mellowness of the ages. Some villages were swallowed up by their neighbours while others became mere suburbs of towns.

BEAULIEU

'Surely there is some profit to be found in coming to a quiet village like this, if it will only give us a glimpse of a life which stands out in such strange contrast to our own.'

John Wise, The New Forest: Its History and Scenery, 1862

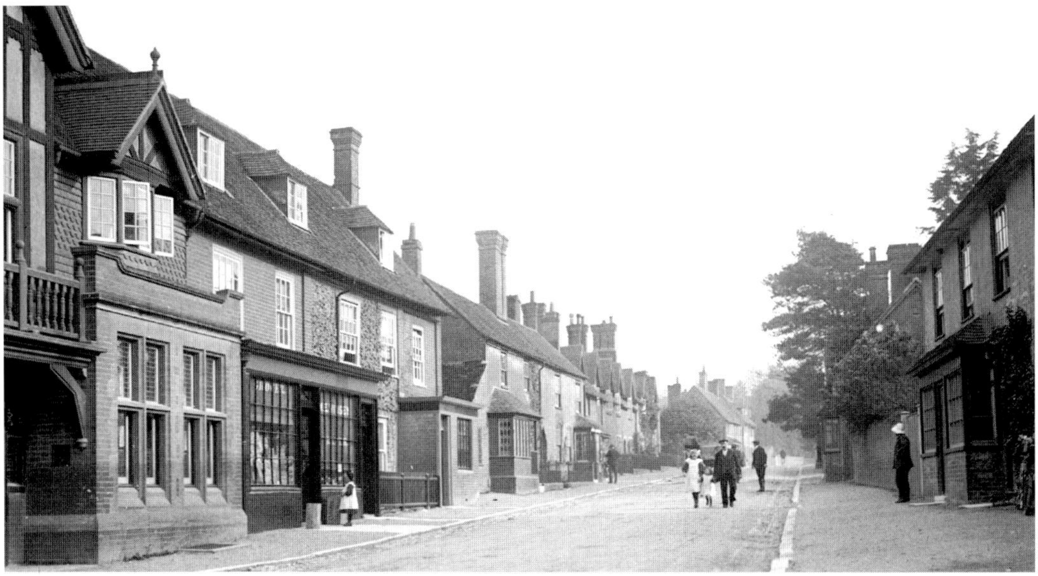

The joys of walking along Beaulieu's streets without the intimidation of tourist traffic!

'Beaulieu has a distinction above all Hampshire villages, and is unlike all others in its austere beauty and atmosphere of old-world seclusion and quietude. Above all is that quality which the mind imparts - the expression due to romantic historical associations.'

WH Hudson, Hampshire Days, 1903

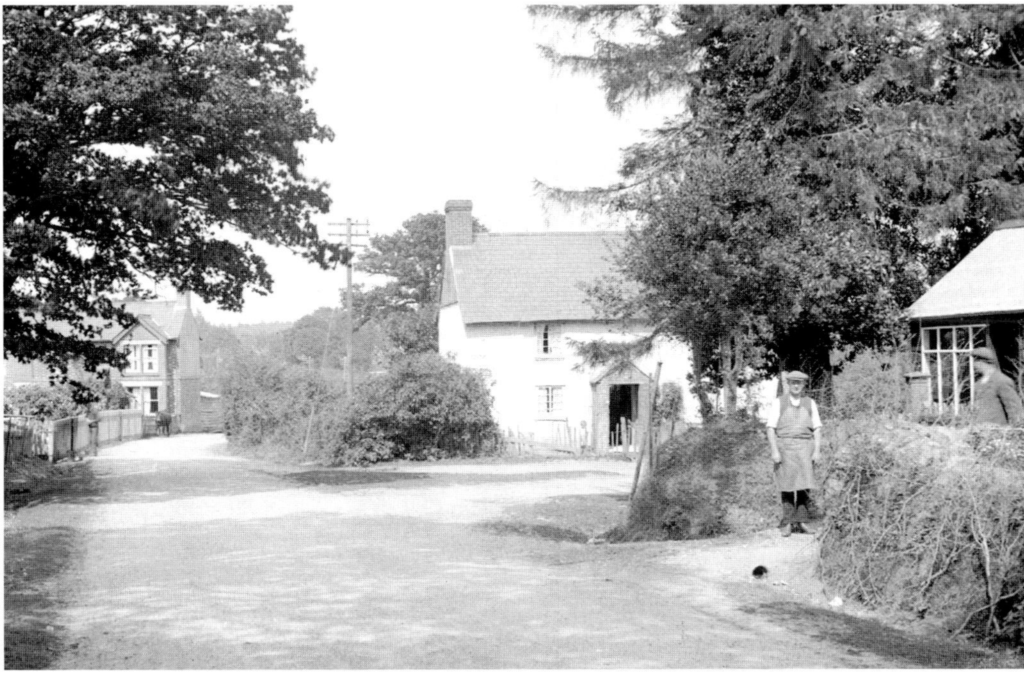

Just one horse in the background here, but for generations Burley was famed for its annual pony fair.

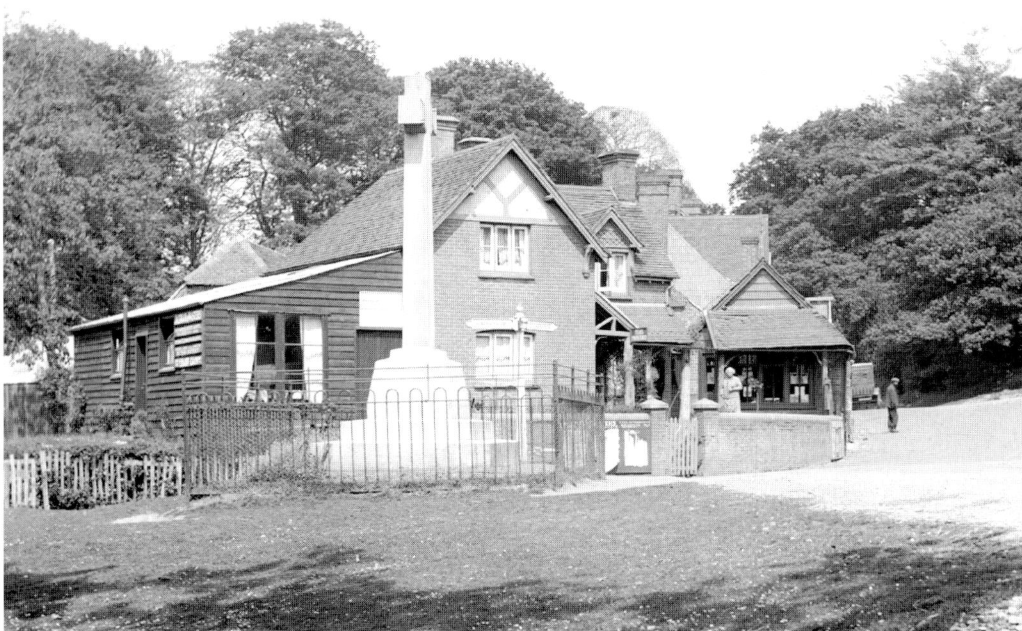

Above Burley at the crossroads: the memorial marks not only those lost in the Great War but also the end of an era of relative isolation.

Next page On the southern edge of the Forest, Ashley's HB Burbridge was a baker and confectioner as well as a postmaster.

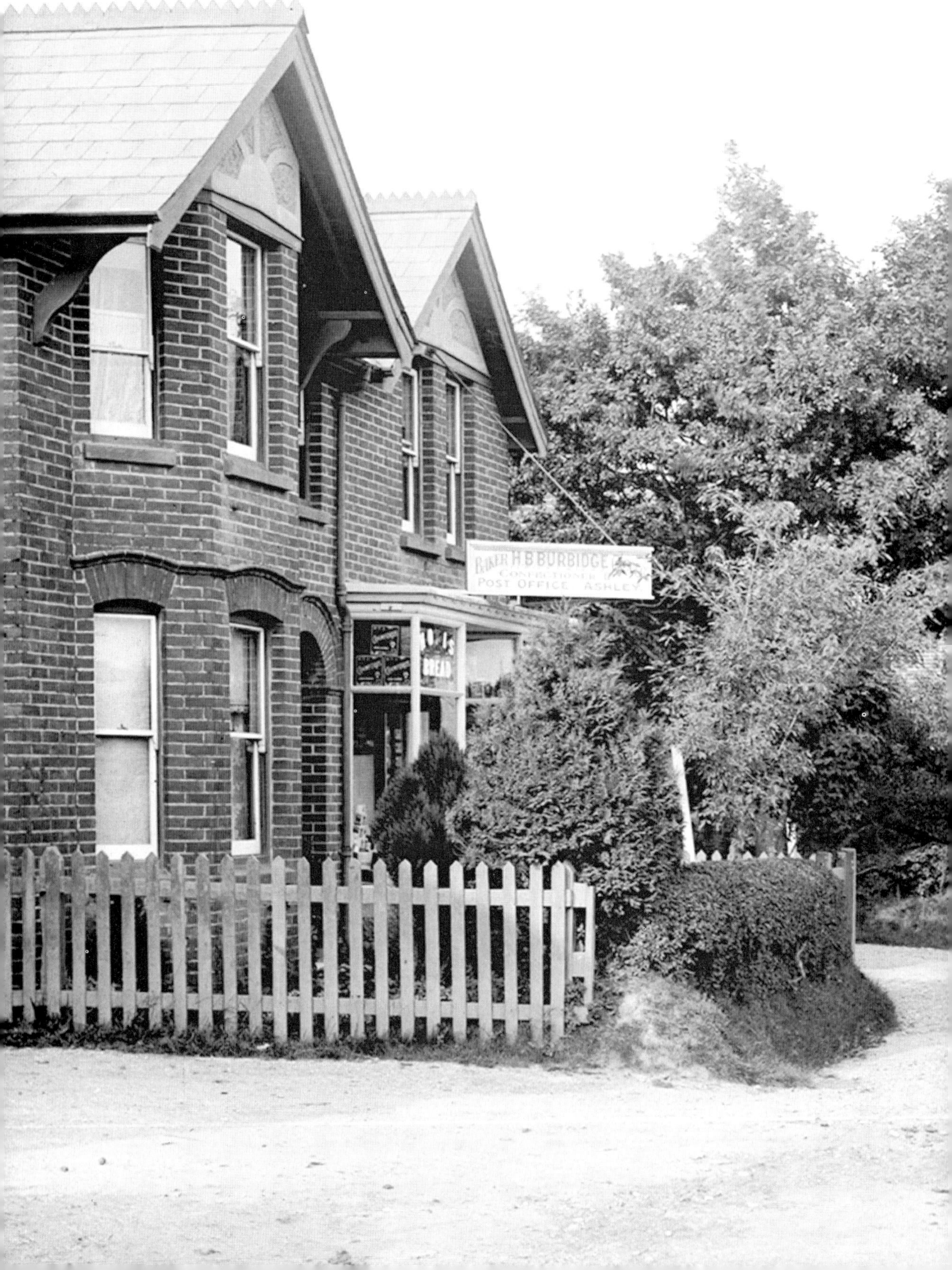
H B BURBIDGE
POST OFFICE ASHLEY
BREAD

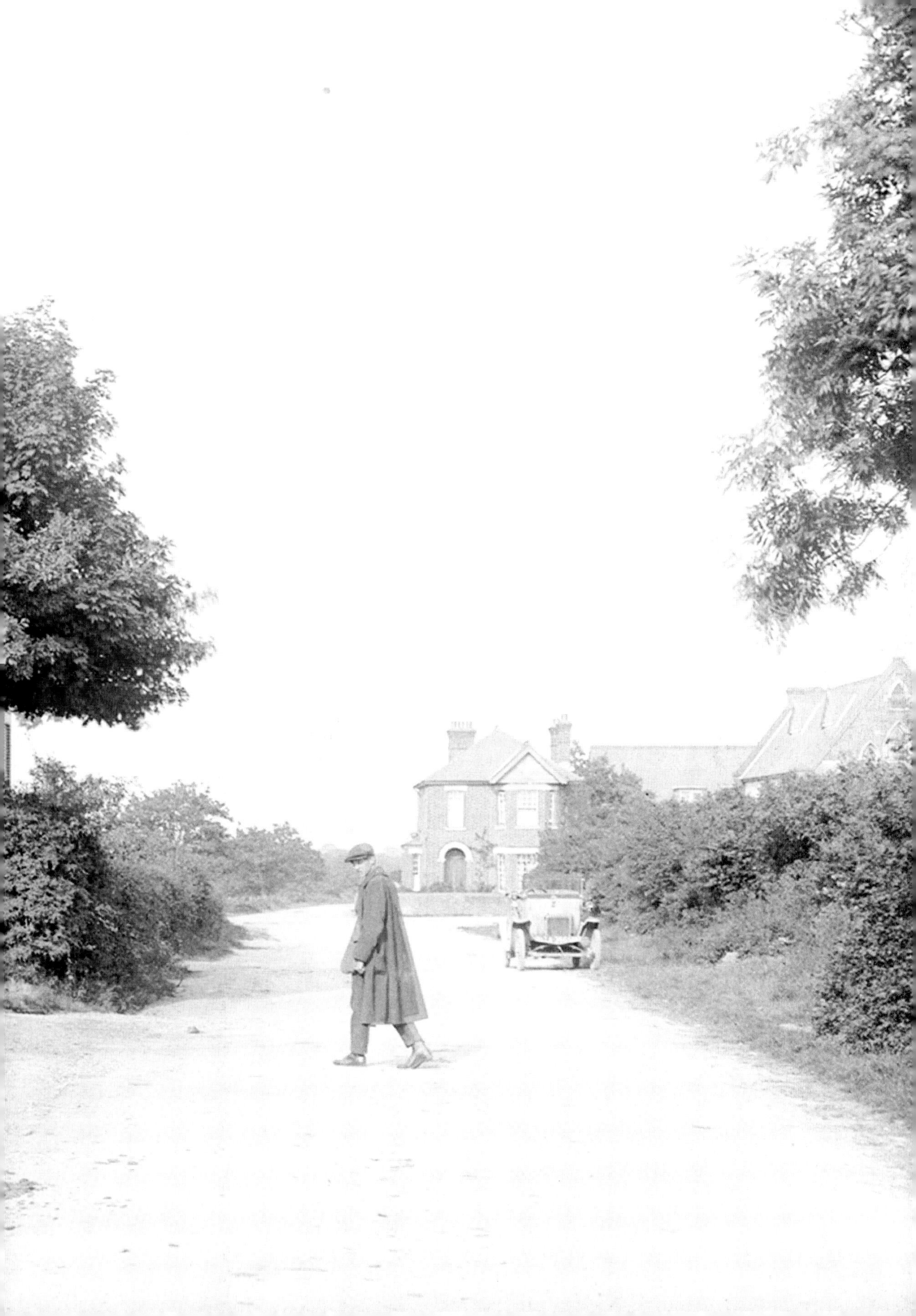

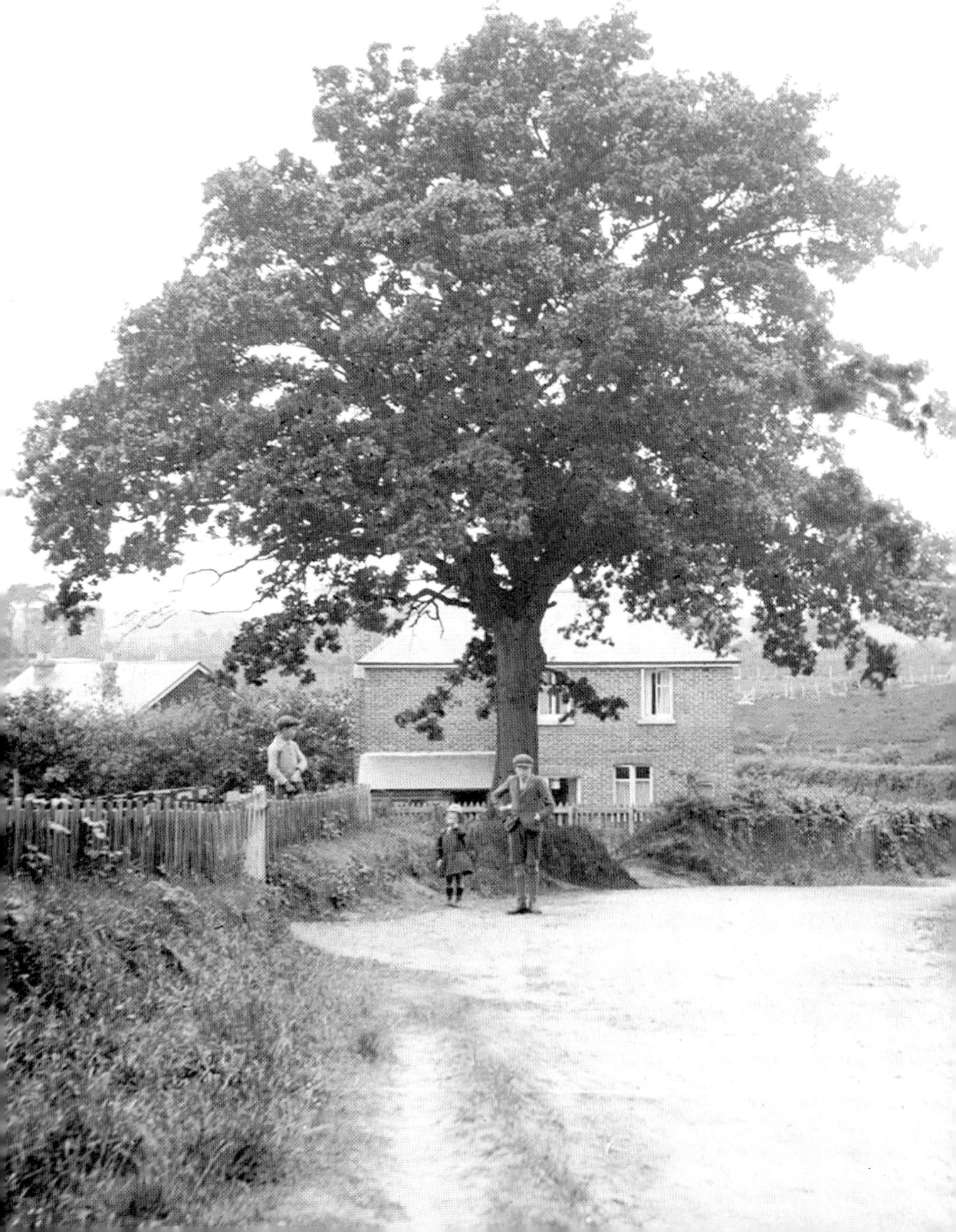

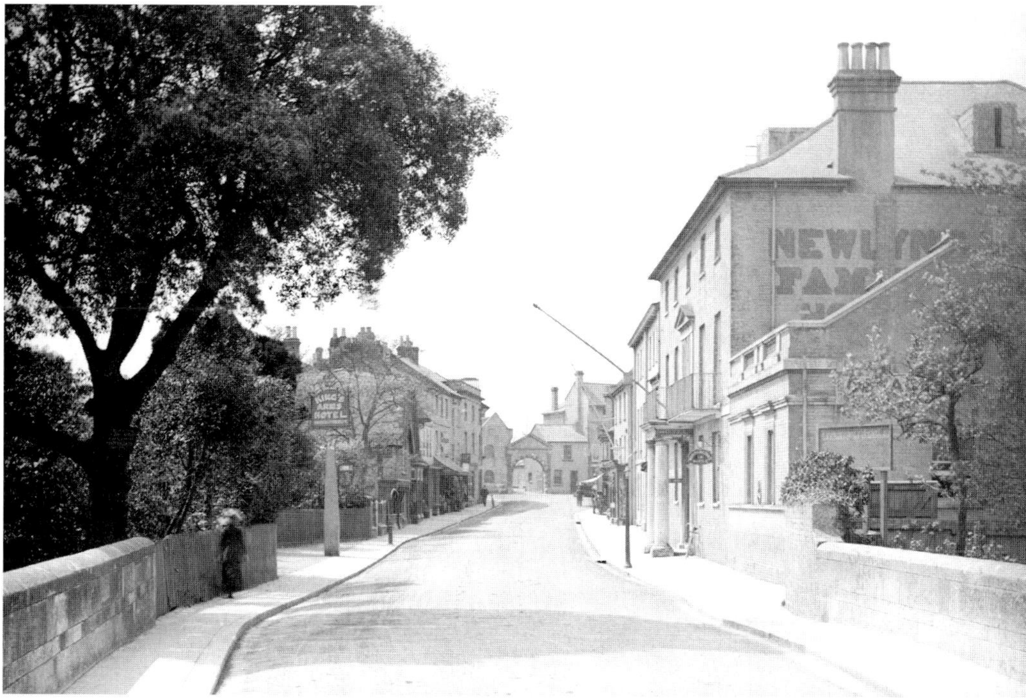

On the estuaries of the rivers Avon and Stour, Christchurch grew up around a priory first built circa 1100.

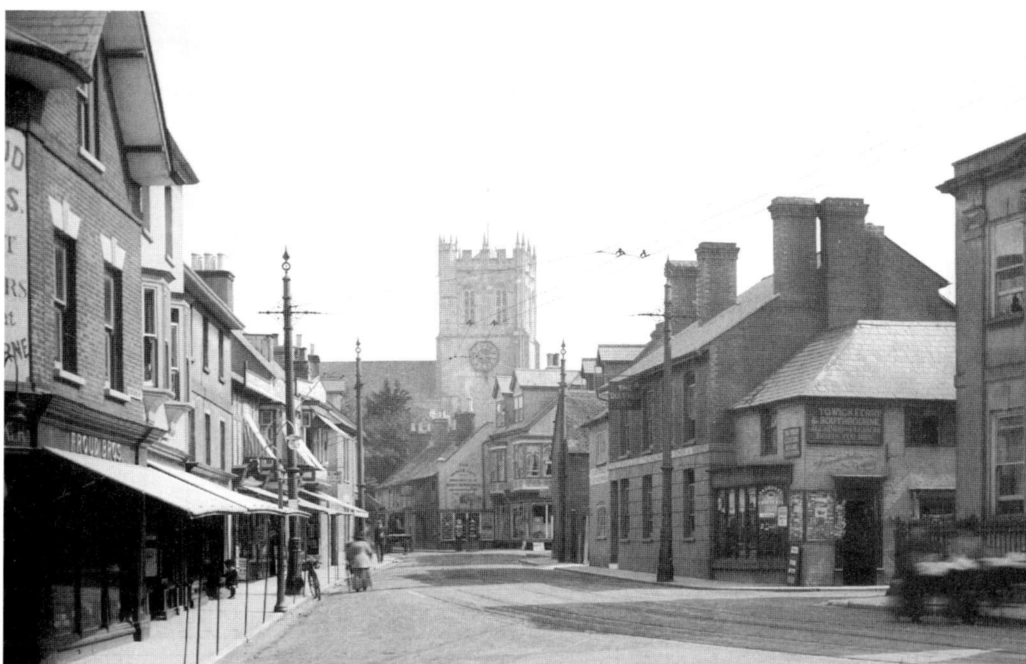

Above Christchurch has long been a great tourist attraction, with its splendid priory church, monument to the poet Shelley and the remains of a Norman castle.

Left 'No! I can't come out to play.' Boys exchanging news at sleepy Verwood.

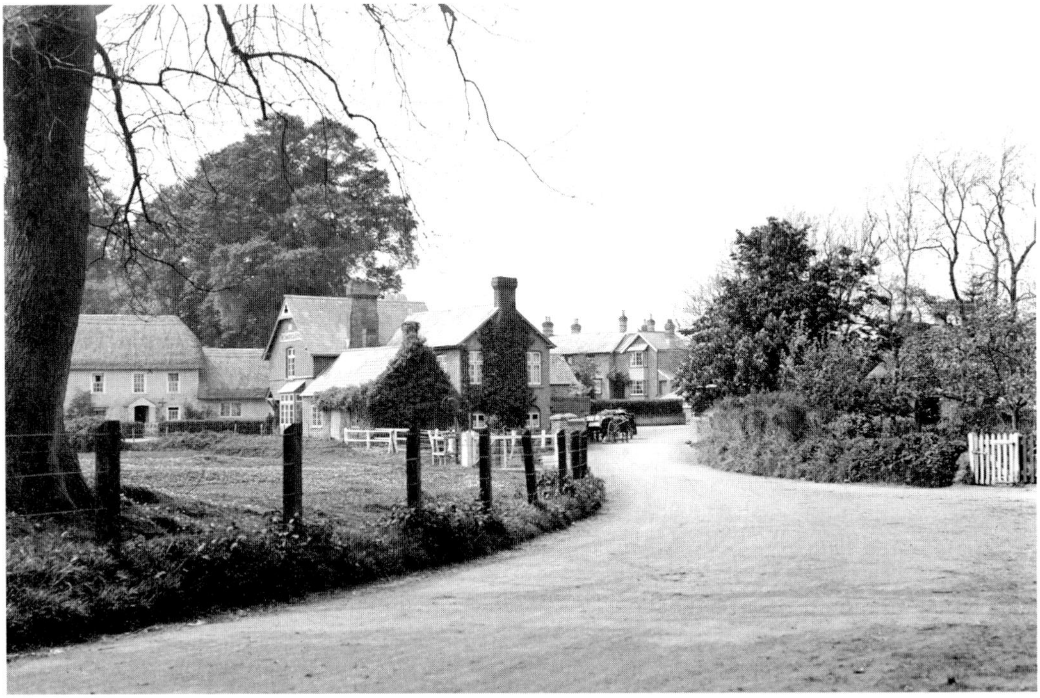

Typical of many Forest villages, in the early 20th Century Sopley still had plenty of thatched roofs alongside the newer tile and slate.

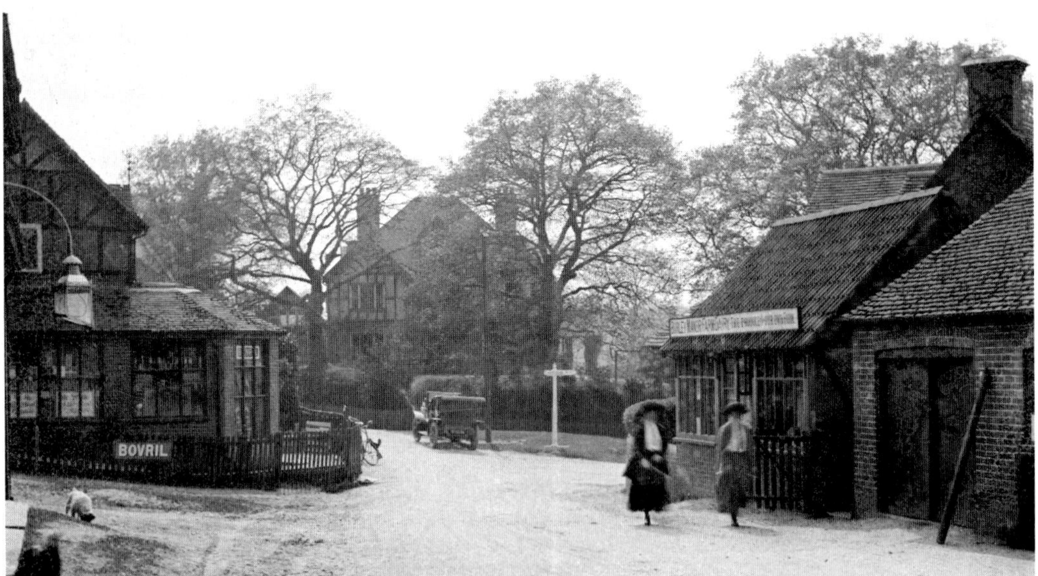

At Burley, Manor Farm Dairy was among the first to promote 'home produce' to a widening, more mobile market.

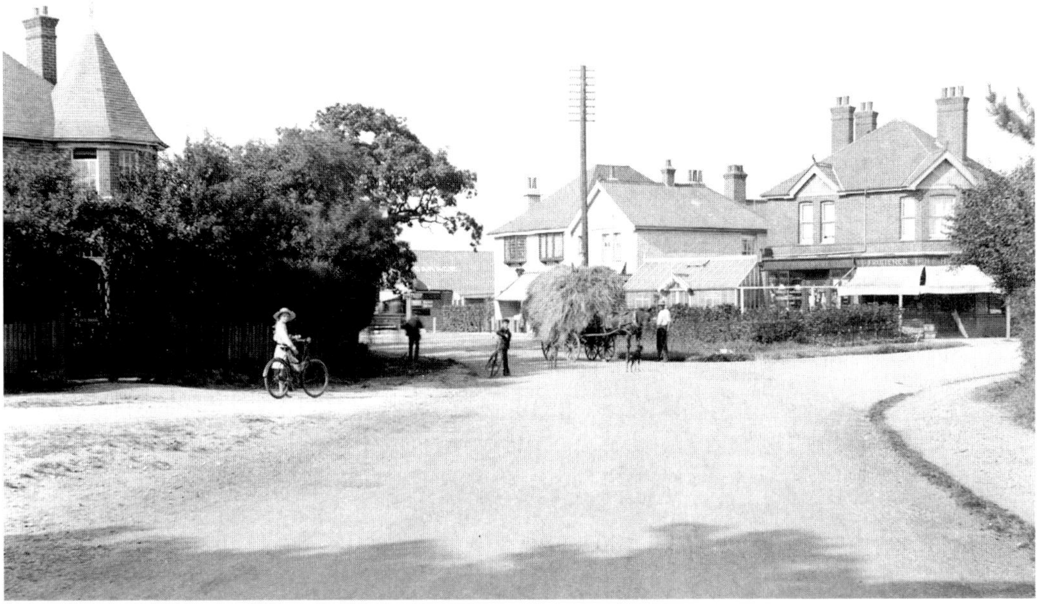

With the latest bike, at New Milton.

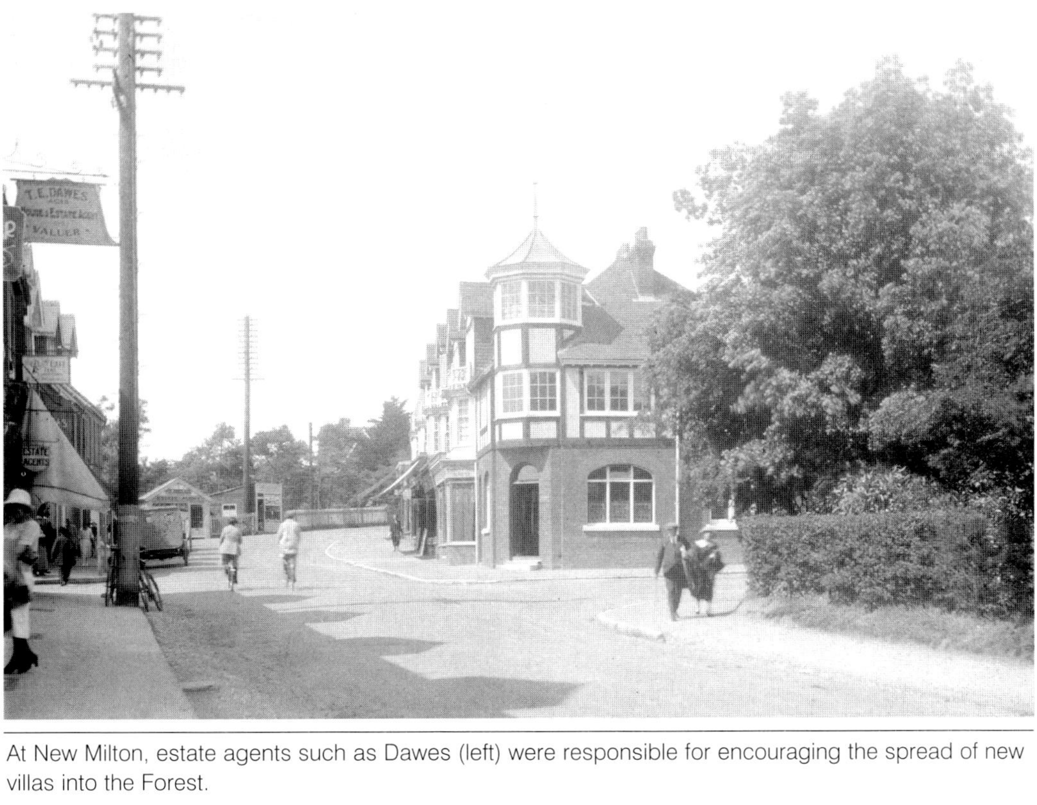

At New Milton, estate agents such as Dawes (left) were responsible for encouraging the spread of new villas into the Forest.

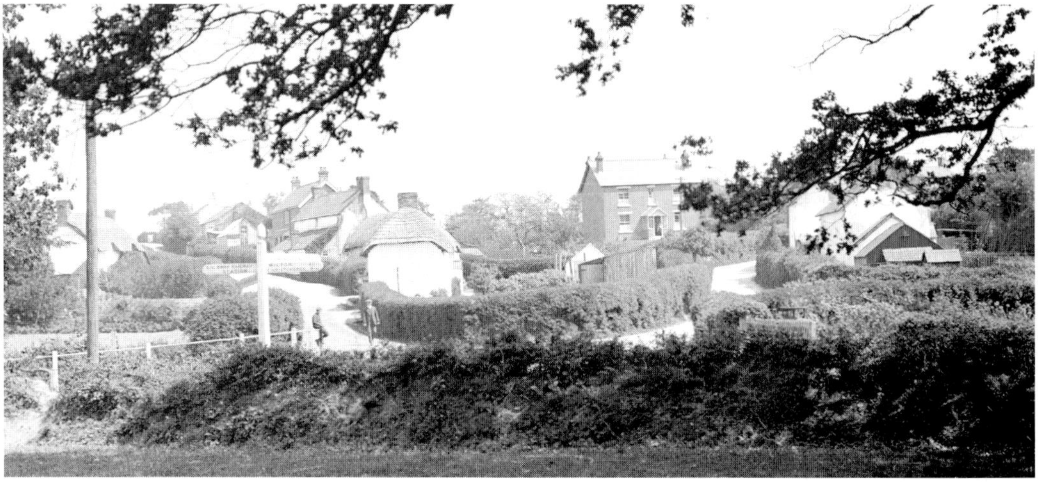

Dating from only 1841, the straggling parish of Sway is but a slice of the once huge parish of Boldre.

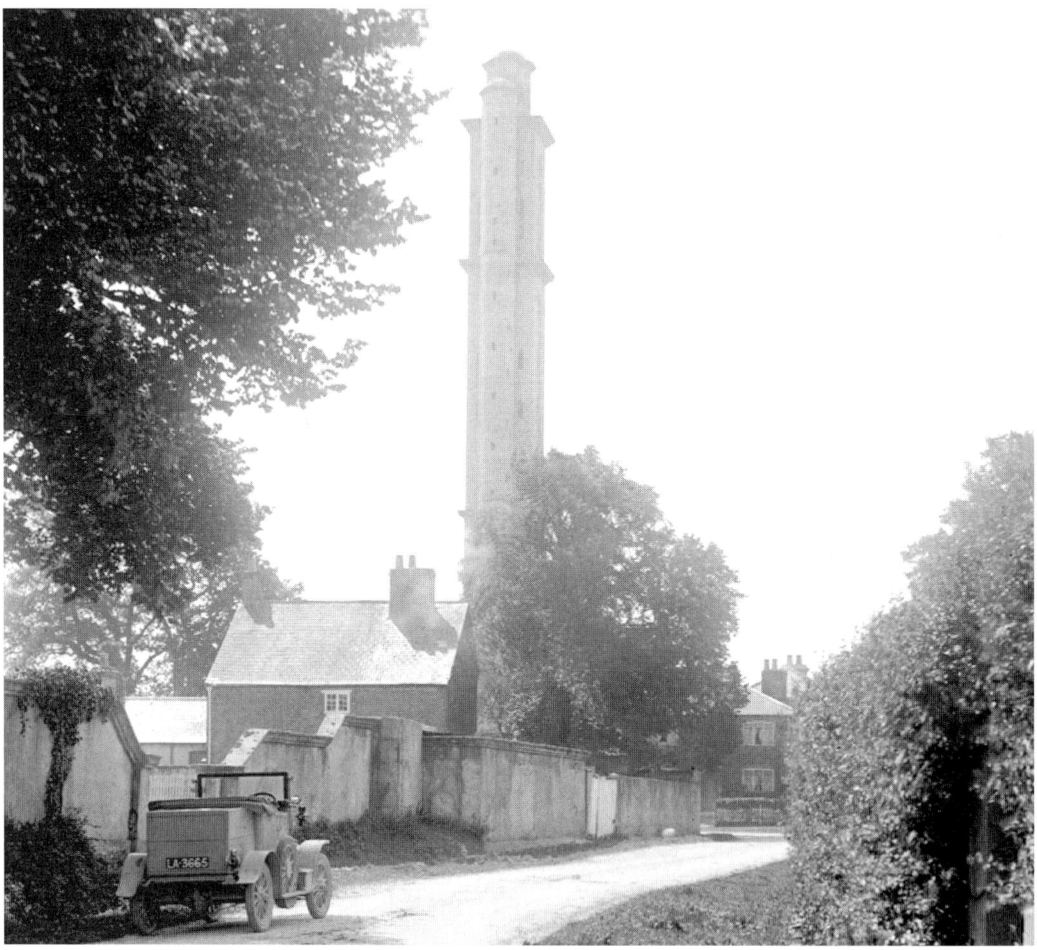

Sway's gaunt concrete tower 'Folly' was built by one Petersen, apparently as a memorial for himself, with a smaller one nearby to keep his wife's memory green!

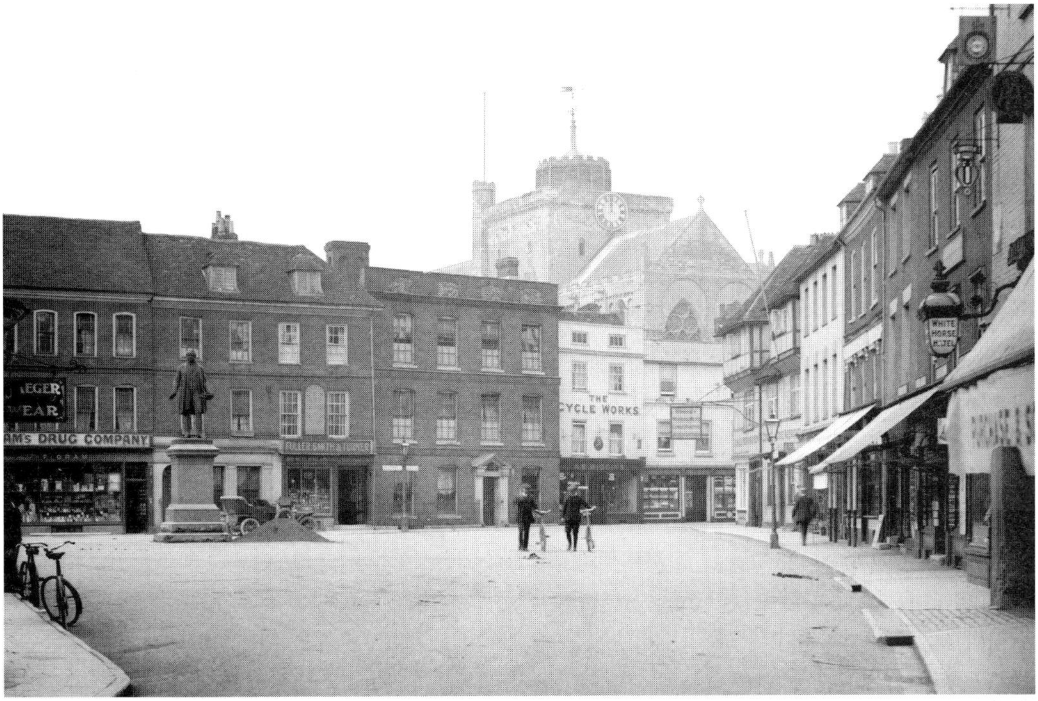

In ancient Romsey the White Horse Hotel (right), despite its Georgian facade, has provided comfortable accommodation on the north-western approach to the Forest since Elizabethan times.

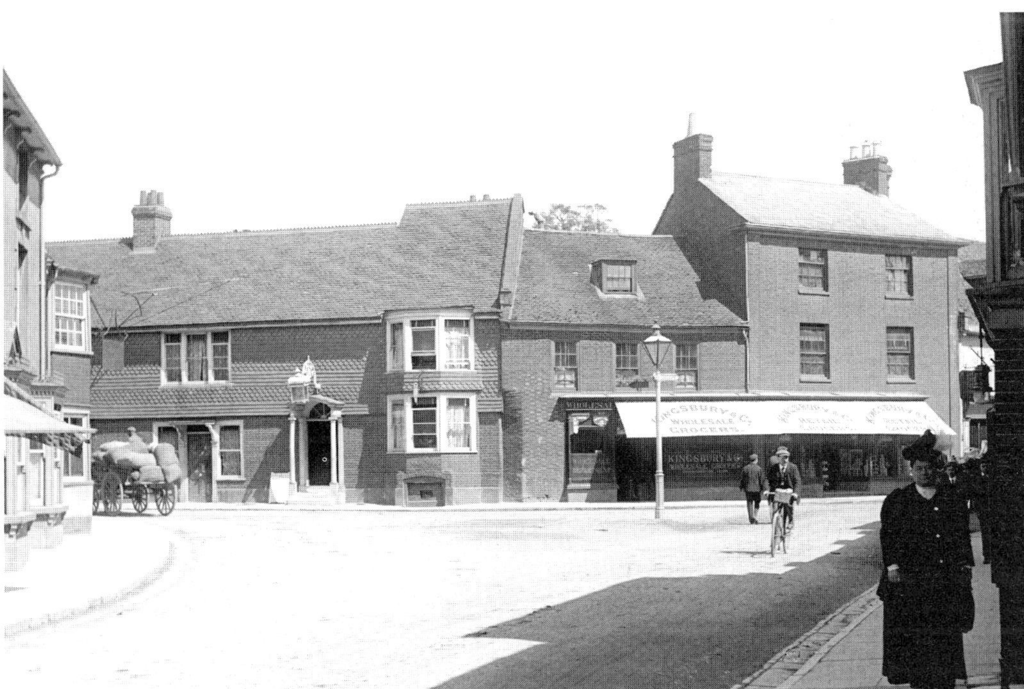

The main town on the western edge of the Forest, Ringwood takes its name from 'wood at a boundary', from the Old English *rimuc-wudu*.

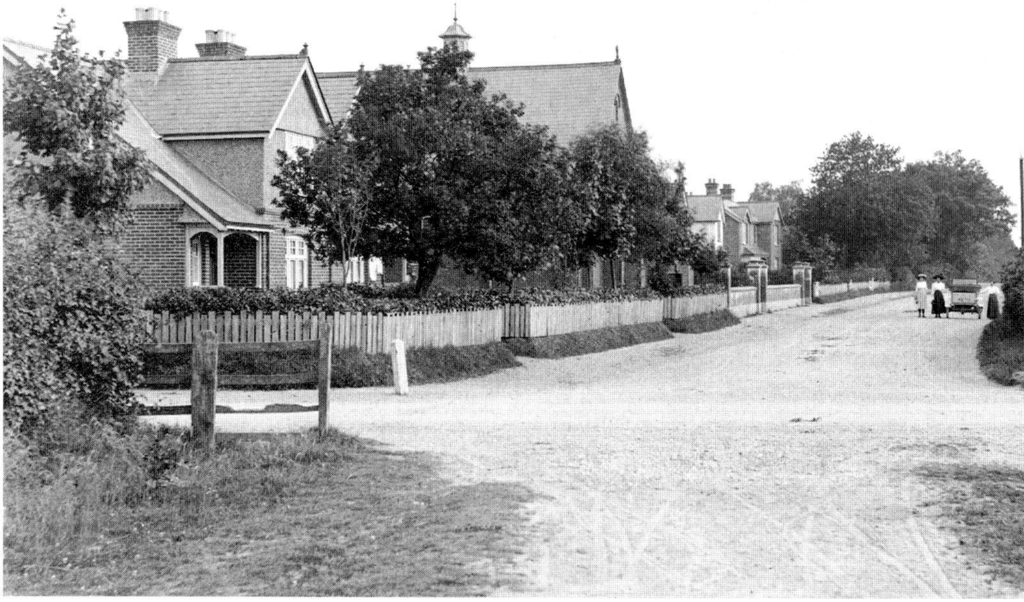

In the early 1900s, at Verwood, having your photograph taken in the street was quite an occasion, especially next to a car!

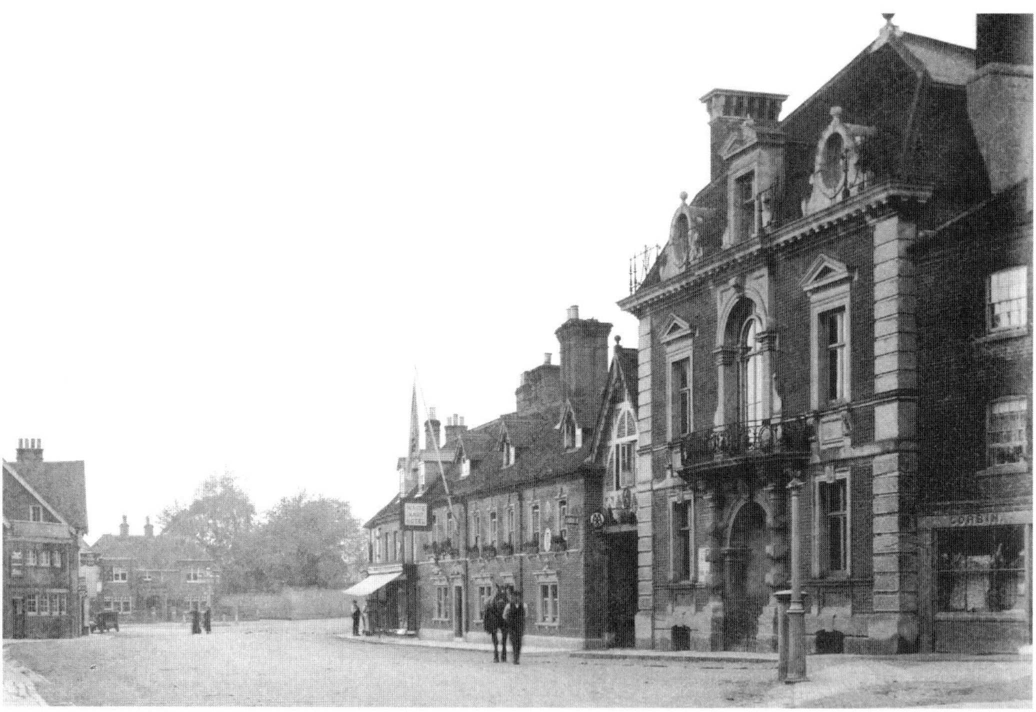

Still retaining many of its attractive old houses, Ringwood is where Monmouth penned his petition for mercy after the 1685 rebellion.

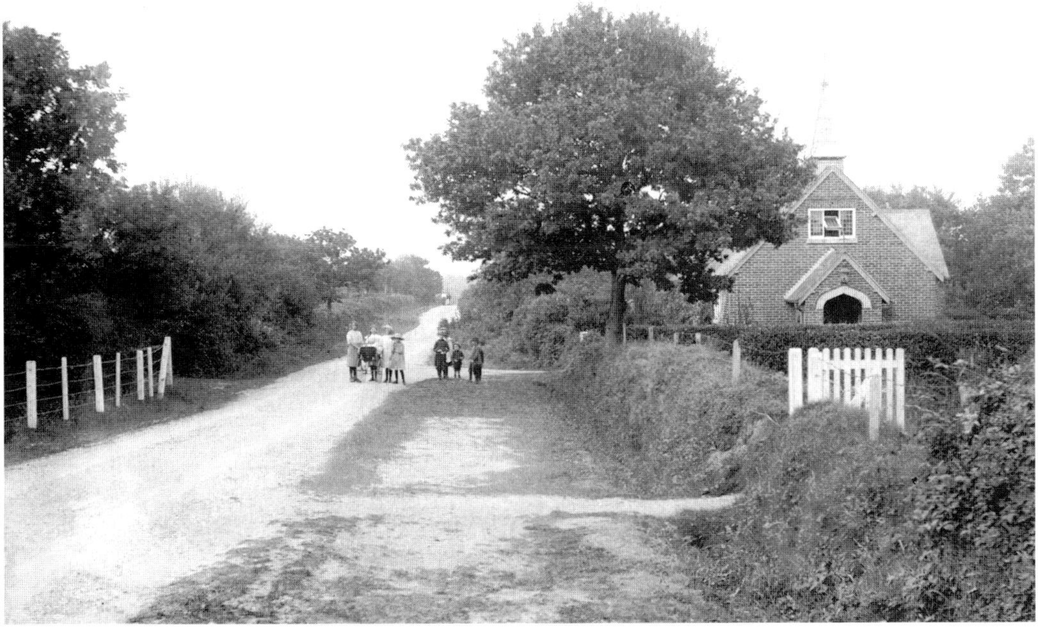

Built in 1907 and a private chapel for three years, St John's Church Bashley came to lose its bell tower but the original bell - from a ship - can now be seen on the wall above the main entrance.

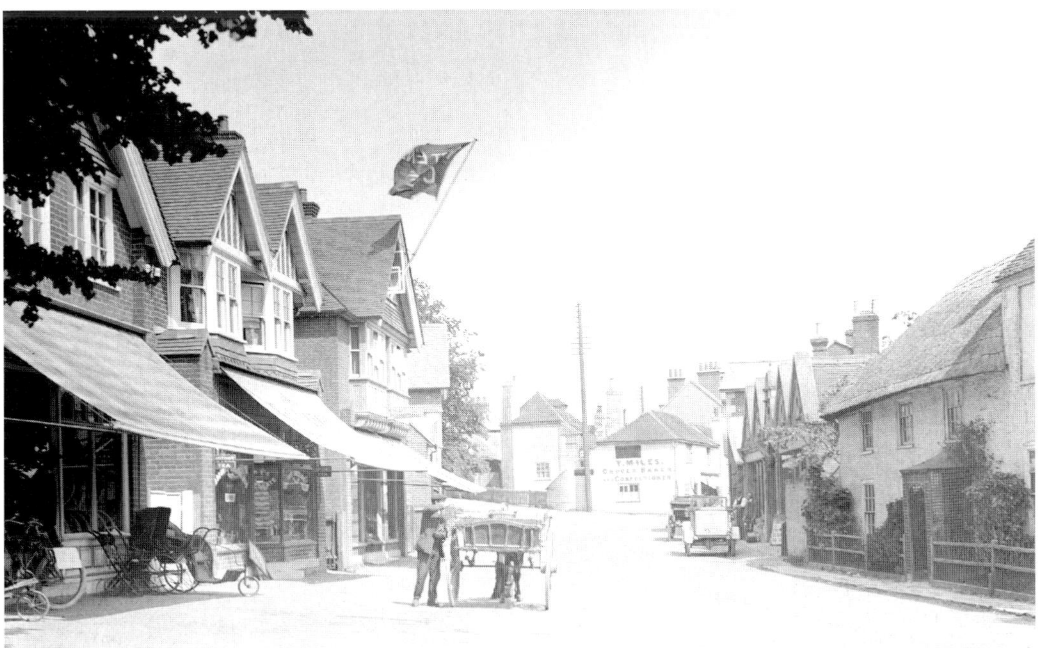

A wide range of transport at Milford-on-Sea, which was already an important corn-grinding centre at the time of the Domesday book, in 1086.

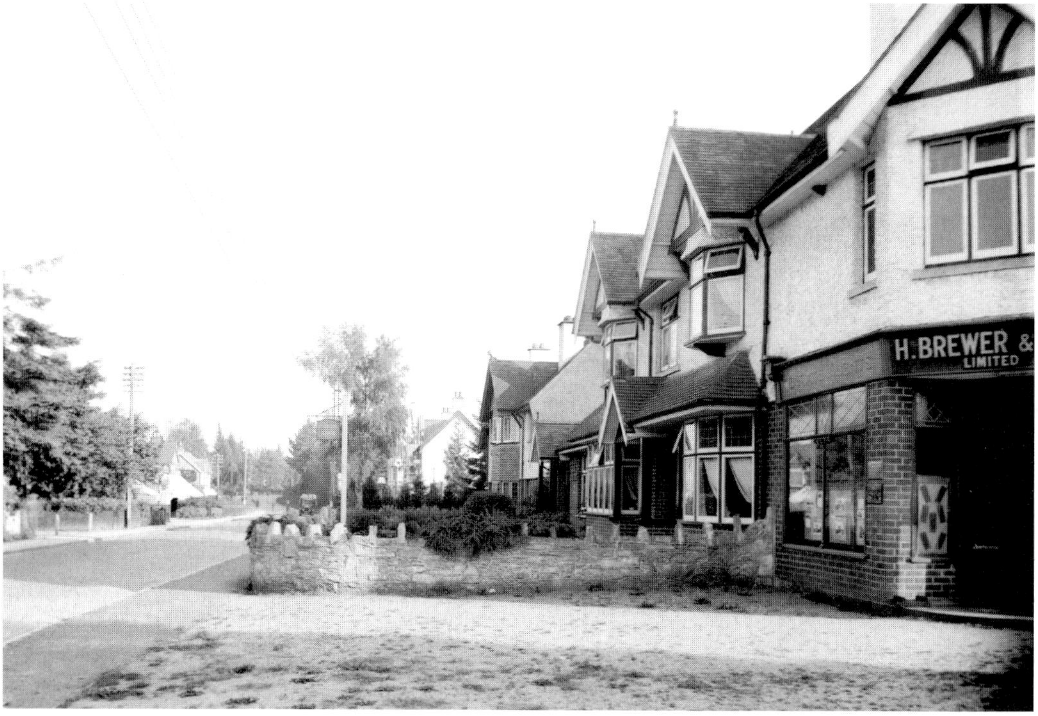

Longham, when the western approaches to the Forest were far quieter than they are today.

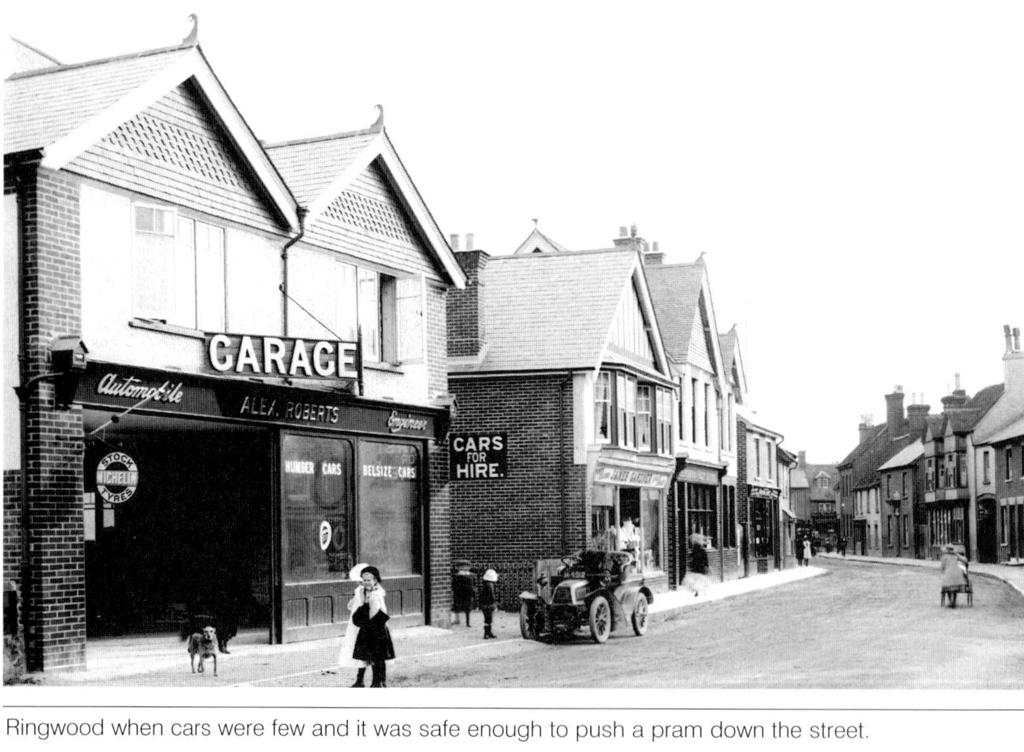

Ringwood when cars were few and it was safe enough to push a pram down the street.

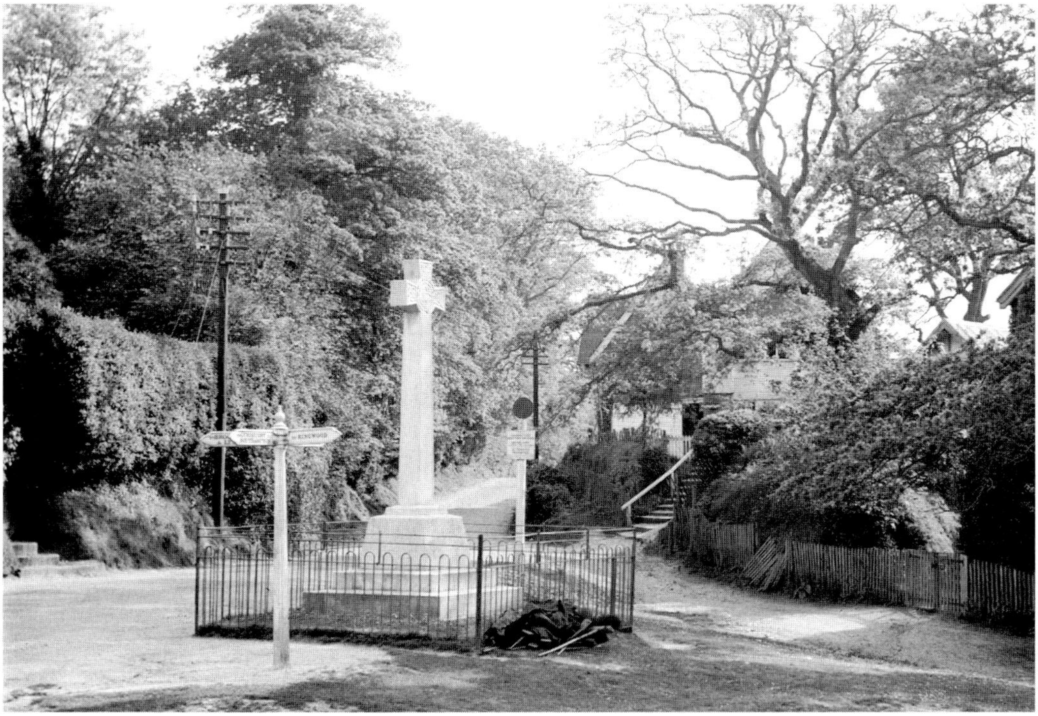

Burley cross, when the roads to Ringwood, Southampton, Lyndhurst, Brockenhurst and Lymington were considerably rougher.

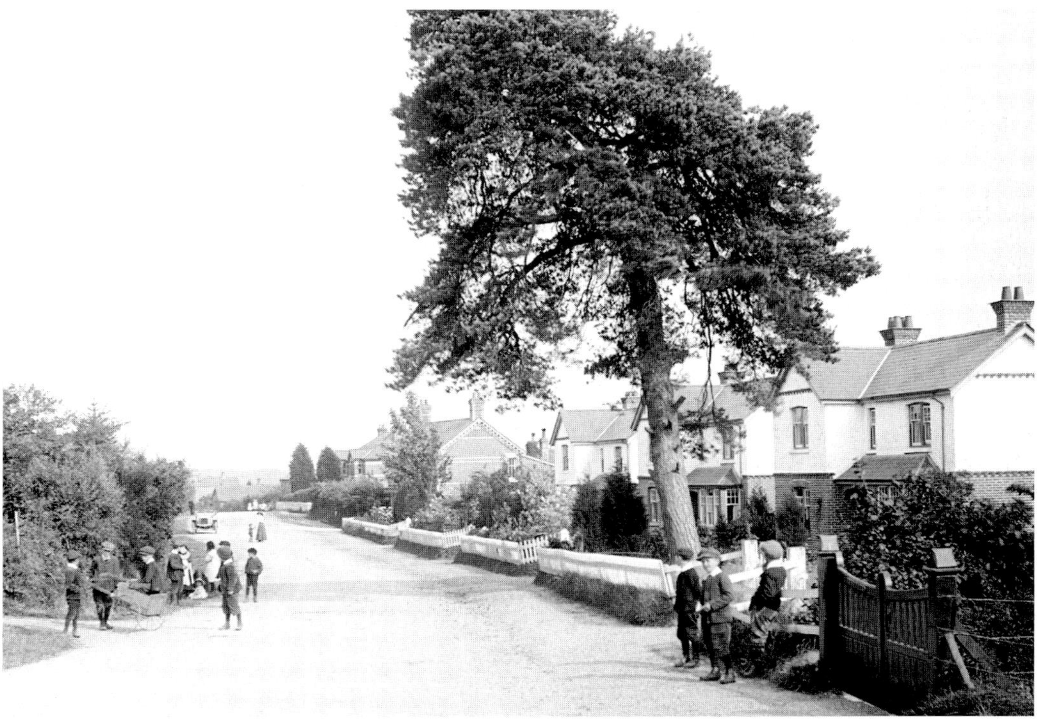

Children of all ages enjoying the peace and relative safety of almost traffic-free streets at Verwood.

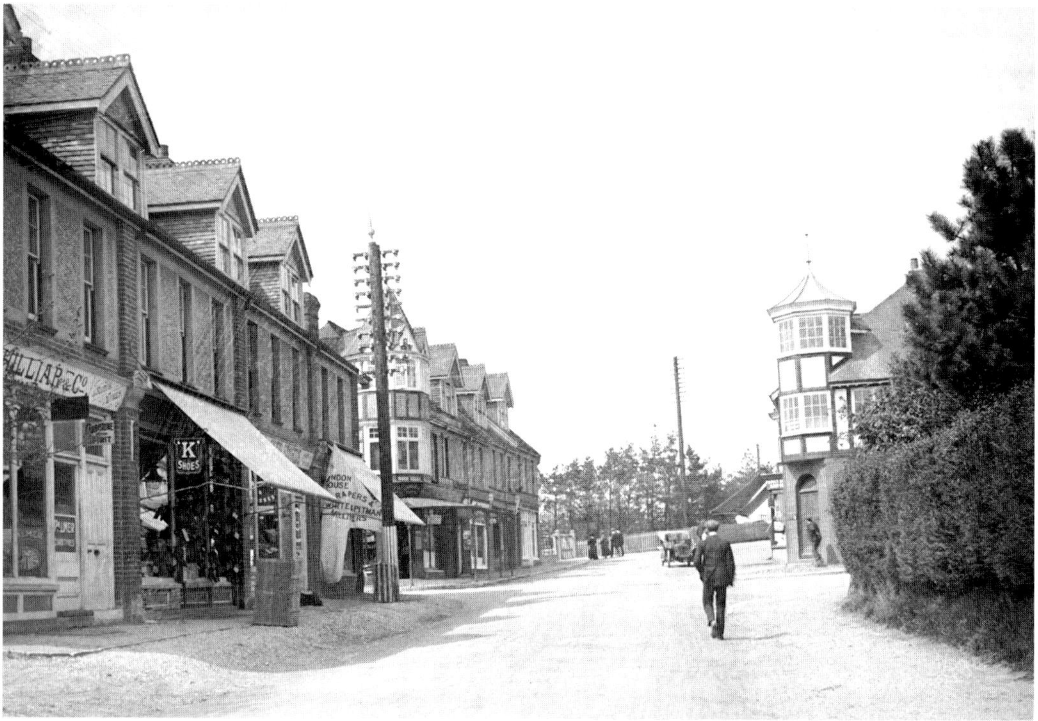

New Milton before the roads were made up. The first shop of Focusing Ltd, the publishers of this book, was yet to be built, in the area behind the hedge to the right.

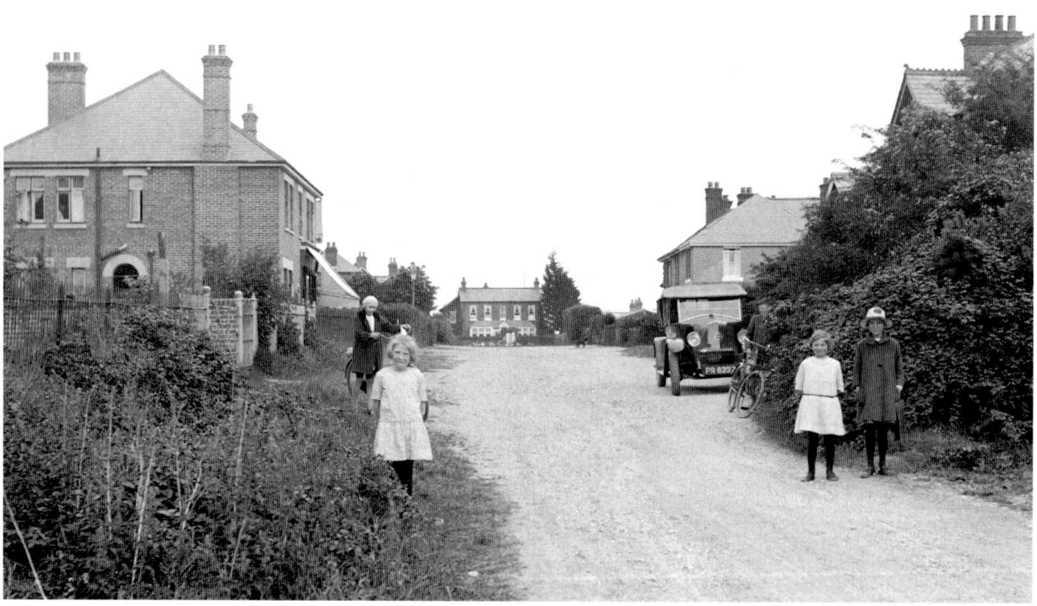

Posing for pictures at Walkford, on the south-western edge of the Forest.

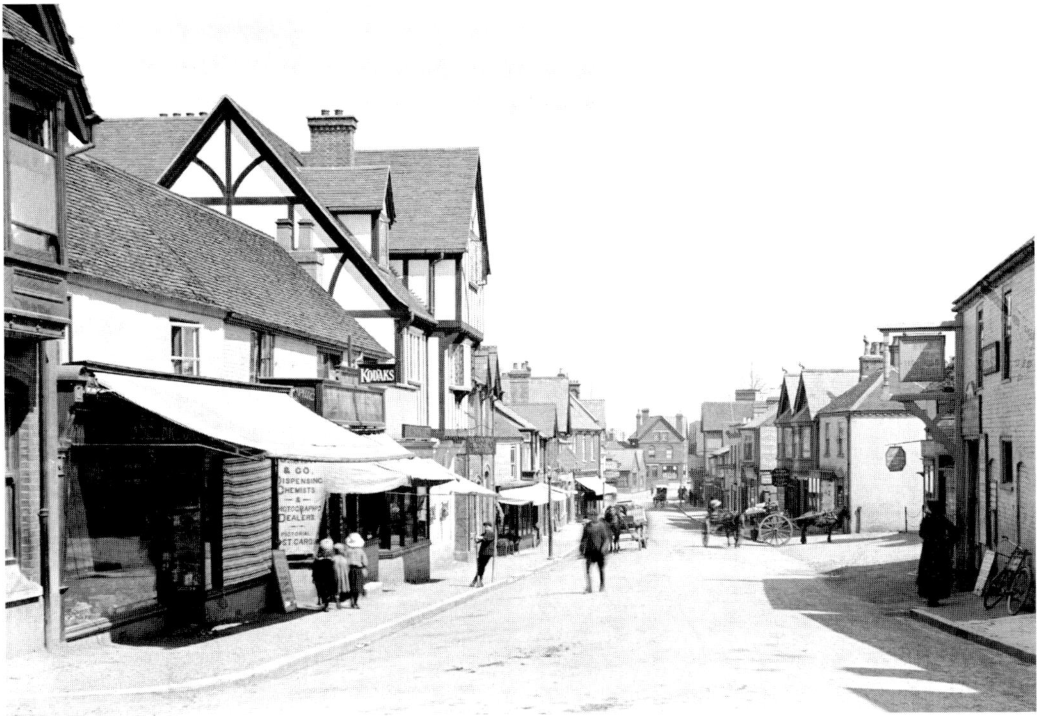

Centrally situated on main roads, Lyndhurst has long been the 'capital' of the New Forest, attracting tourists from far and wide. Note the Kodak and postcard adverts (left).

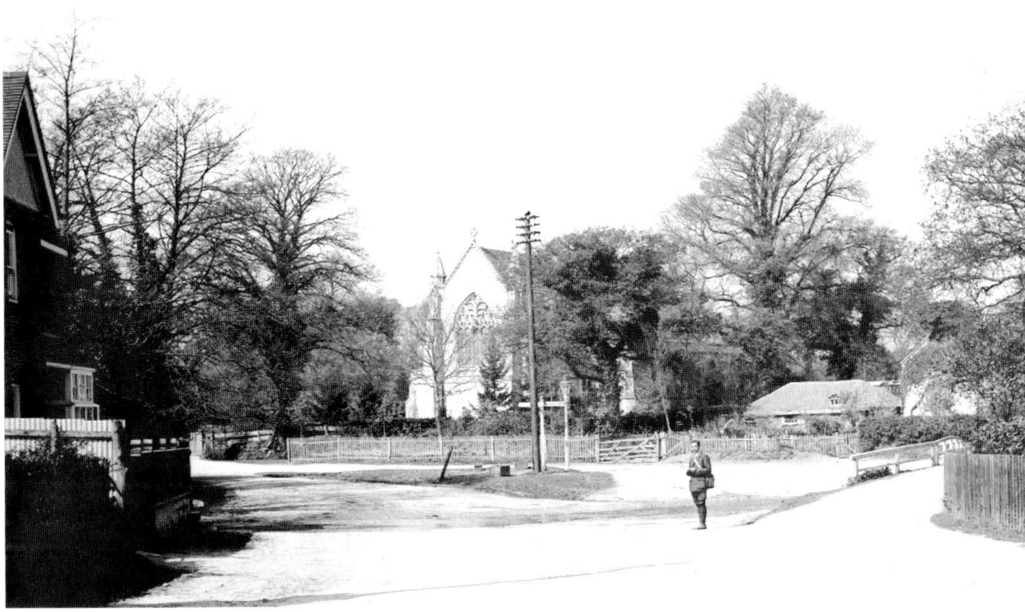

When flooded, the ford at Brockenhurst has long been an obstacle for traffic.

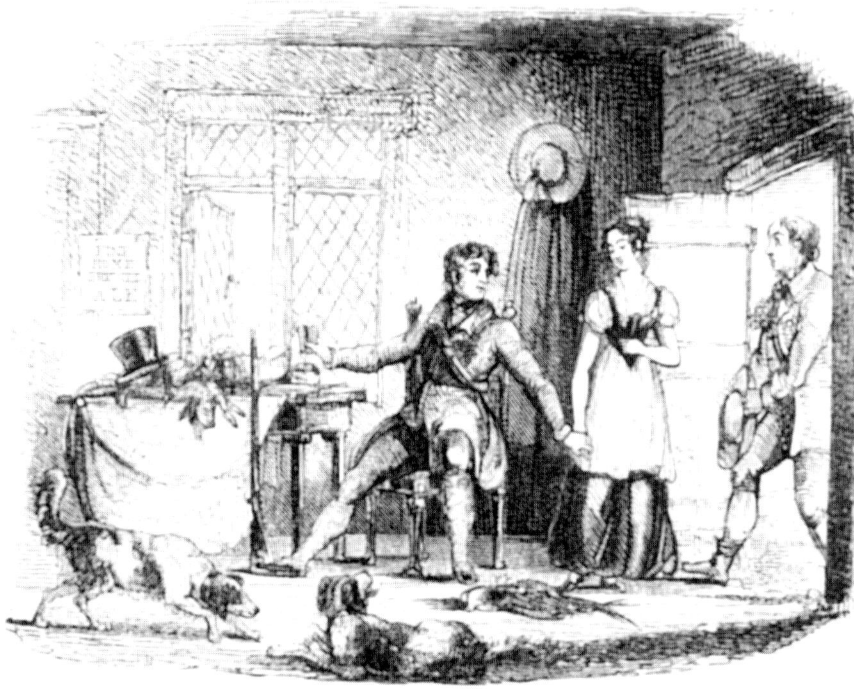

ONE FOR THE POT

'Game, furred and feathered, would not exist at all but for the private estates scattered throughout the Forest, in which game is preserved, and from which the depleted Forest lands are constantly being restocked.'

WH Hudson, Hampshire Days, 1903

IN SPORT & LEISURE

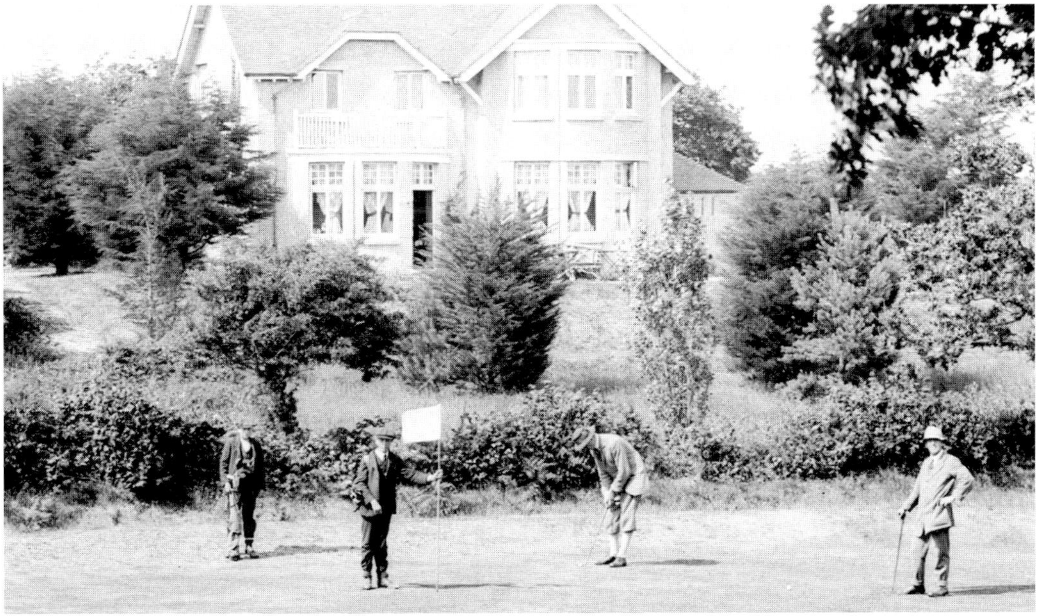

Above Golf at Barton-on-Sea, one of the many leisure activities which enticed the rising middle classes to take up residence in and around the New Forest.

Next page Once described by Brian Vesey-Fitzgerald as 'rather comic but very cheap', Burley's little golf-course became spoilt when 'discovered by Bournemouth'.

For many centuries, while English kings and the nobility hunted the deer and flew falcons at game, Forest peasants were too preoccupied with subsistence to have any concept of sport. A Sunday morning stroll to church, after getting up extra early to tend the stock, would be the only relaxation for many. Even children had to pull their weight, tending animals and carrying out many other chores both before and after school and even at weekends. If they were lucky, they might have played hide-and-seek or bowled a hoop down the rutted road. But as hard Victorian ideals faded, religion relaxed and mass production put a few more pennies in people's pockets, leisure time steadily increased. The middle class was born and their arrival in and around the Forest stimulated the rapid development of fashionable exercise such as riding, gamebird shooting, golf and cricket. The Forest became the headquarters of the Old Hawking Club and meets of the foxhounds and buckhounds always attracted plenty of onlookers. Indeed, in 1836, when the Royal Buckhounds came down to hunt the red deer 2000 people were present. However, most places where humble village boys traditionally dangled a worm over the bridge became the preserve of incomer anglers. Every inch of countryside now had to pay its way. But there was always the nearby coast, where adventurous lads could fish for supper and people of all stations could follow the new fashion for bathing in the sea, at centres such as Barton and Milford. Furthermore, the excellent natural harbours of the western Solent stimulated rapid growth of sailing, especially at Lymington. And, of course, the Forest is ideal for today's legions of ramblers and birdwatchers.

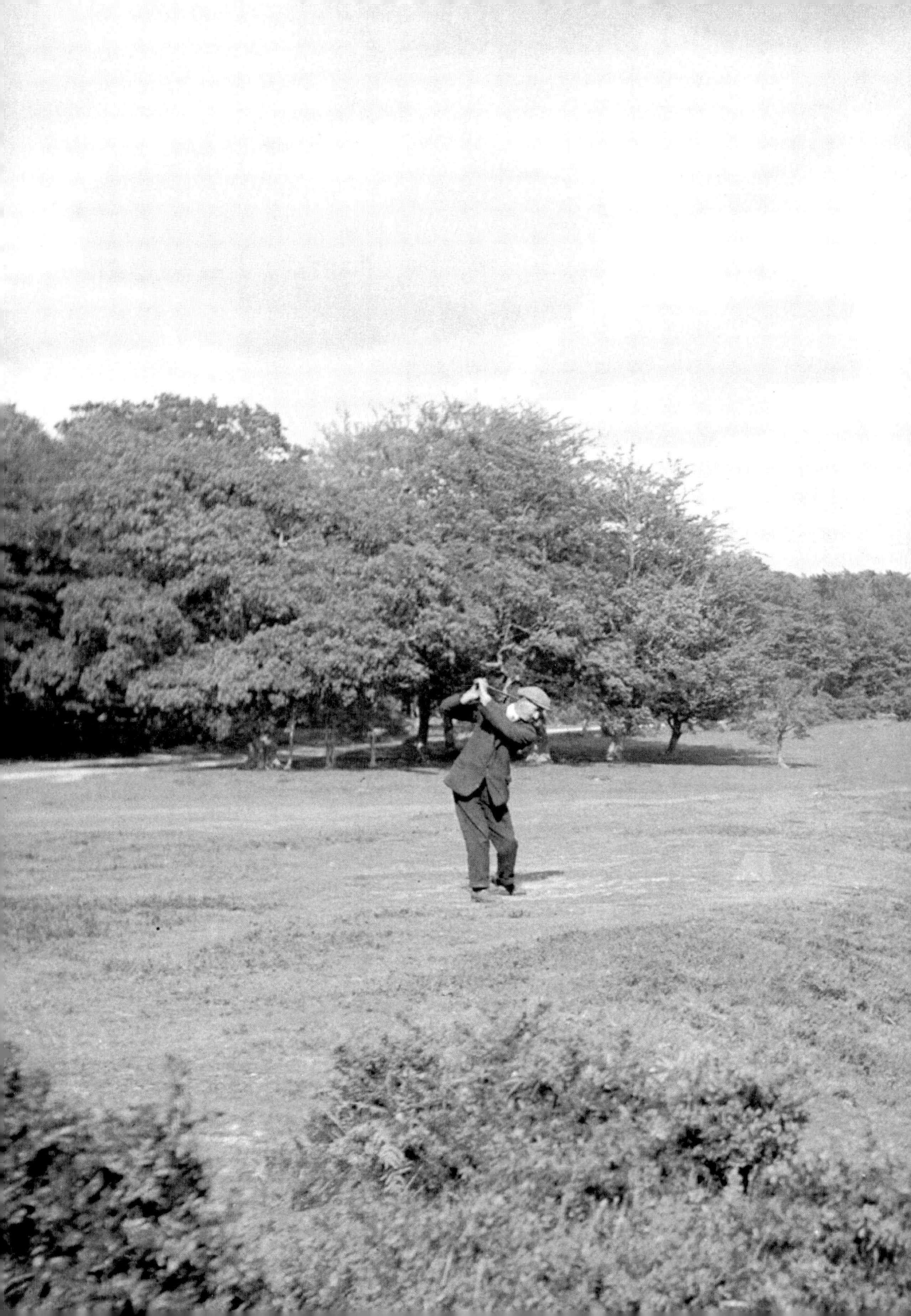

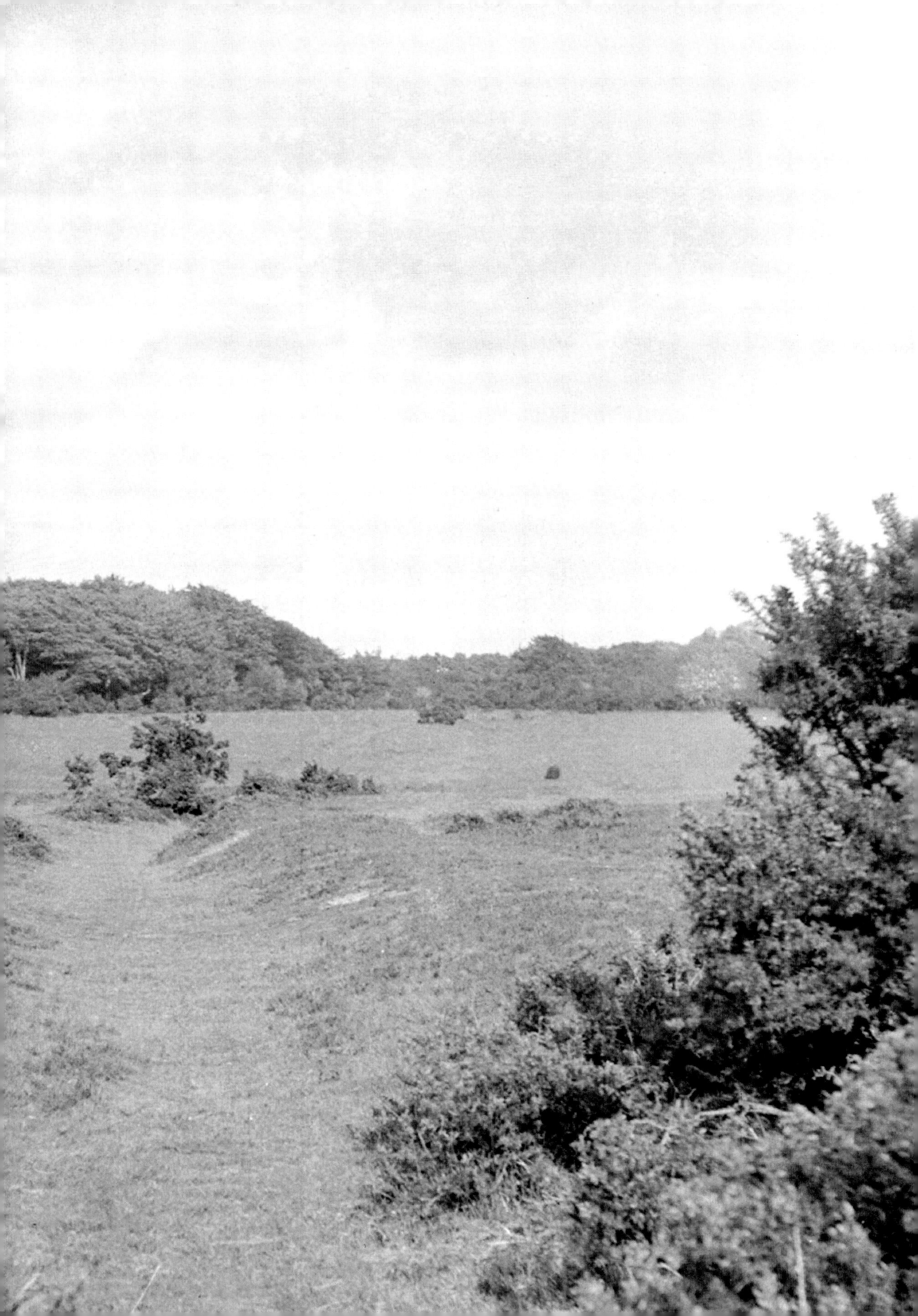

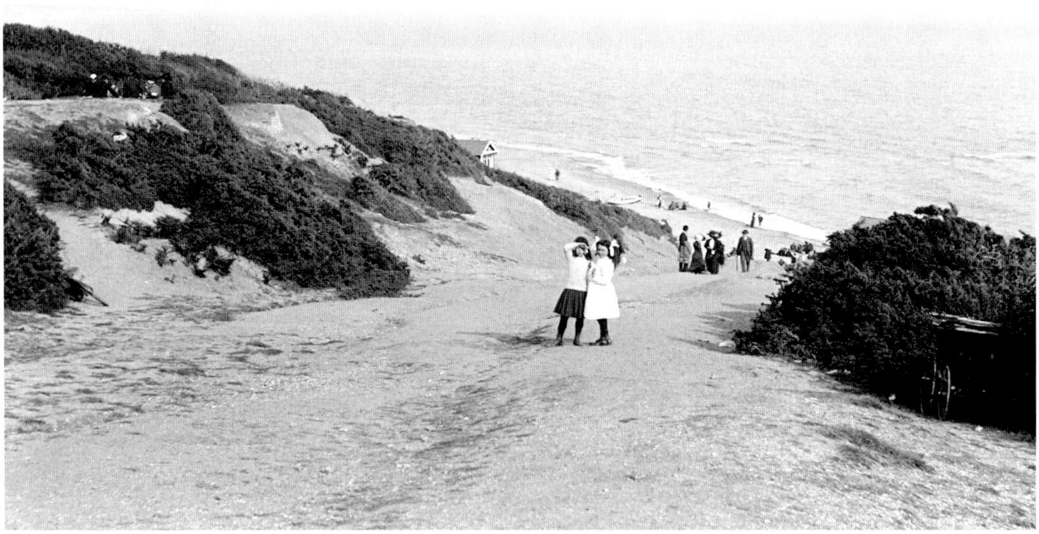

On the southern edge of the Forest, Highcliffe's beach offered welcome refreshment and exercise for the new influx of tourists and residents.

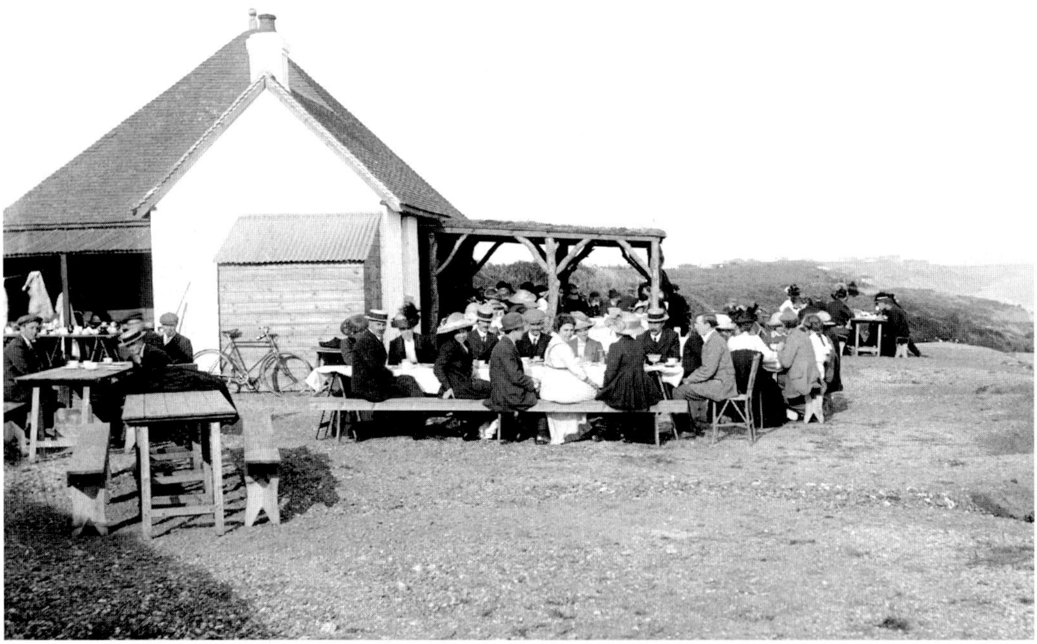

Taking tea on the head at Highcliffe provided the opportunity to show off the latest fashion as well as take gentle exercise.

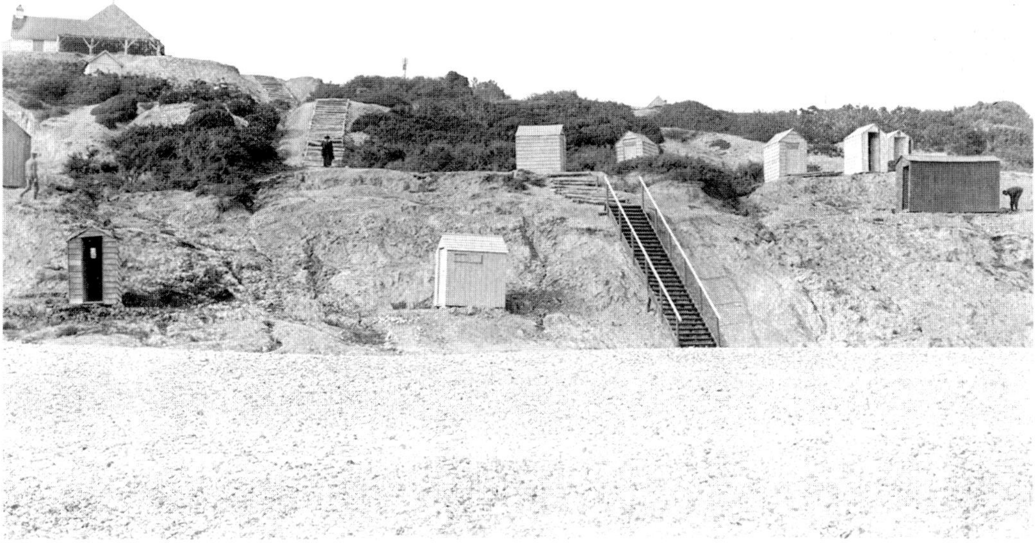

Highcliffe beach huts, built to support rapidly growing interest in sea-bathing during the early 1900s.

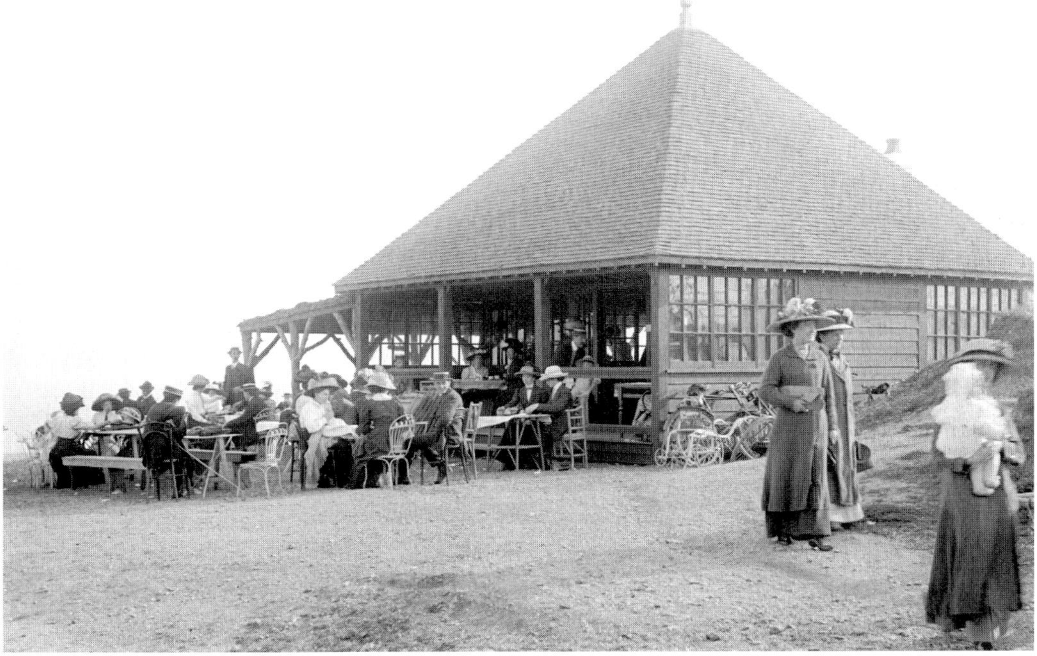

No matter what the weather, visitors to Highcliffe had to dress correctly. Note the admiring gaze from the man seated right.

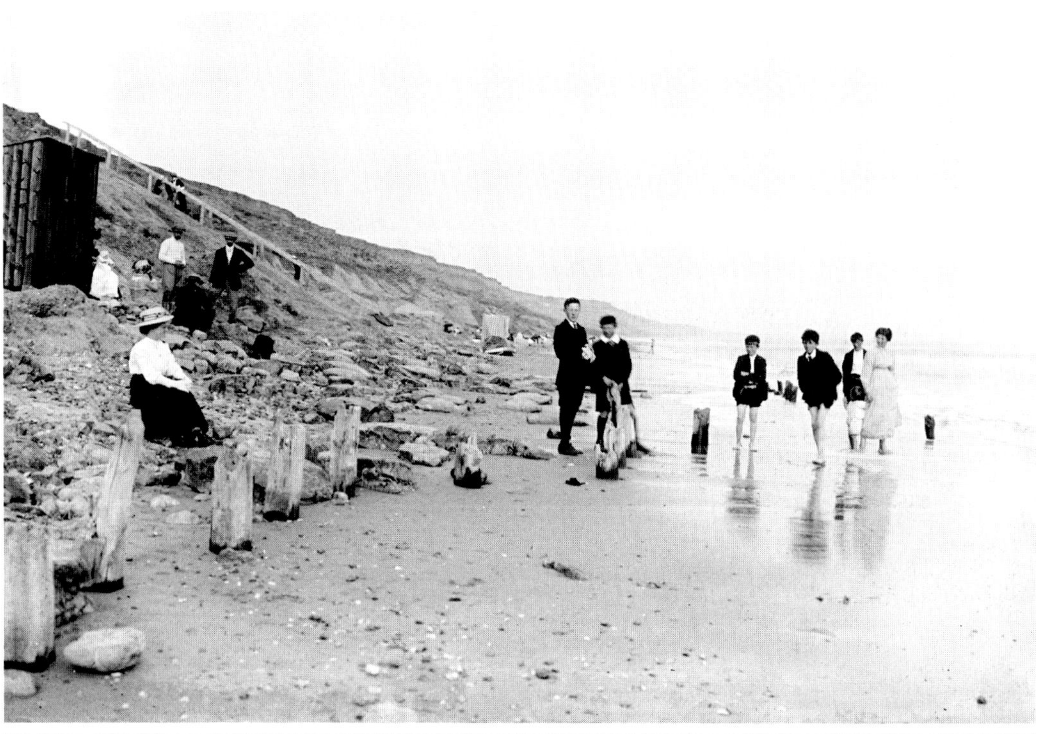

Even when paddling, these boys at Barton-on-Sea retained their ties and caps, while mother barely braved an ankle.

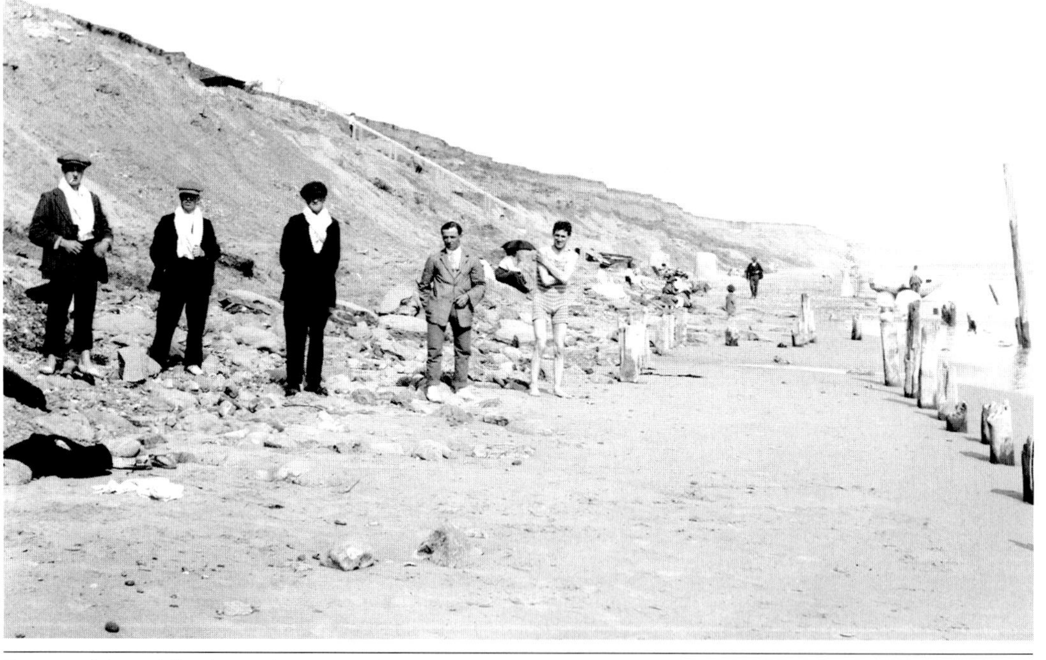

Presumably a chilly day at Barton-on-Sea, with just one shivering bather and companions with scarves!

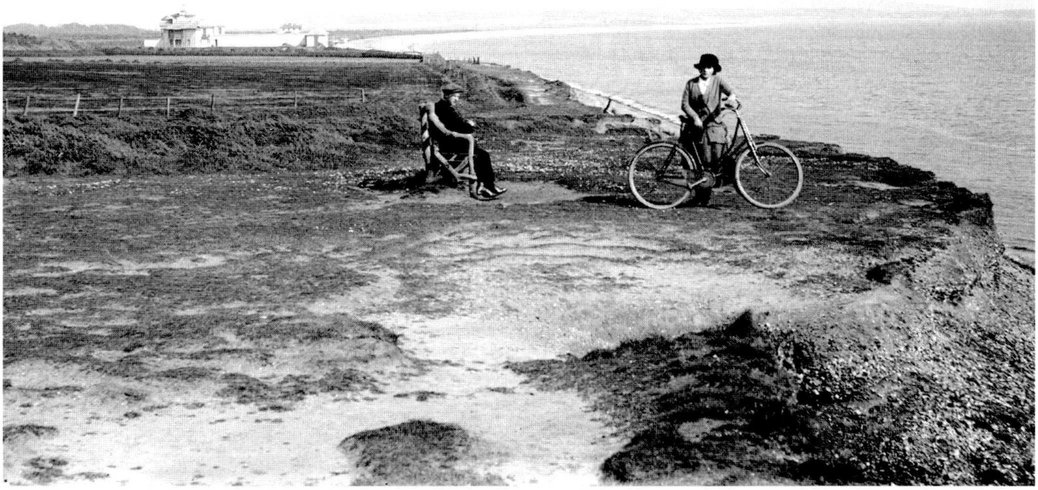

When the coastline at Milford-on-Sea was still very unspoilt. The beach here is mostly shingle.

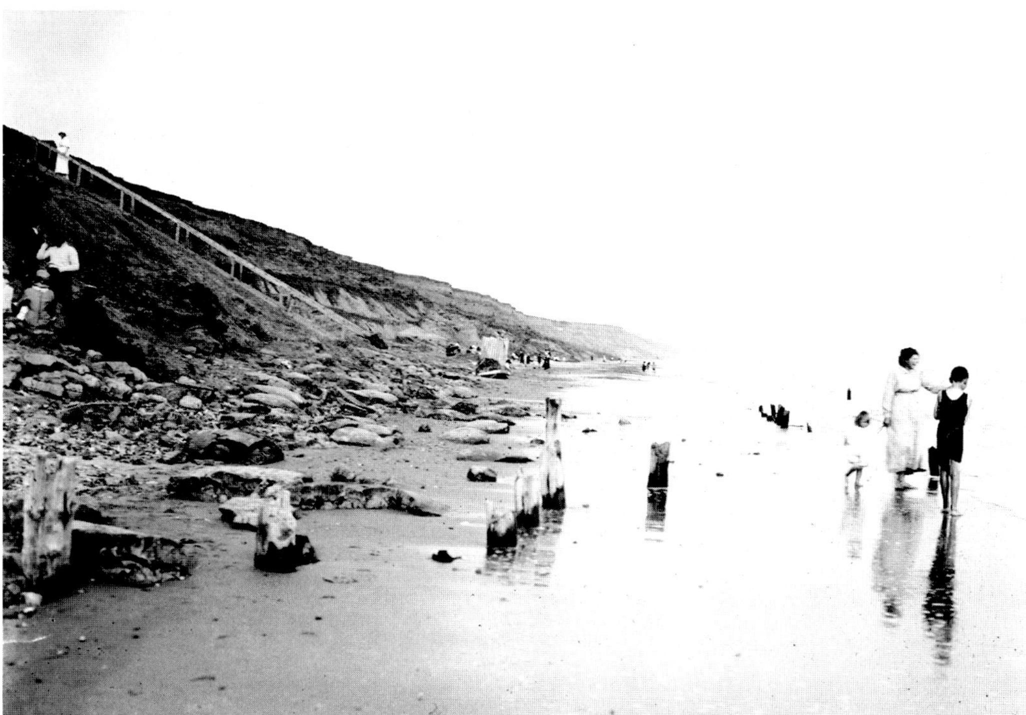

For Forest families, escape to the beach was but a few miles away, at Barton-on-Sea.

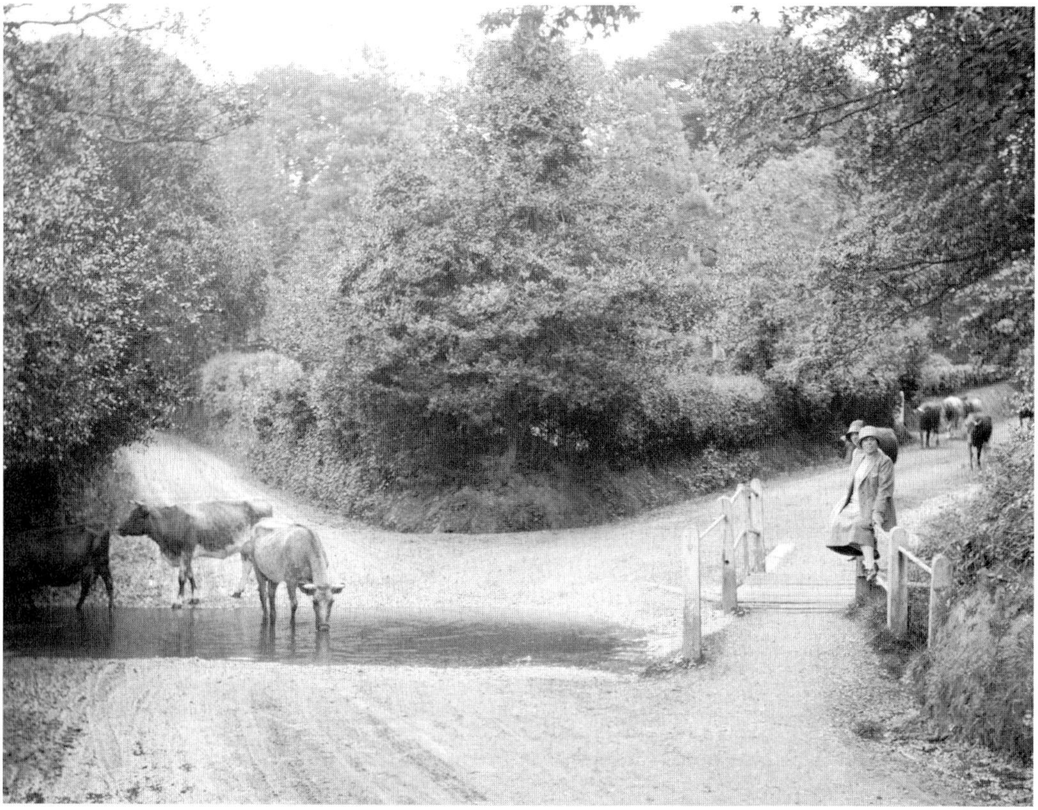

Even when walking, these ladies at Walkford were very fashion-conscious, with shiny shoes totally unsuited to muddy lanes.

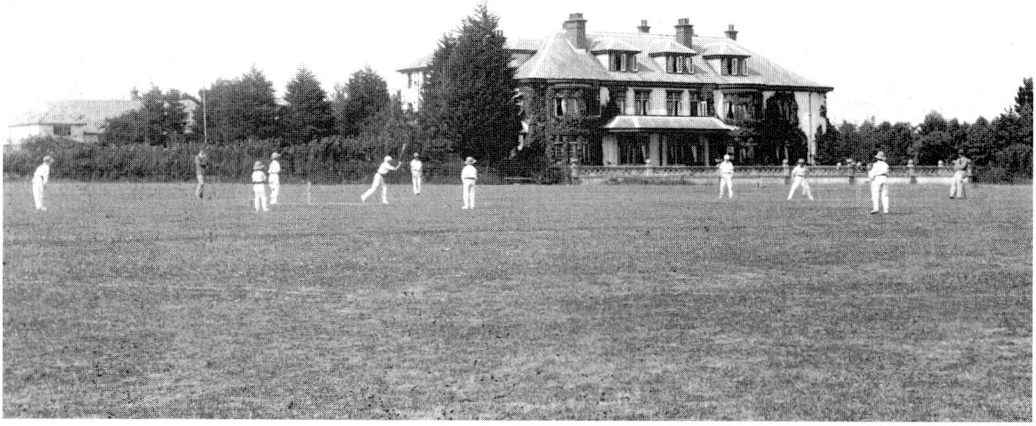

At New Milton, as in so many parts of the kingdom, cricket has long had a keen following.

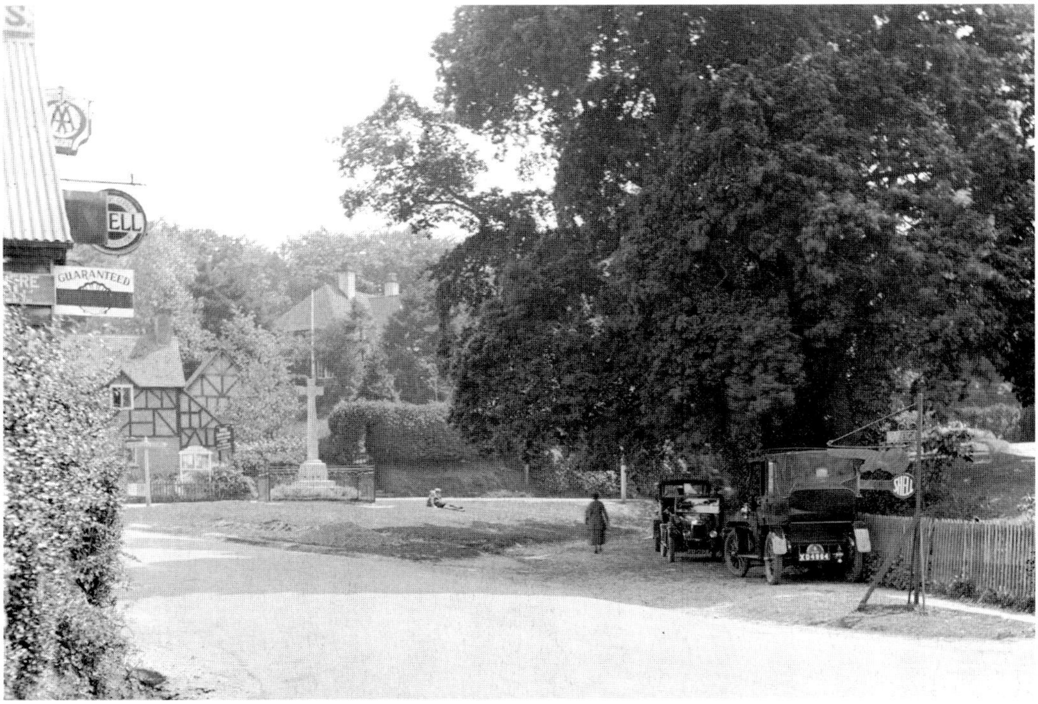

In the early 1900s, families lucky enough to own a car could venture out from nearby towns on excursions to still relatively remote villages such as Burley.

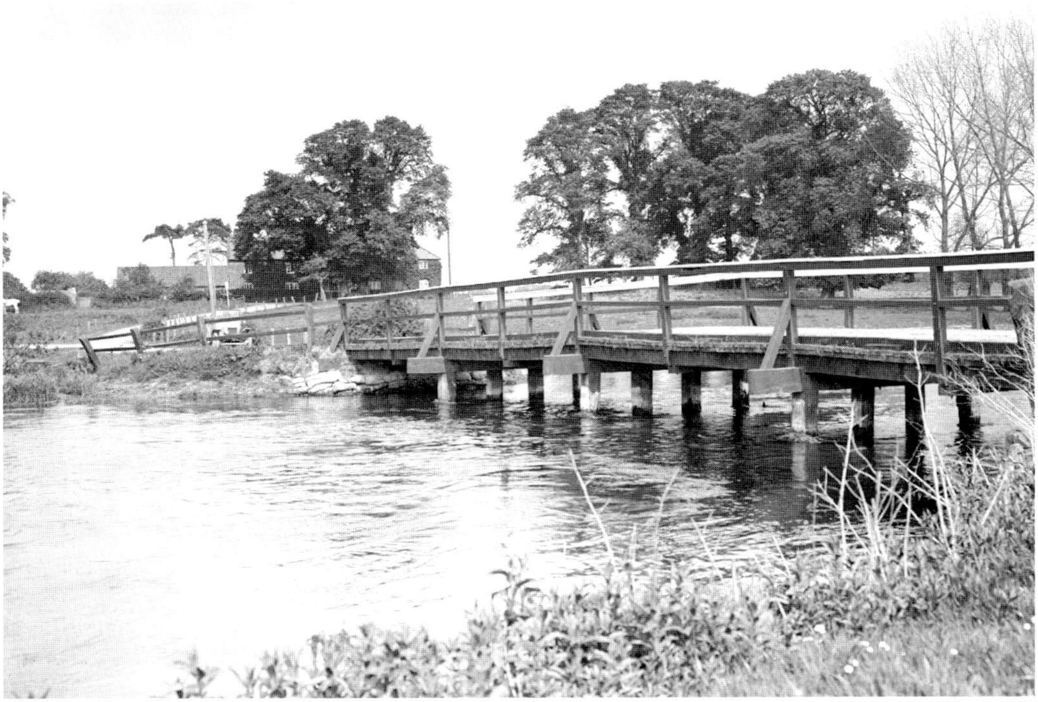

Renowned for angling, the Avon has been important to Sopley since the Domesday Book of 1086, when the mill was valued at 10 shillings and provided 875 eels a year for the lord of the manor.

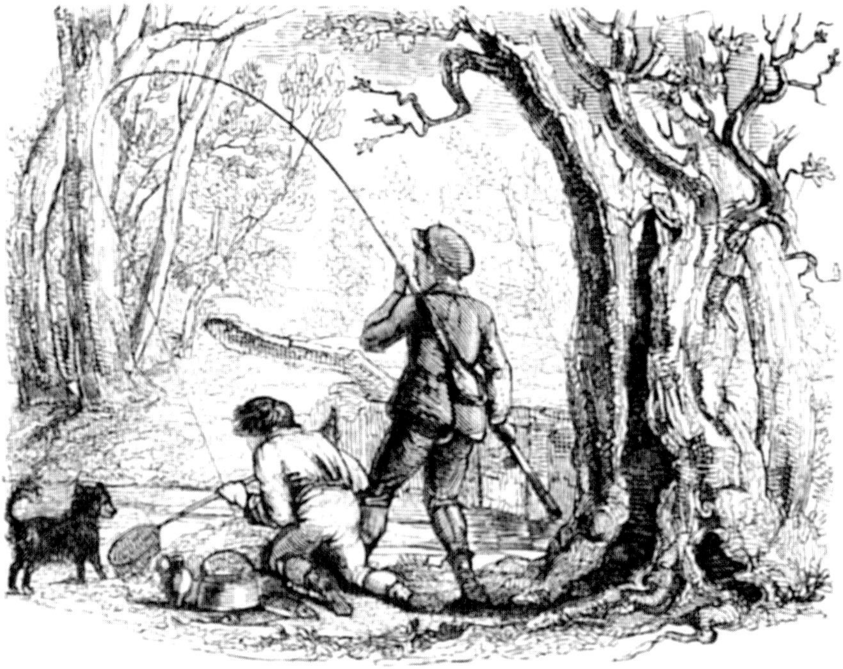

'Thou that hast loved so long and well
The vale's deep quiet streams,
Where the pure water-lilies dwell,
Shedding forth tender gleams;
And o'er the pool the May-fly's wing
Glances in golden eves of spring; -
Oh! loved and lovely haunts are thine!'

Mrs Hemans

IN QUIETEST CORNERS

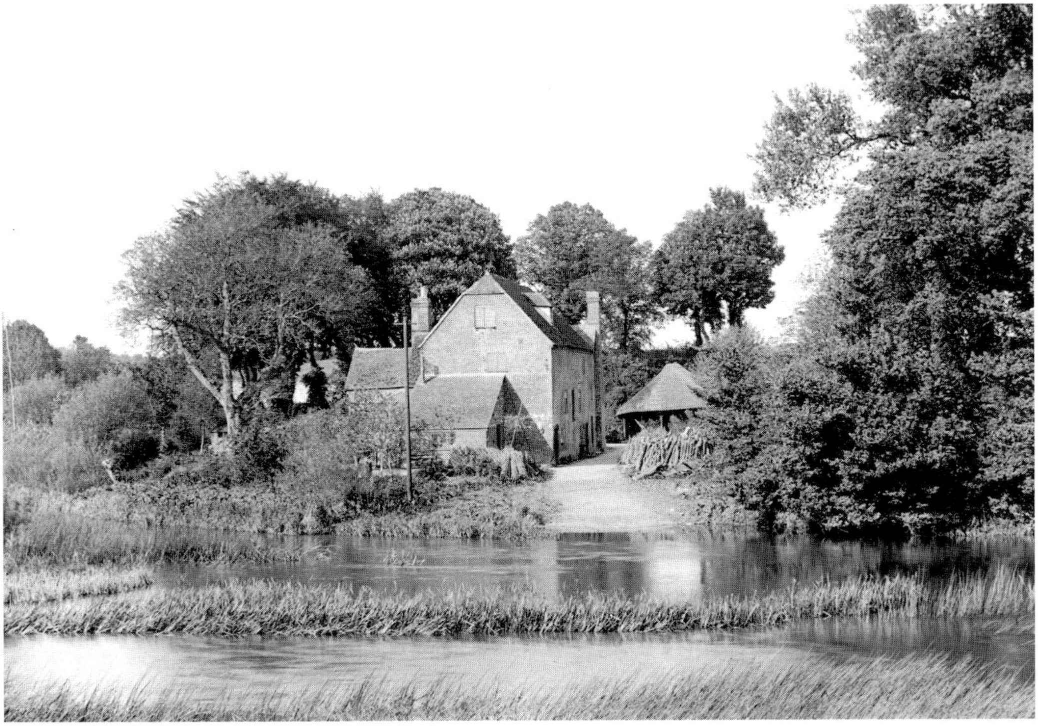

The perfect setting at Sopley, on the banks of the Avon, fringed with mature trees.

Today, in much of the Forest, at 'honeypot sites' and against the constant drone of traffic, we can only dream of how deliciously peaceful it once was. For many centuries the only sounds of the Forest were all what we would now regard as immensely pleasing, ranging from the gentle thud of the woodman's axe and the creak of a cart to the whinnying of horses, snuffling of boar and roaring of stags. Yet, such is the size of the Forest and so varied its habitat and landscape, even at the start of the 21st Century there are occasions when we can find perfect peace in the quietest of corners. Whether through being unfashionable places in which to live or having difficult access, some hamlets retain more than a vestige of antique calm. Here and there, in woodland clearings and secret backwaters, you will find unspoilt old cottages and farmhouses with unspoilt old owners who have resisted the tide of change and continue to live in harmony with nature. Mercifully, there are still many places where the car cannot reach and the internal combustion engine cannot spoil your temporary illusion of escape. Here we can be alone to share the unwritten language of the great trees as they whisper in balmy breezes or creak and crash angrily in a gale. Here, too, are endless rivulets and streams away from the paddling hordes, places where the silence is broken only by the rising of fish or water rippling over a pebbly bed. And although we have lost so much wildlife, both in variety and number, many species have been encouraged by organised conservation and remain to serenade us with song or beguile us with beauty.

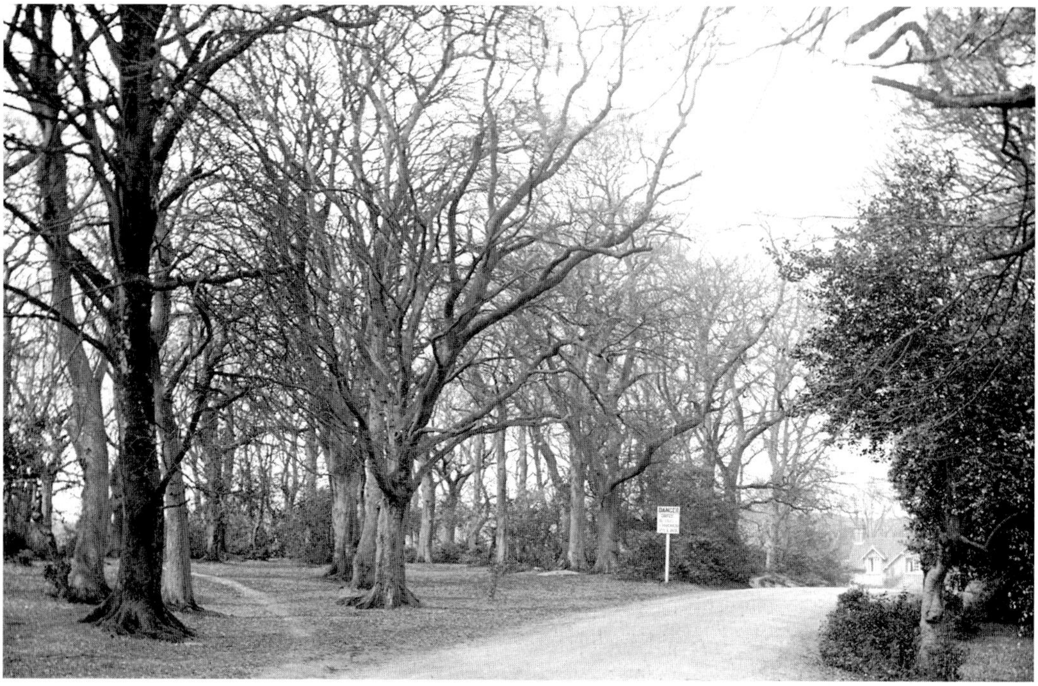

Although most tourists enjoy Forest trees in the full flush of summer, winter woodland architecture also has its charm, as seen here at Burley. Note the early traffic calming notice.

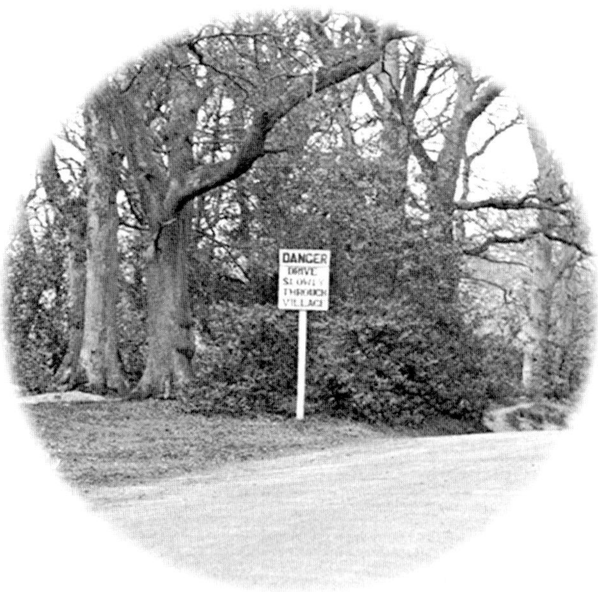

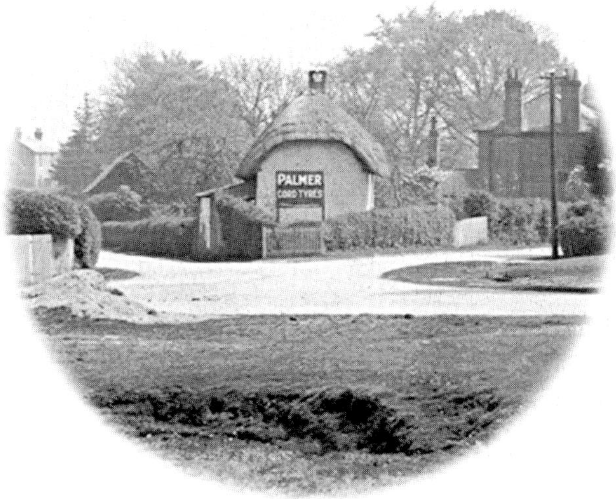

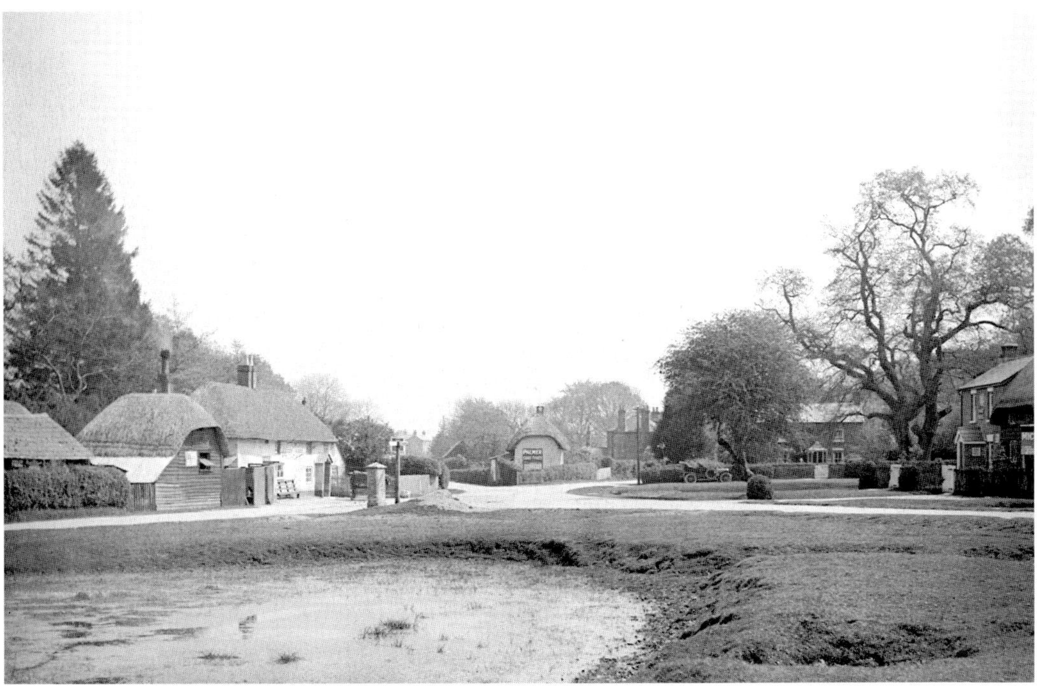

At first sight, time seems to have stood still at picturesque Bransgore, with neatly thatched pub and cottages, but note the car and sign (centre) for Palmer cord tyres above.

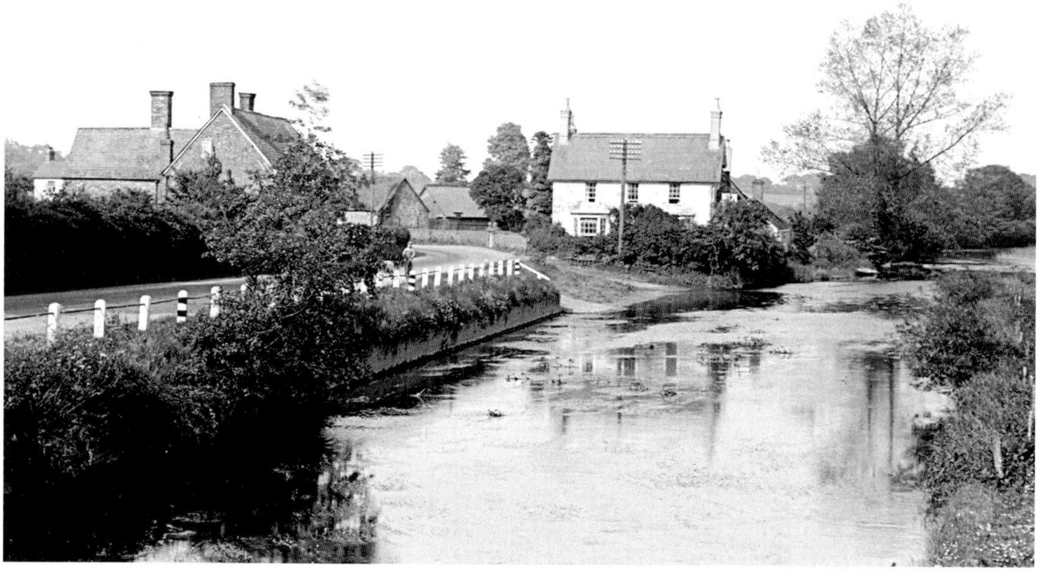

The Stour glides gently past Longham.

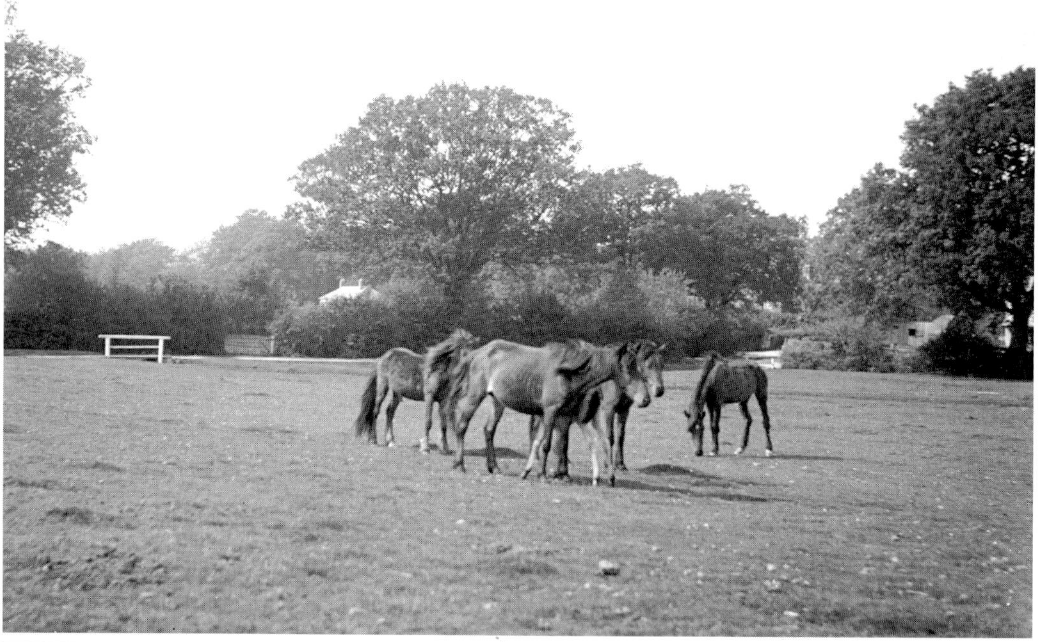

Above Semi-wild ponies, such as these at Burley, have long been the most characteristic inhabitants of the Forest.

Right Bridges and streams have always had a special attraction for both tourists and locals, such as here at Verwood.

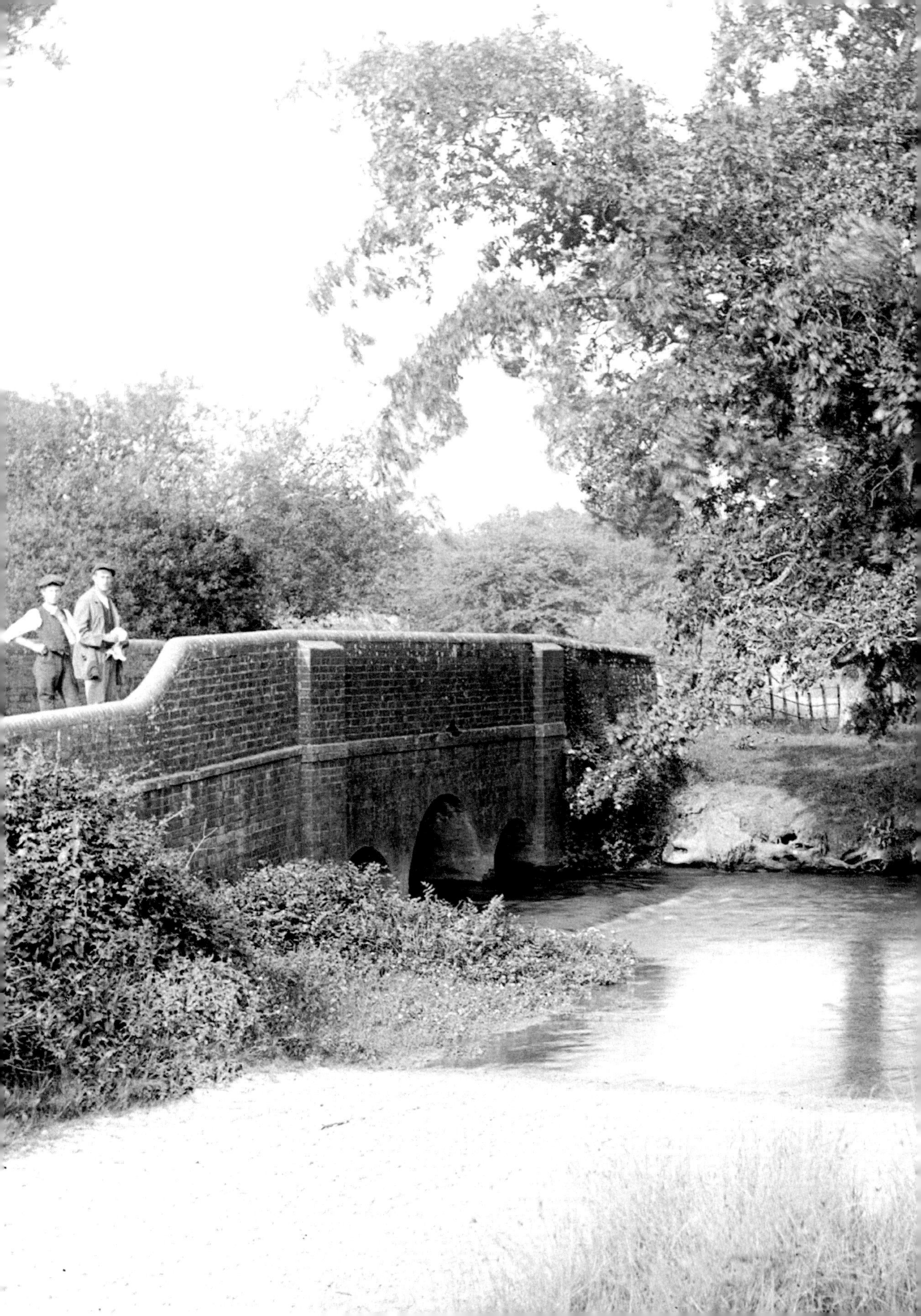

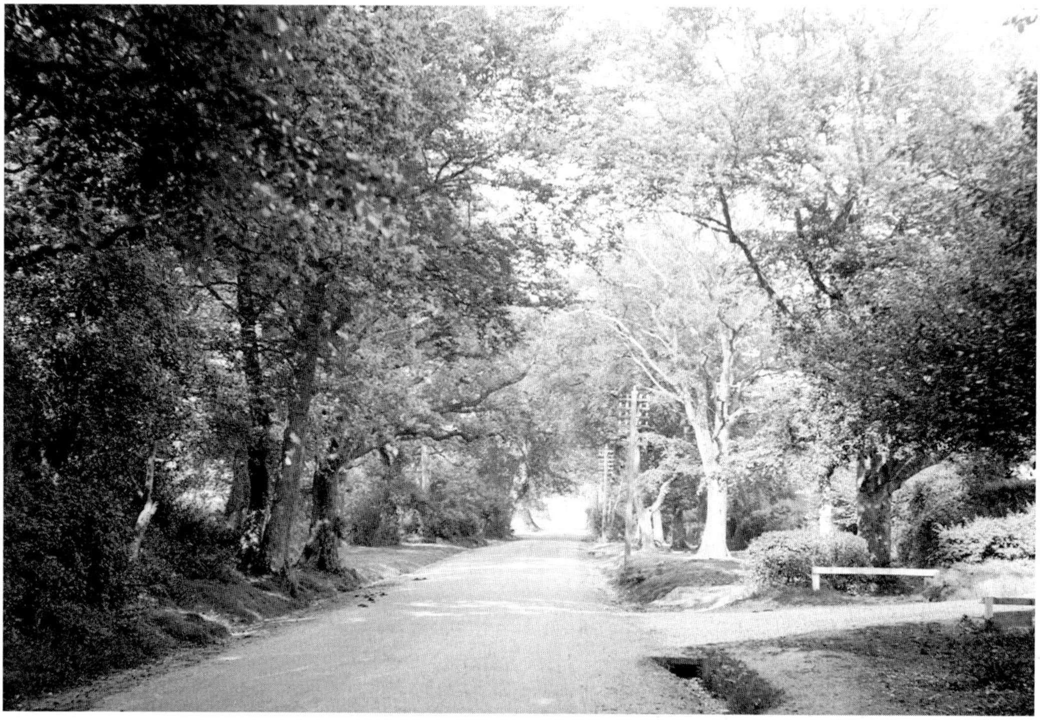

Many of the lanes and footpaths in and around Burley are blessed by a welcome variety of trees.

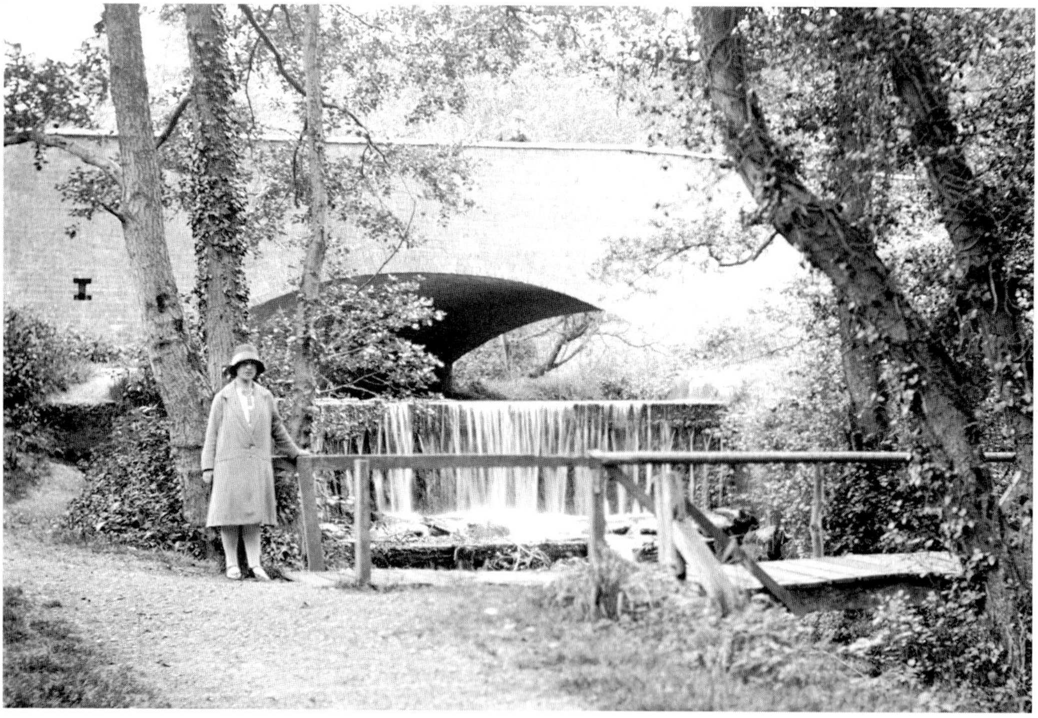

Posing by the waterfall at Highcliffe, while an admirer looks down from the bridge.

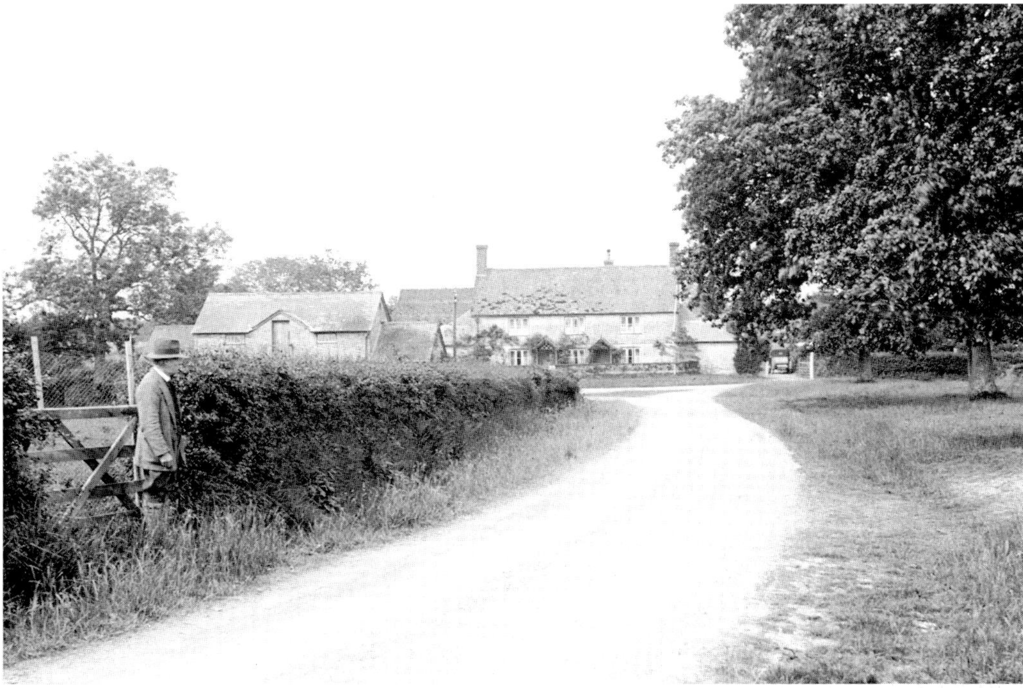

No need for the sign 'Beware tractors turning' in this very peaceful part of Verwood.

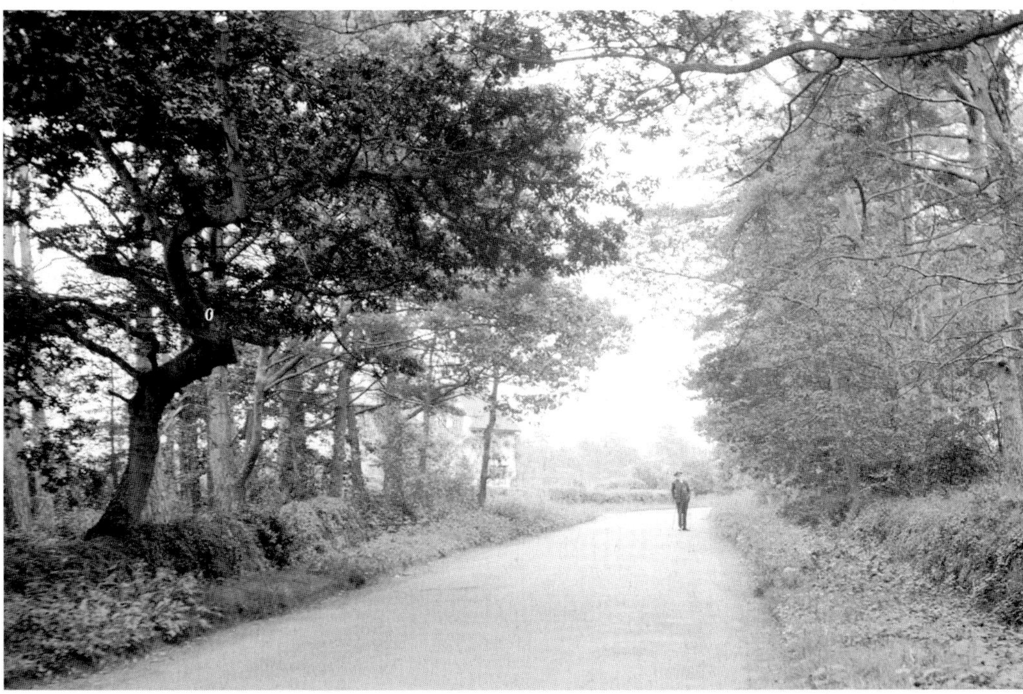

Above An elderly inhabitant finds plenty of peace in a stroll along the quiet lanes of Bransgore.

Next page Typical, tranquil Forest scenery at Burley, where dense woods are interspersed with open, scrubby grazing.

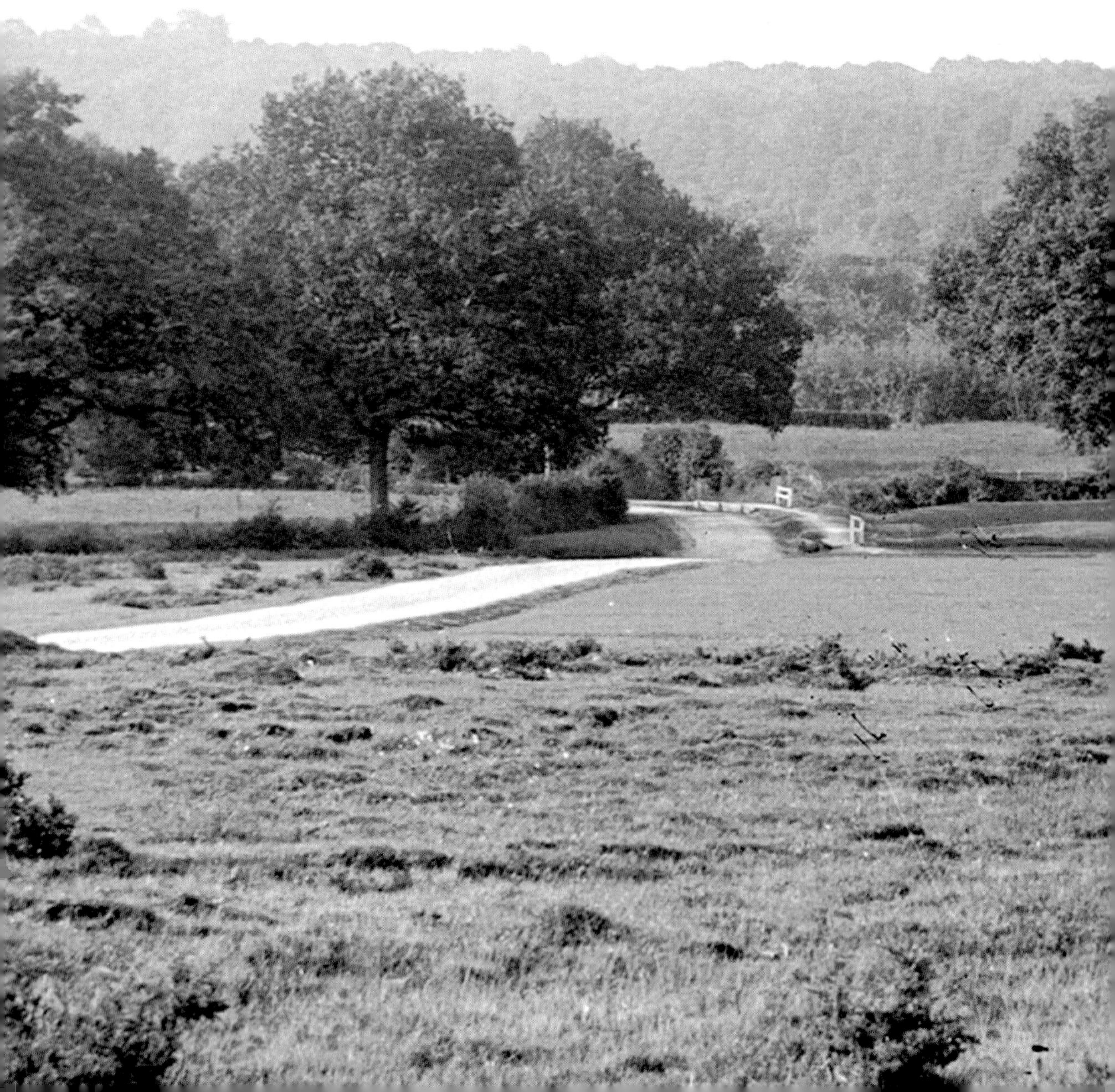

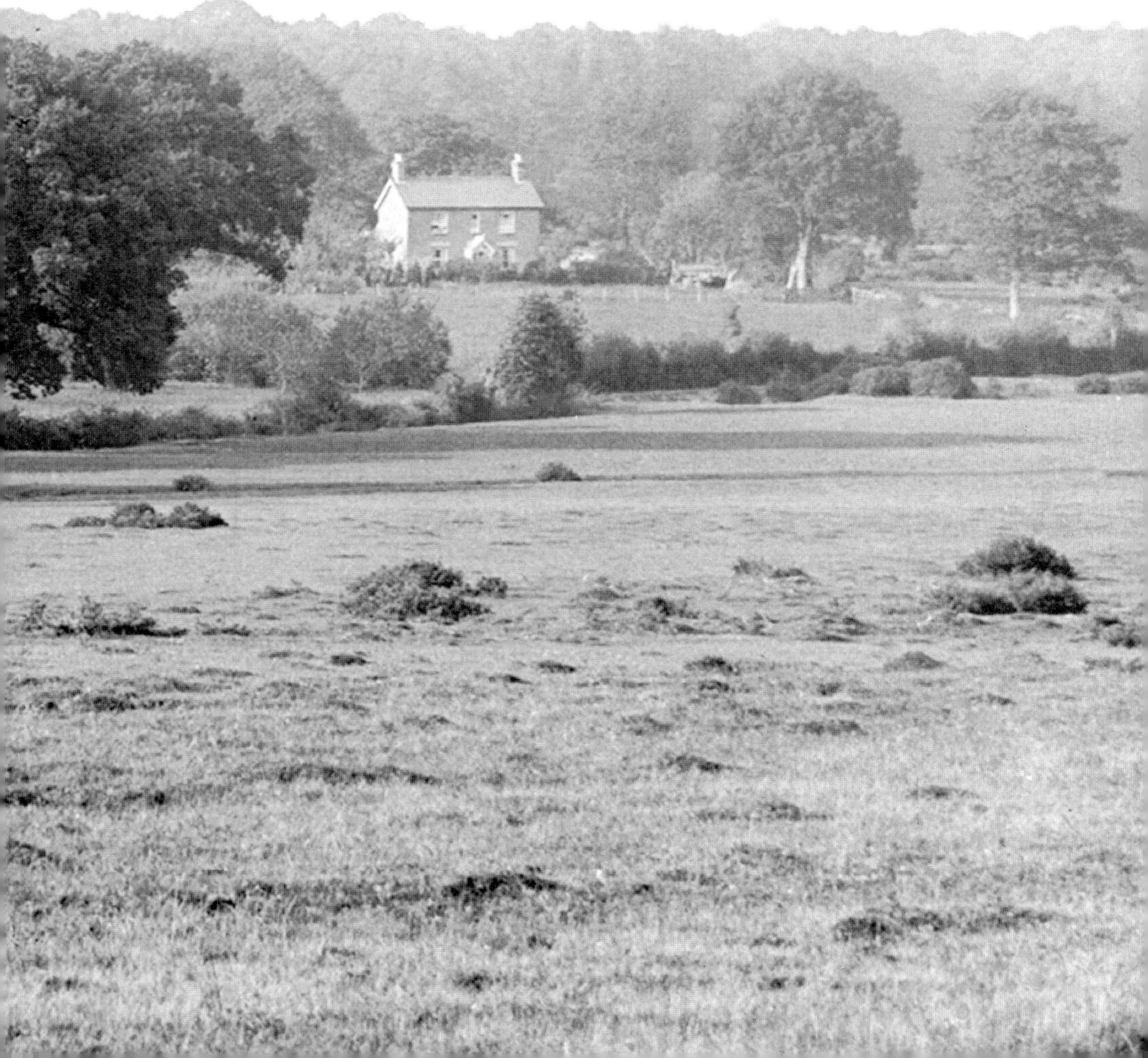

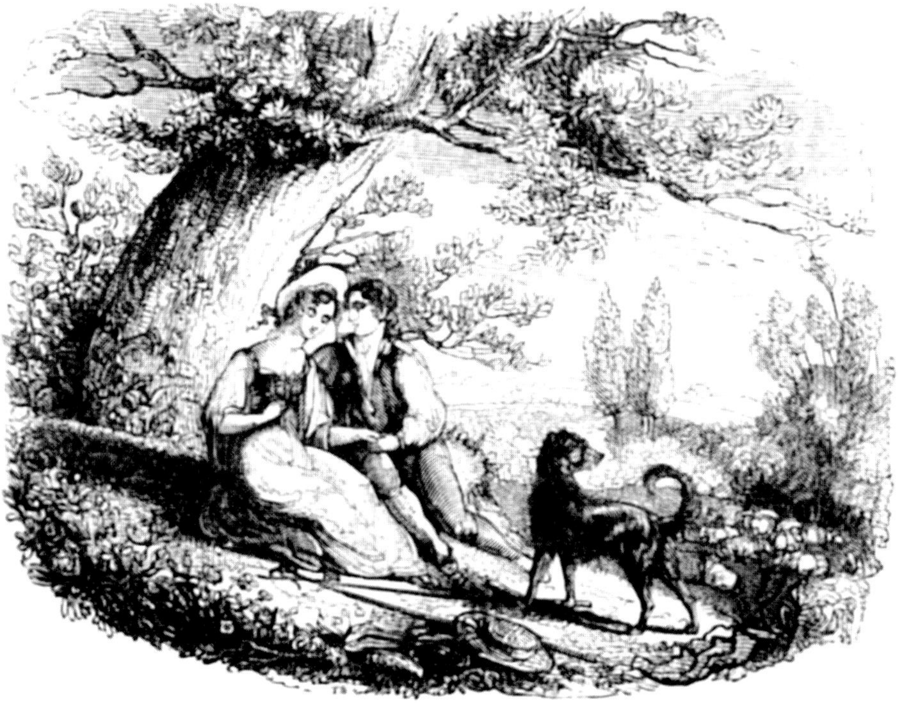

'Oh God! methinks it were a happy life,
To be no better than a homely swain.'

Shakespeare

ON HIGHWAYS & BYWAYS

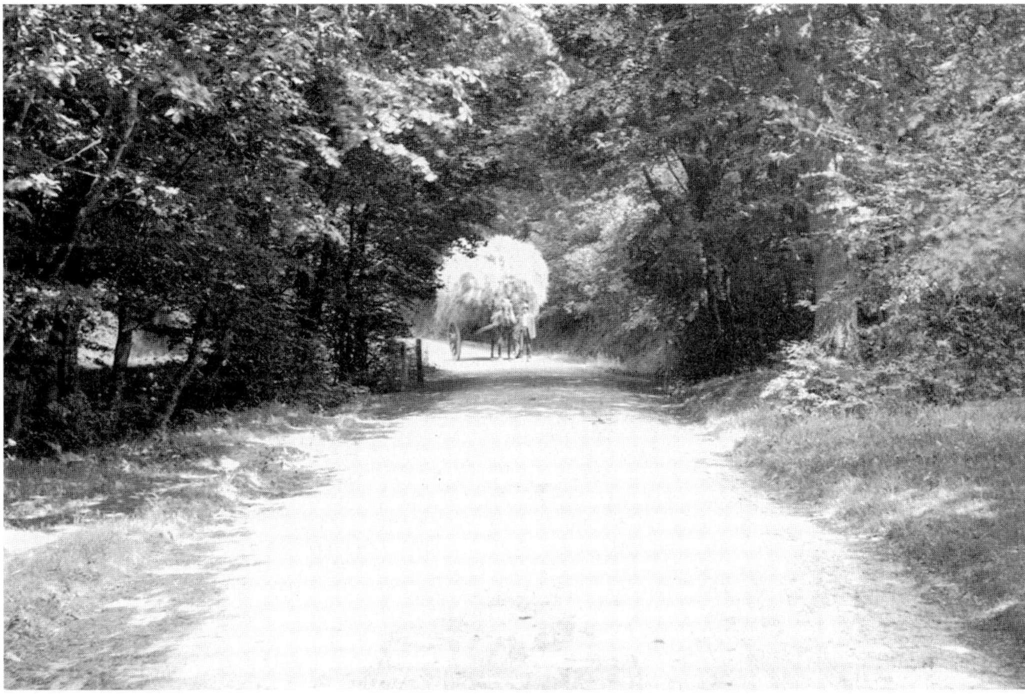

For more than a millennium the horse was the mainstay of Forest transport, in farming and forestry.

Even Hampshire 'Hogs' who lived as recently as the early 20th Century could never have imagined that the day would come when Forest folk think nothing of commuting daily to London. Get up early and see how even the quietest side-road disgorges its fleet of frustrated limos through the best 'rat runs', while some residents use unnecessarily powerful, 'statement' 4x4s which will never go off-road to make unnecessary journeys such as extremely short school runs. Quite a contrast from the days when Dad cycled ten miles each way to earn £3 a week on the forestry, when Grandad walked five miles for a meagre ten bob on the farm and children commonly walked three miles to school. But for today's city slickers the aggro of modern travel is worth every penny and minute for the few daylight hours they may spend in the Forest, for the chance to live in an environment supposedly more suited to healthy family life. Nowadays, at weekends they ride horses simply for pleasure whereas in Grandad's day the only people who took to the saddle for fun were the 'toffs' out hunting. For the majority the horse was the mainstay of the community, in pulling the plough, extracting timber and taking the cart to market. Admittedly we had an in-between period, when steam powered early agricultural machines and introduced Sleepy Hollow to the railway, but that mere 100 years from the mid-19th to mid-20th centuries is long gone, consigned to the dream time. Whether it's in the air over the Forest, on the sea bordering it or on road and rail through it, the new God is six-cylindered and, despite new speed restrictions, ponies still die on Forest roads.

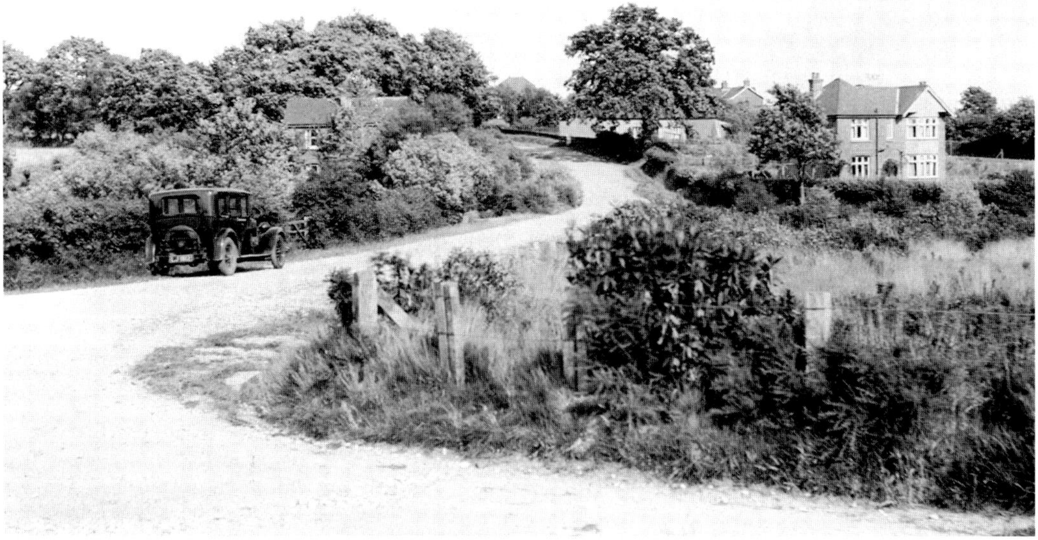

With each section cared for by a lengthman, unsurfaced roads, such as here at Verwood, coped well with the light traffic of the early 1900s.

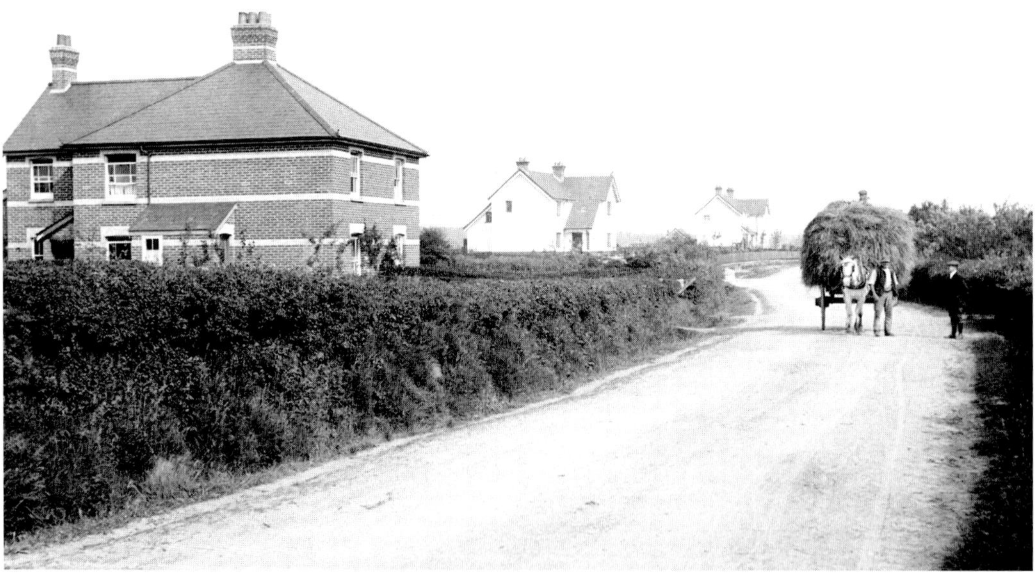

A ride on the haycart, on the way home to Verwood.

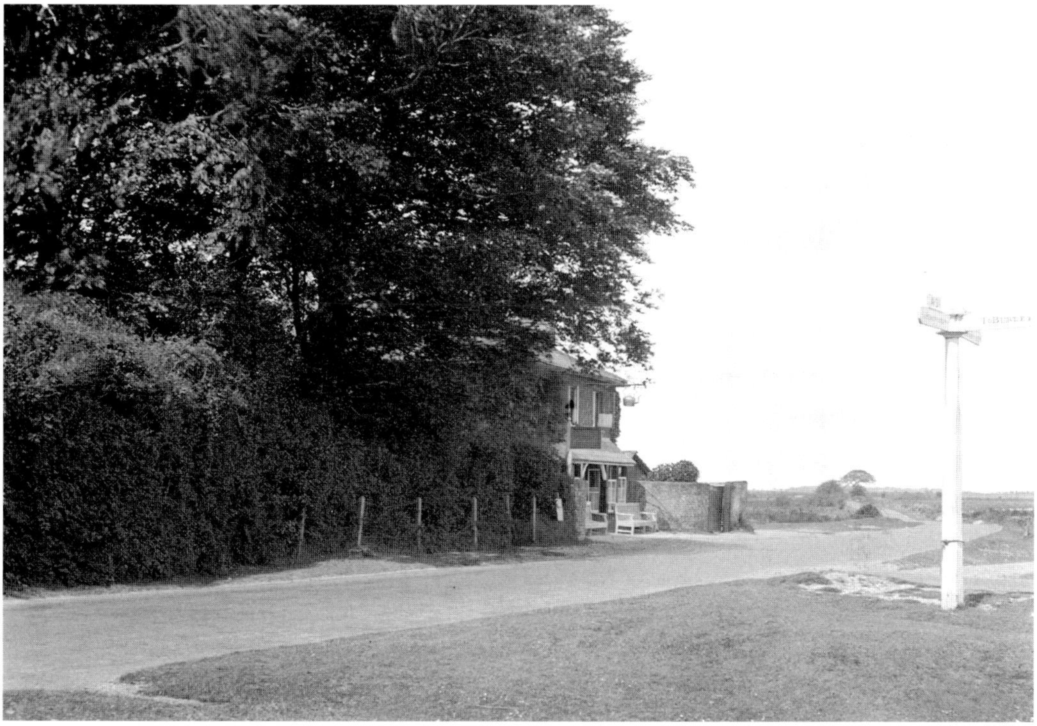

Intriguing sign and seats at Picket Post, suggesting that tea might be taken on the run in to Ringwood.

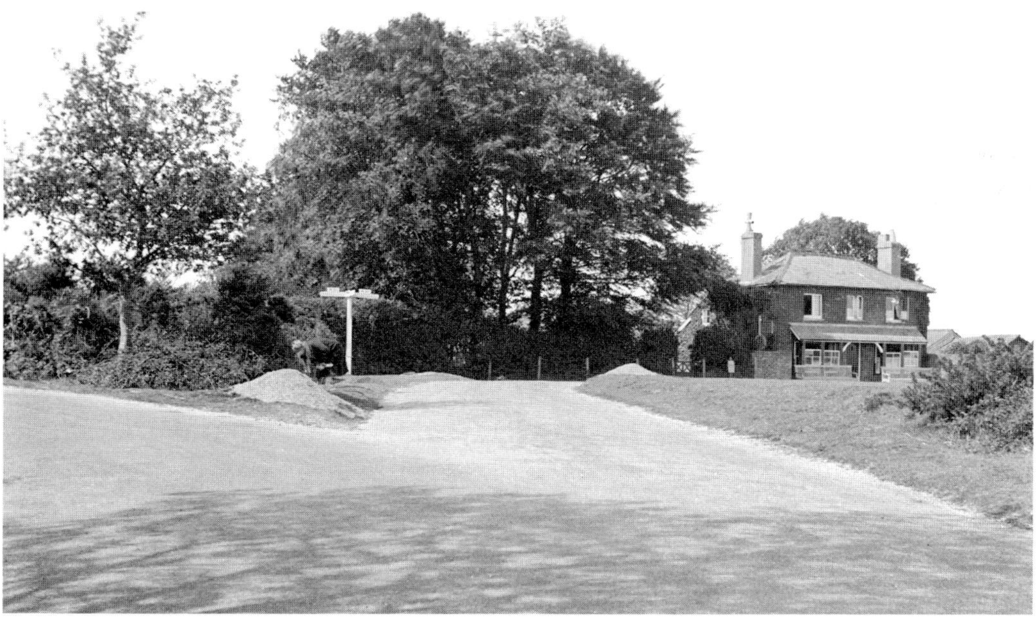

As the Forest was opened up roads were improved and better maintained, such as here at Burley.

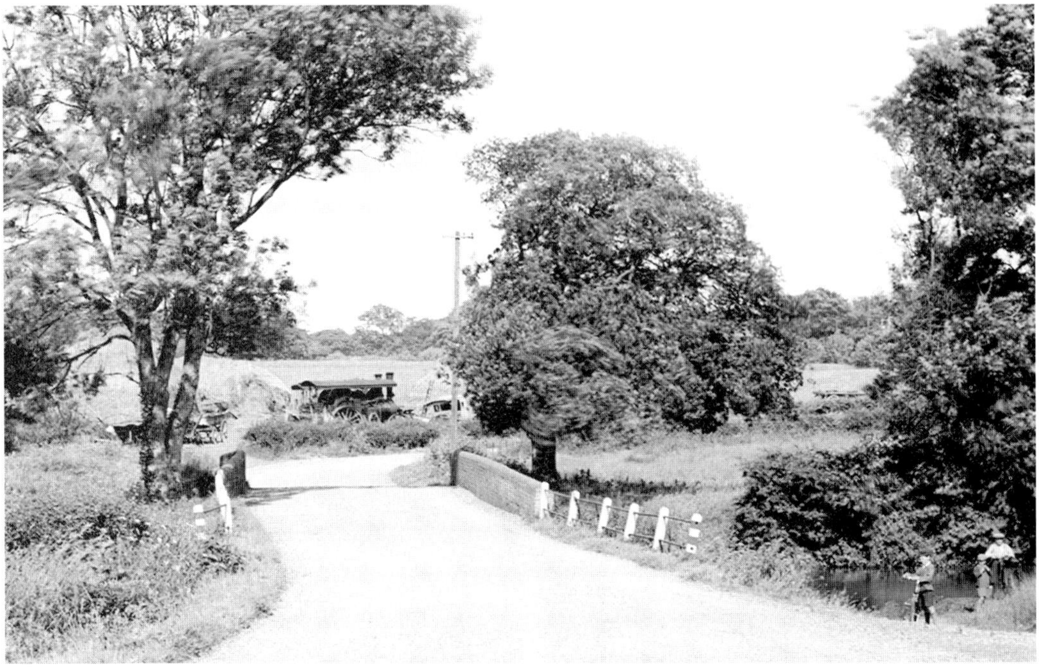

Boys cycle out to play by the stream at Verwood, while early steam-driven farm machinery grinds away in the background.

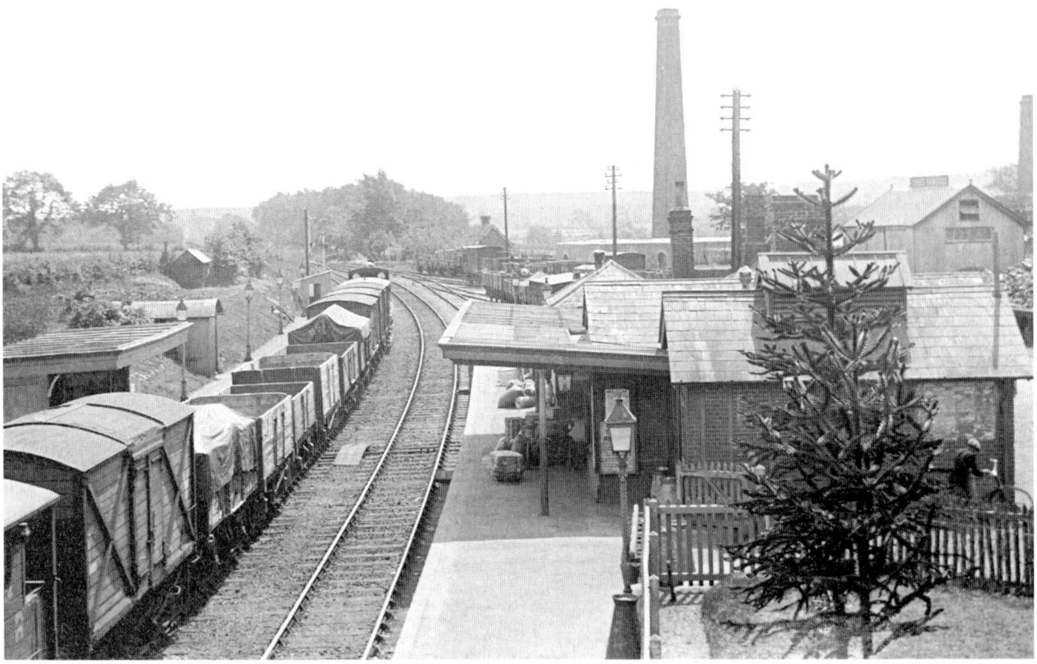

Above The arrival of the railway, in the 19th Century, brought rapid change to villages such as Verwood, nurturing land development and the birth of commuting.

Right Pause for a chat at Verwood, when most country folk still thought nothing of walking miles every day.

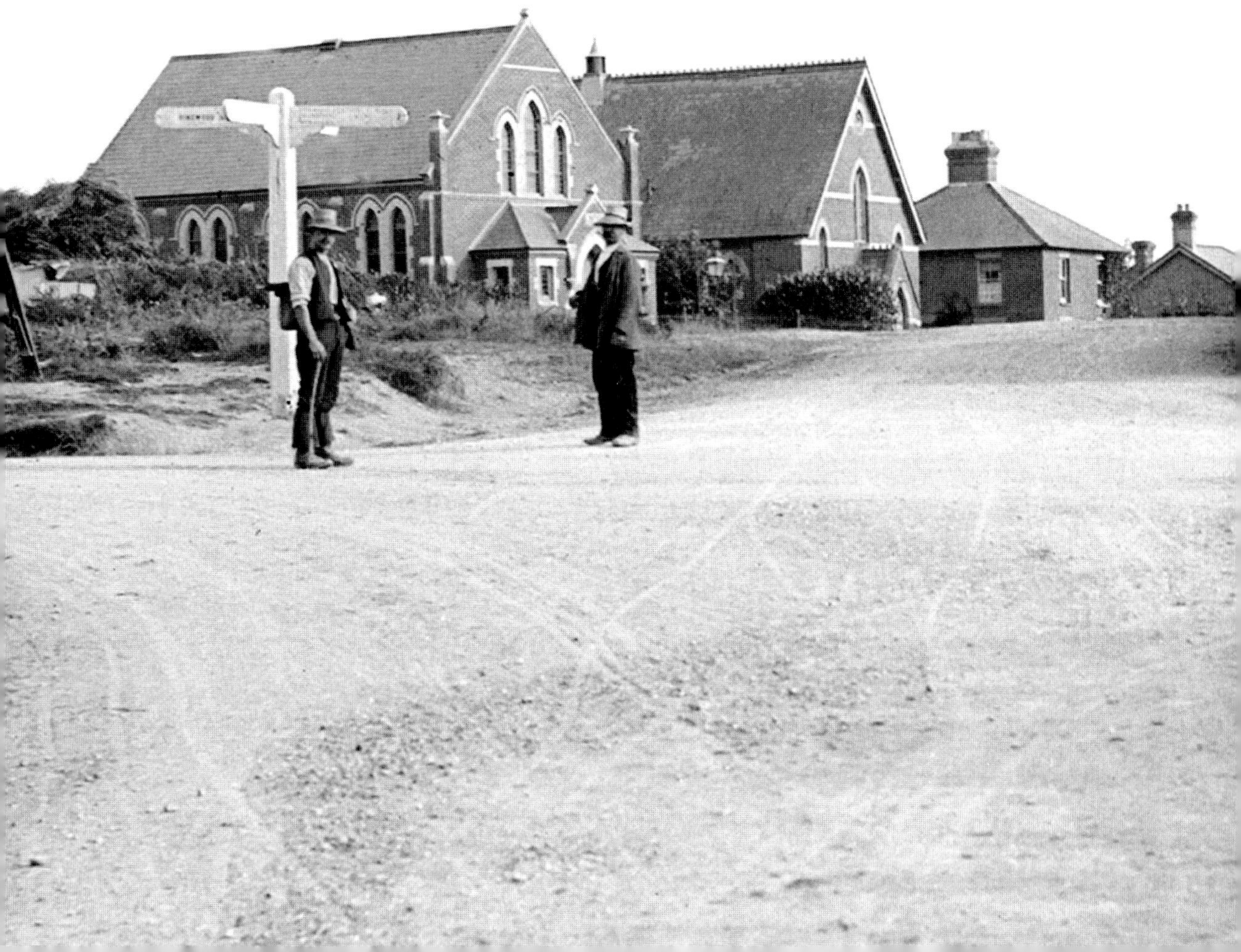

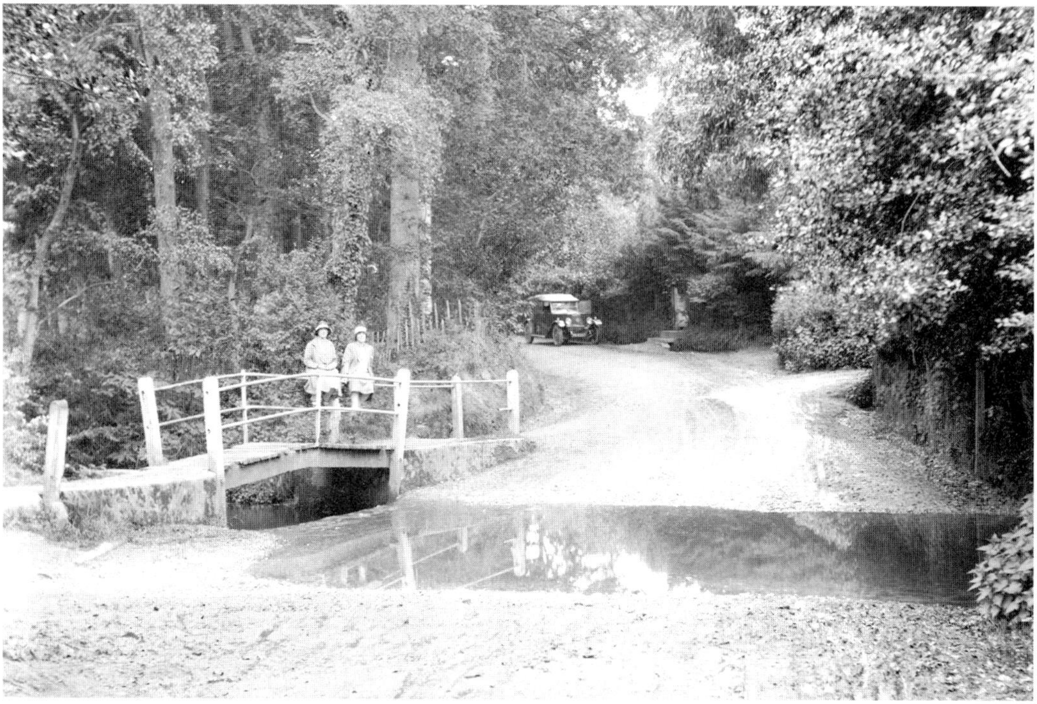

Fords, such as here at New Milton, have long posed a problem to motor traffic, especially earlier, less well-sealed cars.

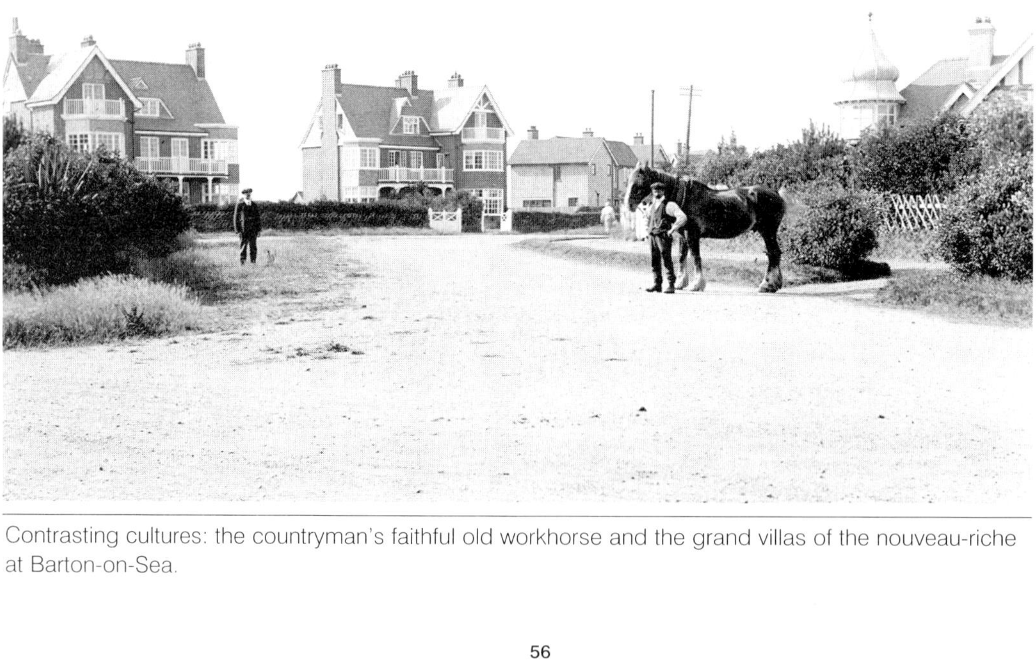

Contrasting cultures: the countryman's faithful old workhorse and the grand villas of the nouveau-riche at Barton-on-Sea.

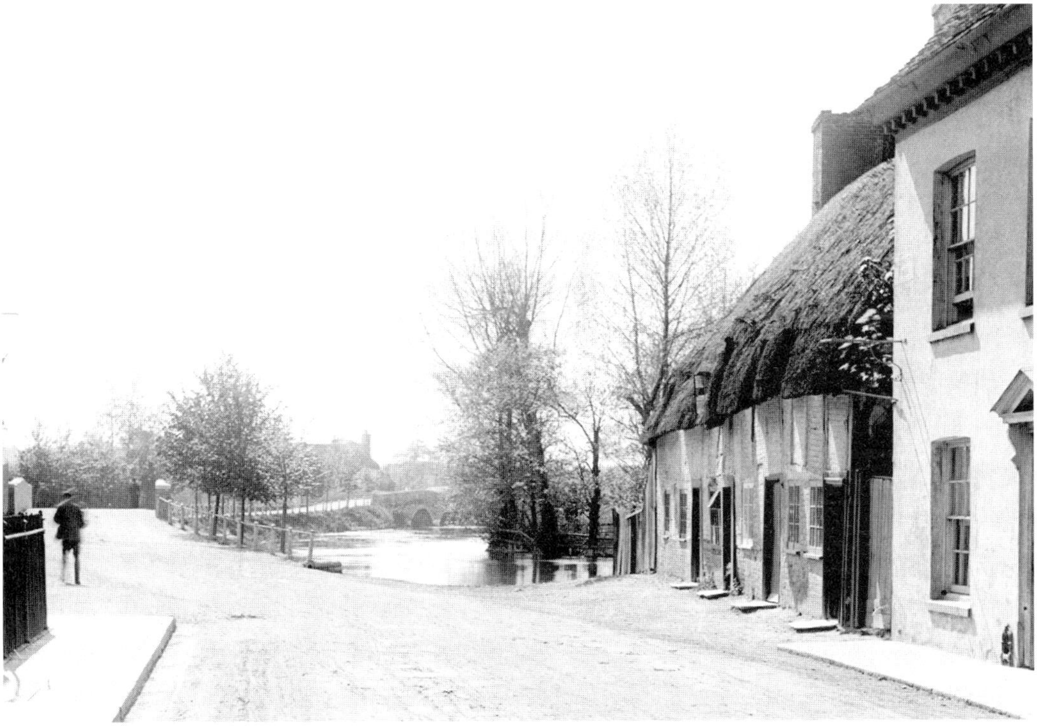

By the Avon at Ringwood, when thatch was common and even town roads were still unsurfaced.

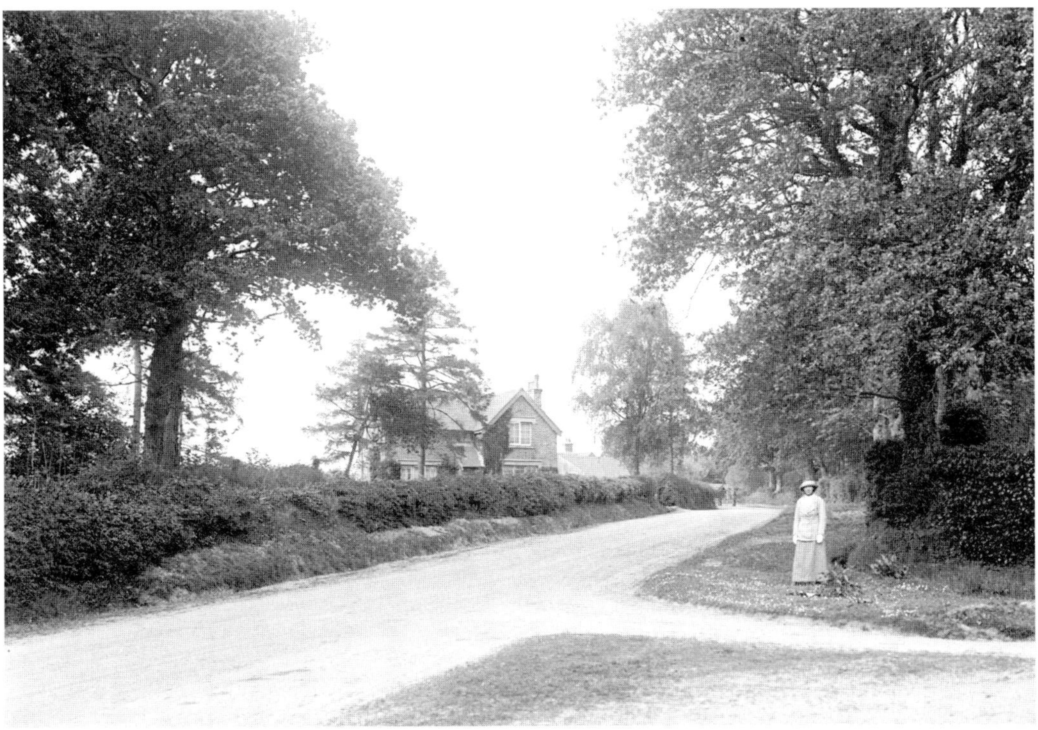

Was this the photographer's wife helping to focus on Bransgore?

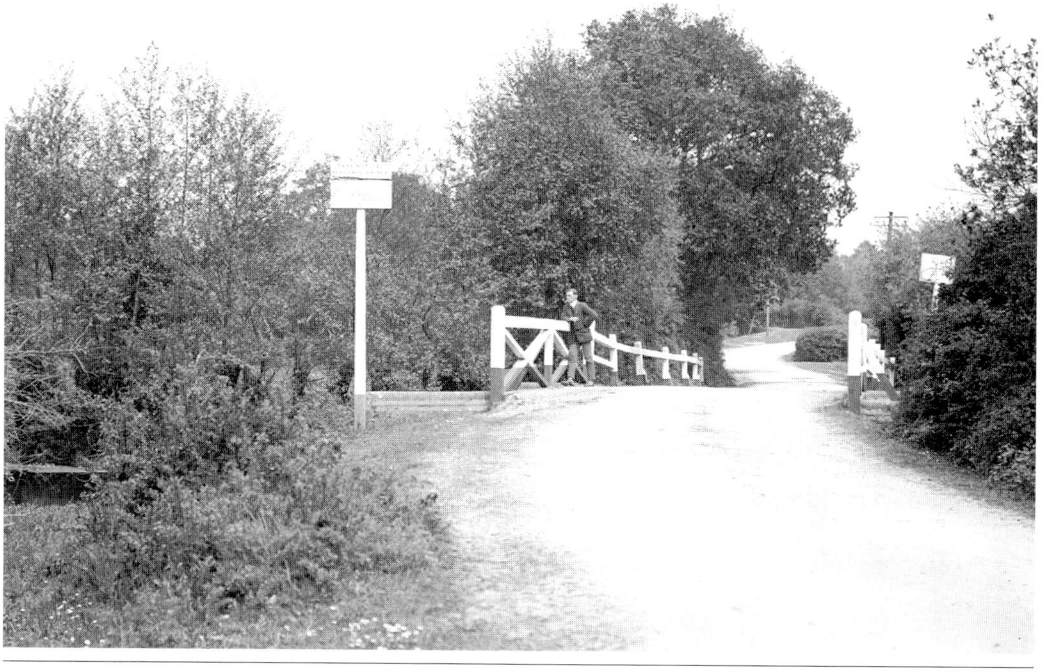

Early bridges, such as this one at Mead Ends, Sway, could not have coped with the weight of modern traffic.

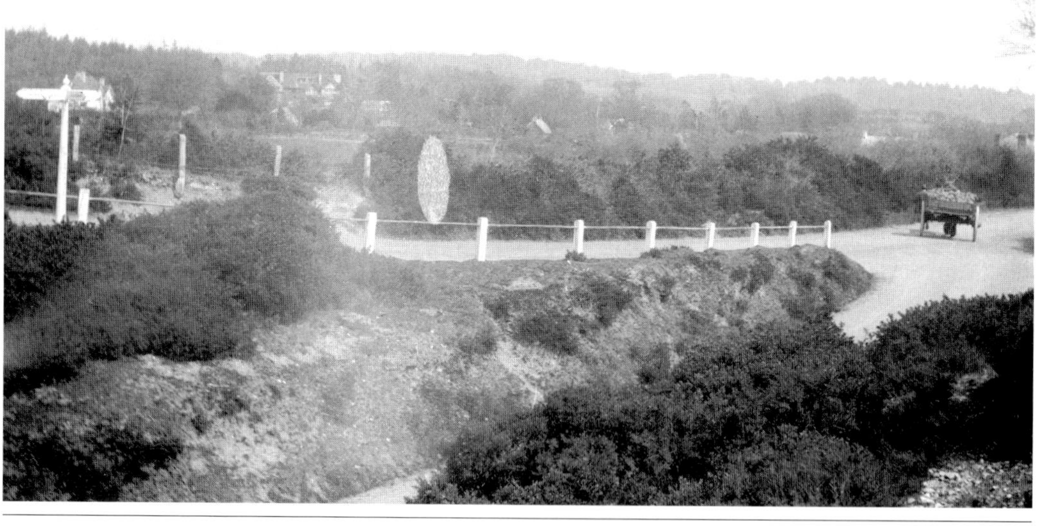

The village of Burley takes its name from Saxon words meaning 'the fortified village in the clearing', referring to an Iron Age camp on Castle Hill.

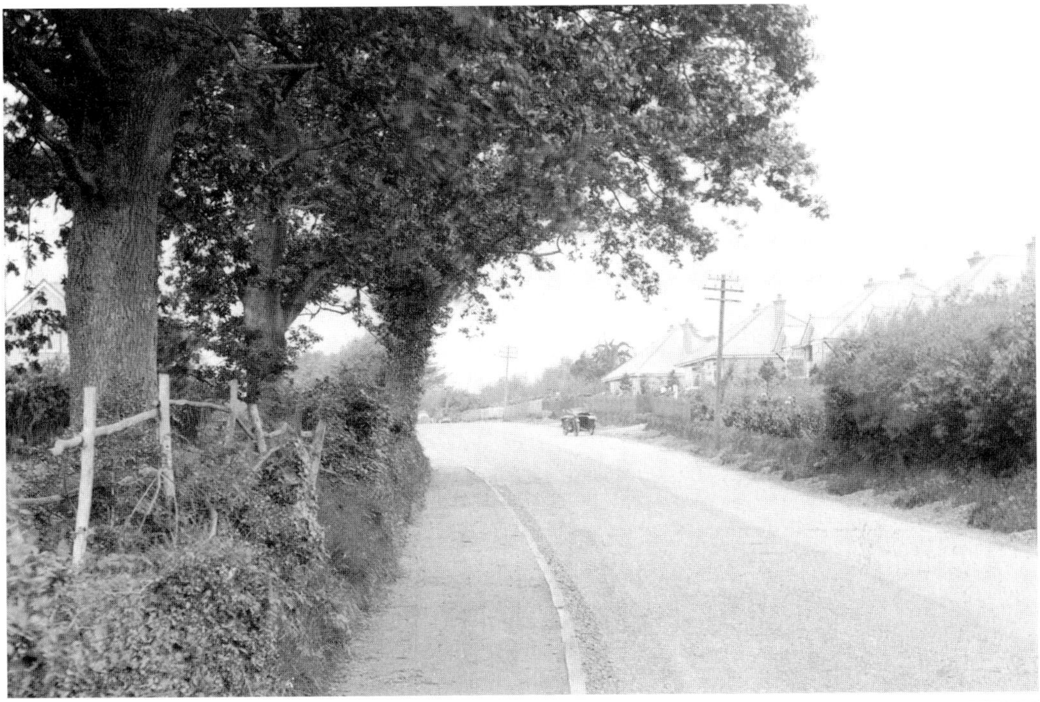

Seen here at Verwood, the motorbike and sidecar became a popular means of transport between the wars.

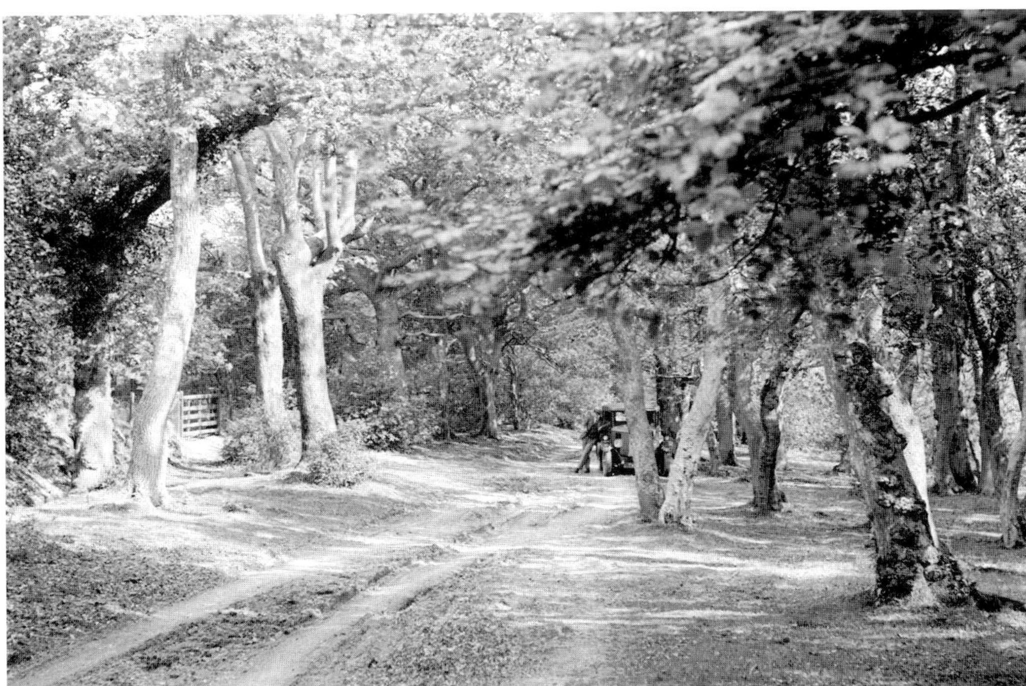

The introduction of the motor car enabled the curious to explore more deeply the ancient woods and byways.

'The mighty roar
That rushes through the forest hoar
When winds are piping loud.'

Miss Bowles

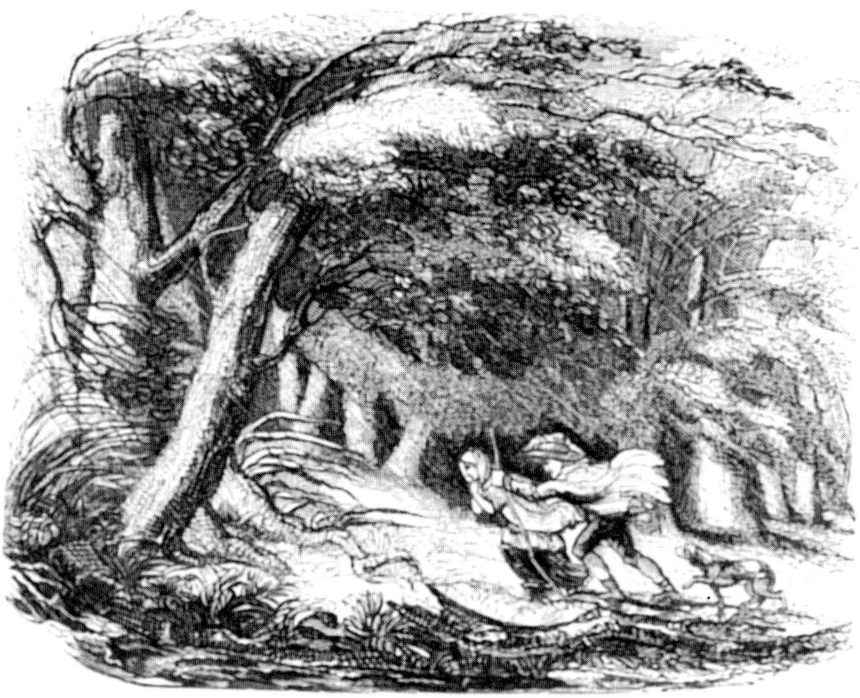

FROM PUBS TO PULPITS

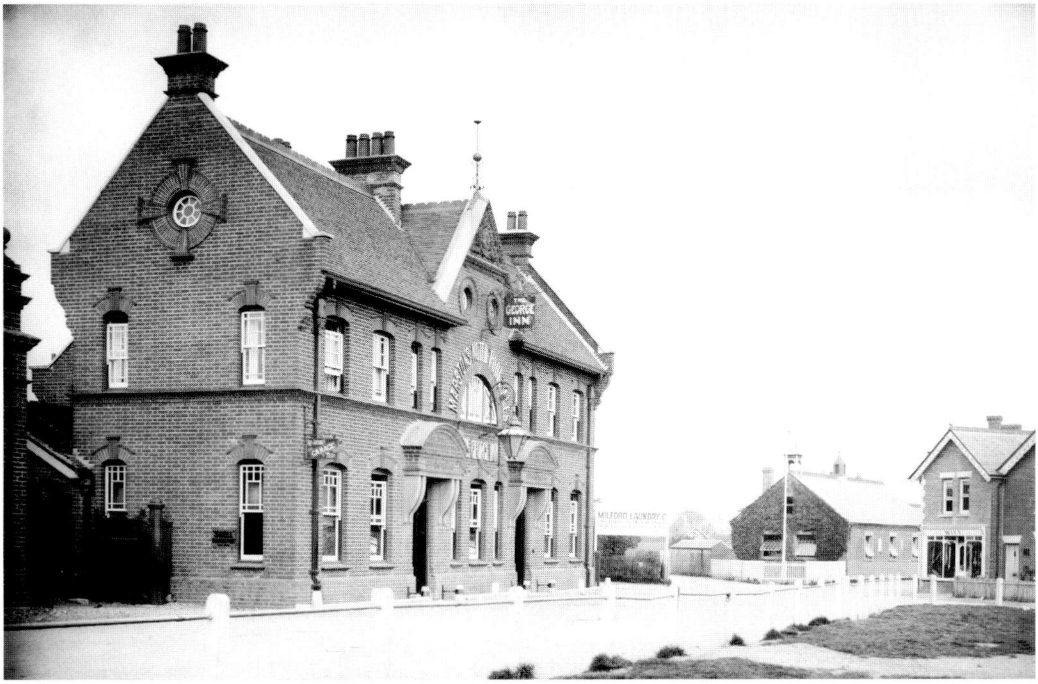

The splendid George Inn at New Milton, a listed building, is now closed.

Although not particularly grand, the Forest area certainly has an interesting architectural heritage, dating back well over a thousand years. Some of the churches pre-date the Domesday Book and establishment of the Forest itself, when the district was known by the Saxon name of Ytene, meaning a furzy waste. Traces of Roman occupation are found on the borders but no Roman villa has been unearthed within the Forest itself; suggesting that, despite proximity to the coast, its wilds were never attractive enough for significant early settlement. There appears to be no truth in the legend that William the Conqueror destroyed many villages and manors to make way for hunting. Indeed, it is likely that the number of churches and villages remained much the same right up to modern times, when many have been swamped by neighbouring towns. Some were spoilt by rapid development at the beginning of the 20th Century, when so many ancient thatched cottages were demolished to make way for hotels and ostentatious villas, erected to meet the sudden demands of tourism and settlement by the nouveau-riche. Fortuitously, some of the oldest cottages have survived through becoming pubs. Infilling continues, of course, but at least we have increasingly better controls. Among surviving treasures are the almost pure-Tudor village of Breamore, whose church dates back to early Saxon times. At Lyndhurst - virtually the capital of the Forest - is the King's House built by Charles II on the site of an earlier one. Adjoining it is the old Court House where, ominously flanked by a mediaeval dock, Verderers meet regularly with the Deputy Surveyor to sort out disputes between Crown and commoners.

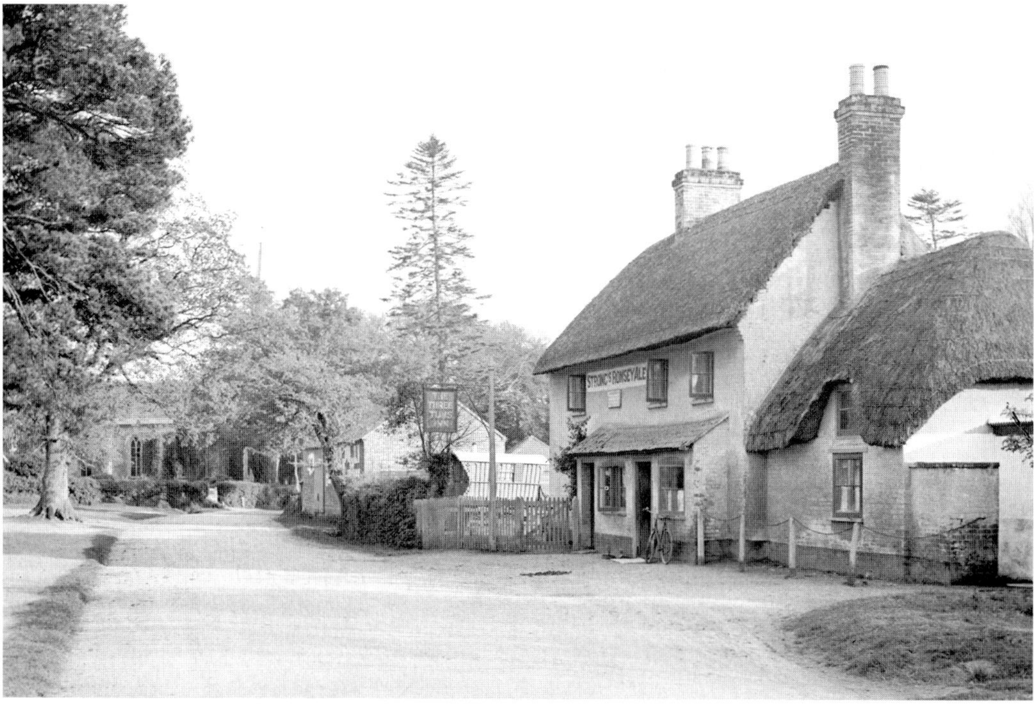

The pretty Three Tuns at Bransgore, where beer used to be made on the premises, has been a pub since the 1600s, or possibly earlier.

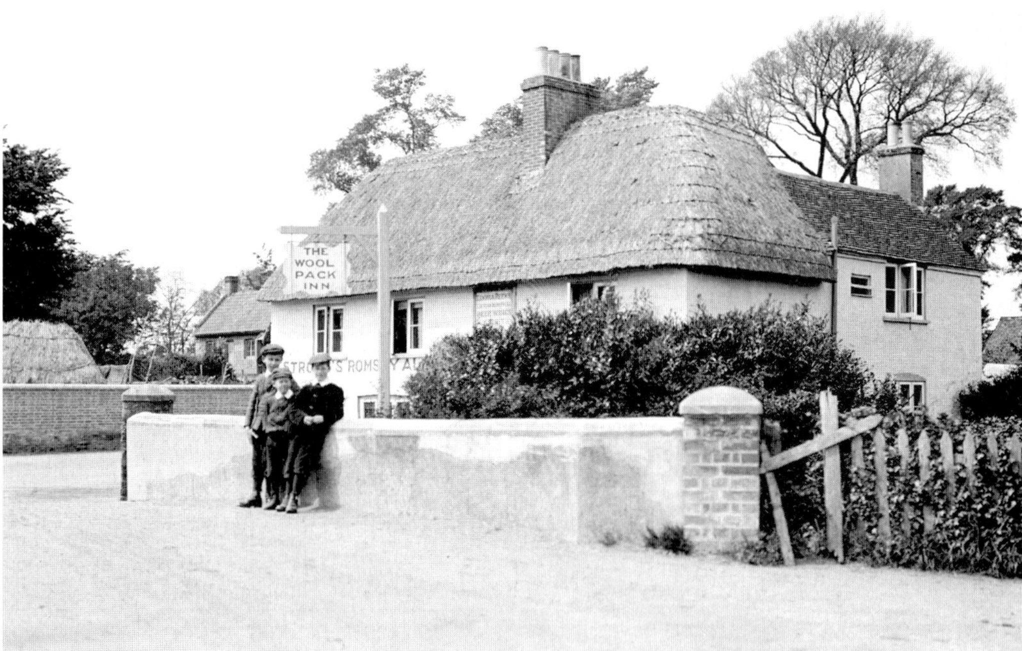

Originally a private house, the Woolpack, Sopley, became an inn in 1725. Among its many famous visitors was Greta Garbo, and Winston Churchill met Roosevelt there during the War.

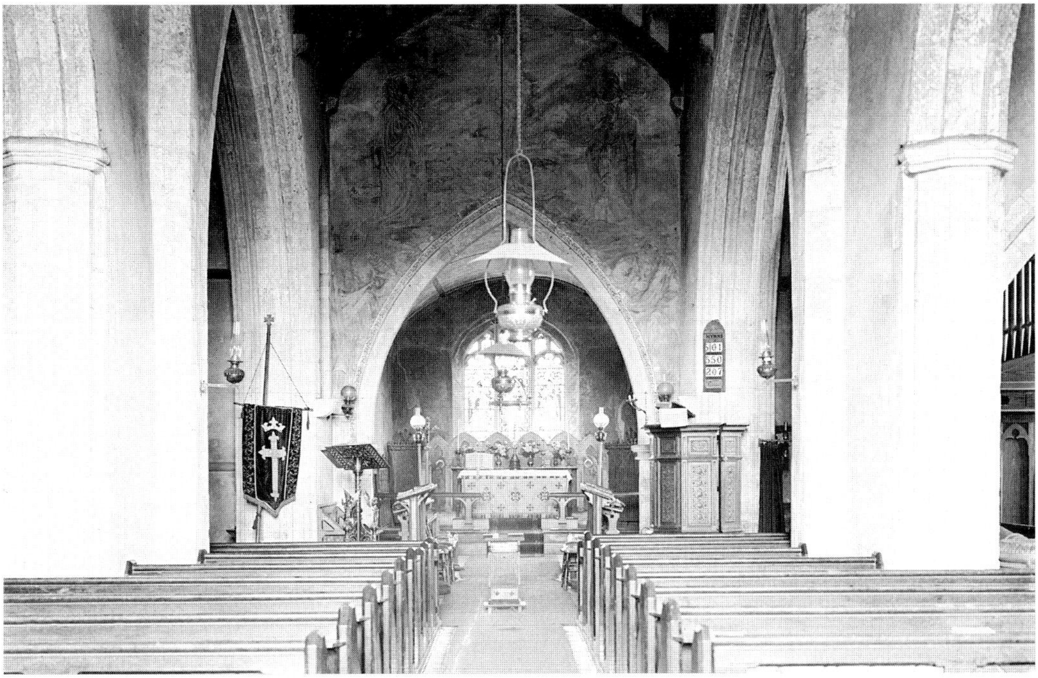

Built in the 13th Century on the site of a Saxon church, The Church of St Michael & All Angels, Sopley, has a fine 1604 strapwork pulpit.

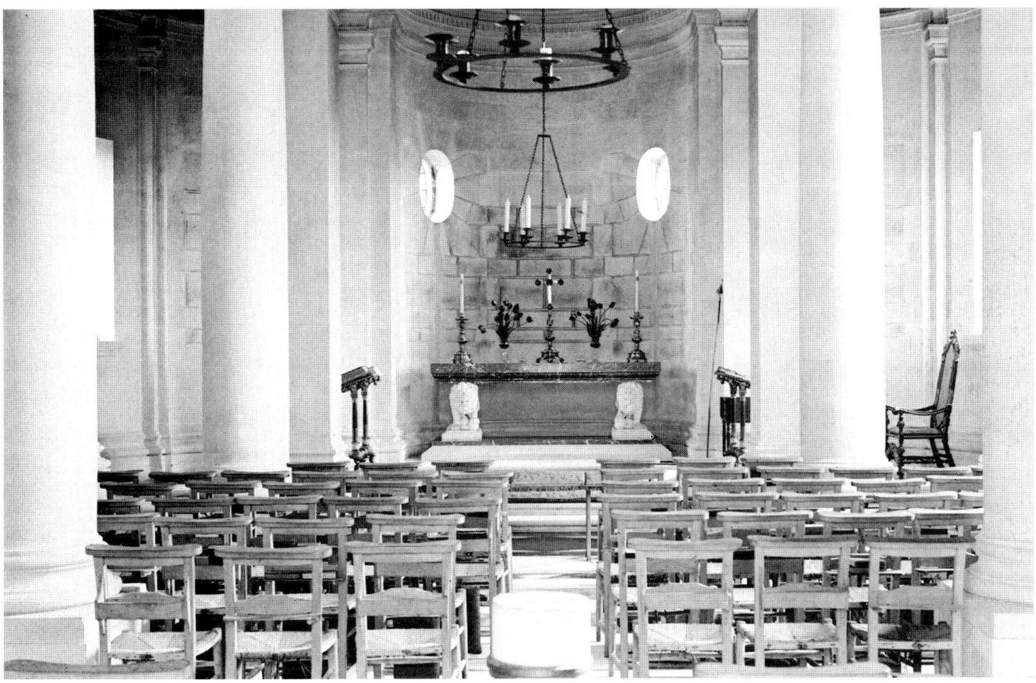

Above The Baroque-style church of All Saints, Thorney Hill, was built in 1908 by the 3rd Lord Manners at the considerable cost of £5,601; in memory of his daughter.

Next page The handsome Crown Hotel at Lyndhurst was built in 1897, but an inn has stood on the site since the 1600s.

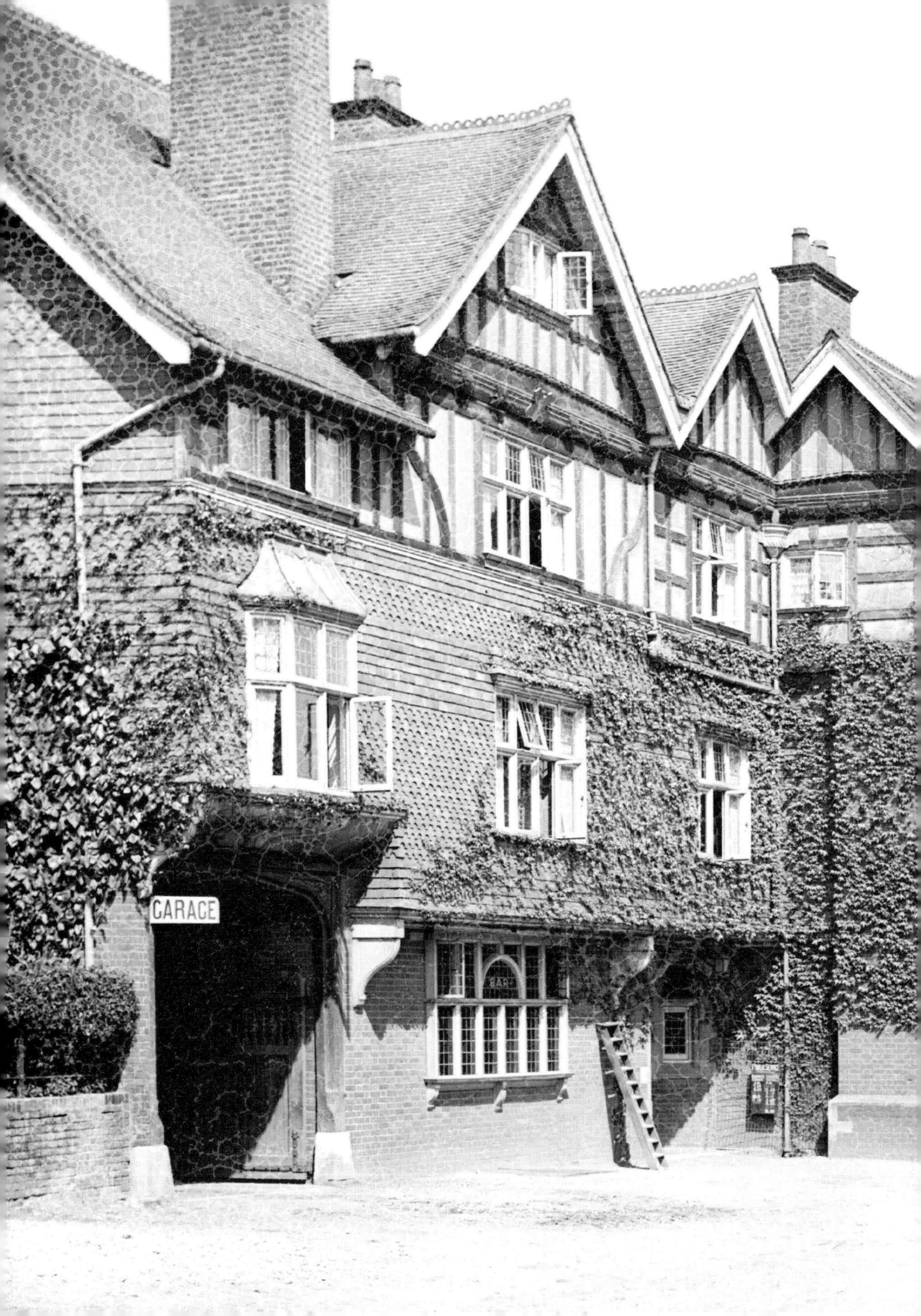
GARAGE
BAR

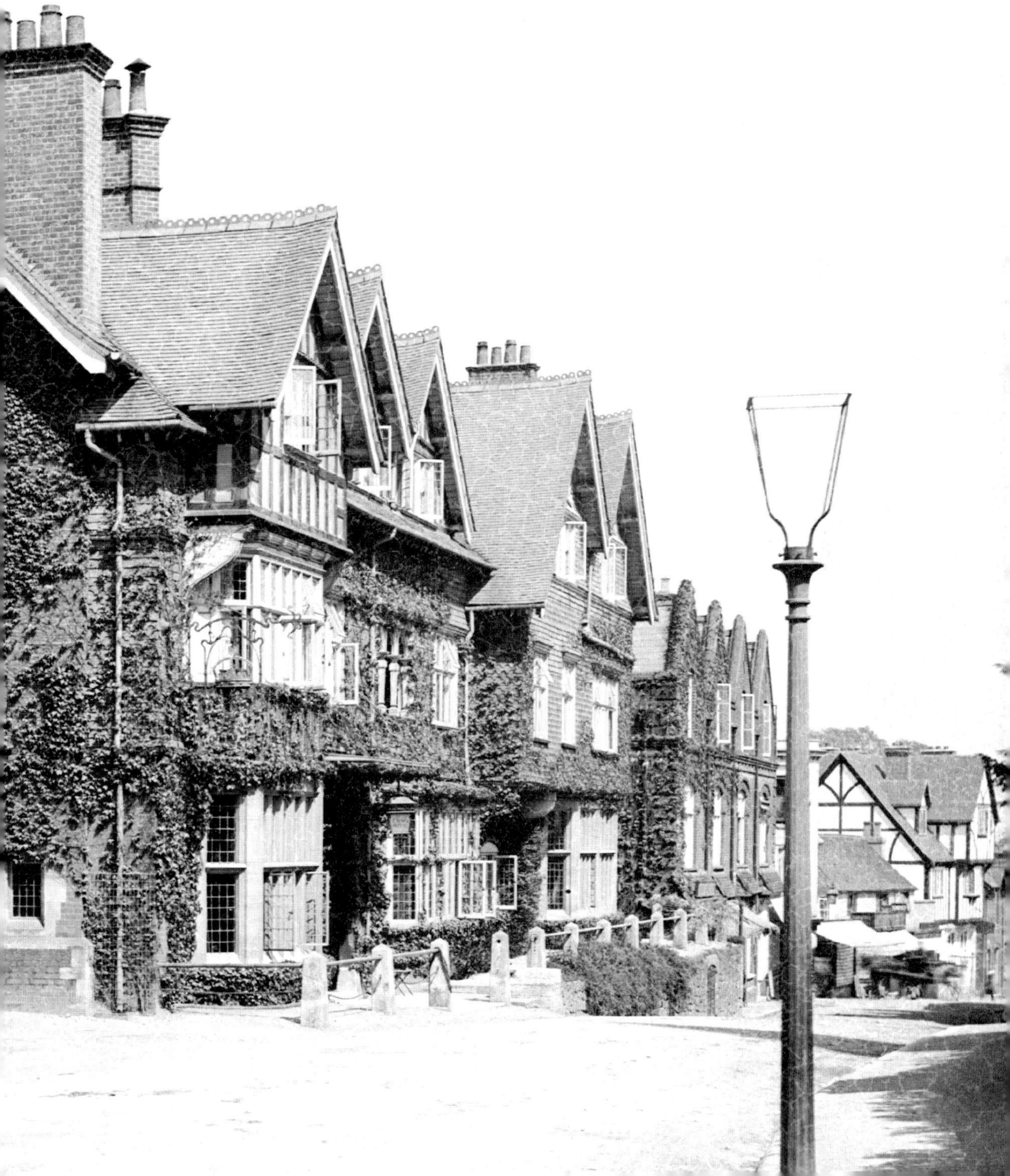

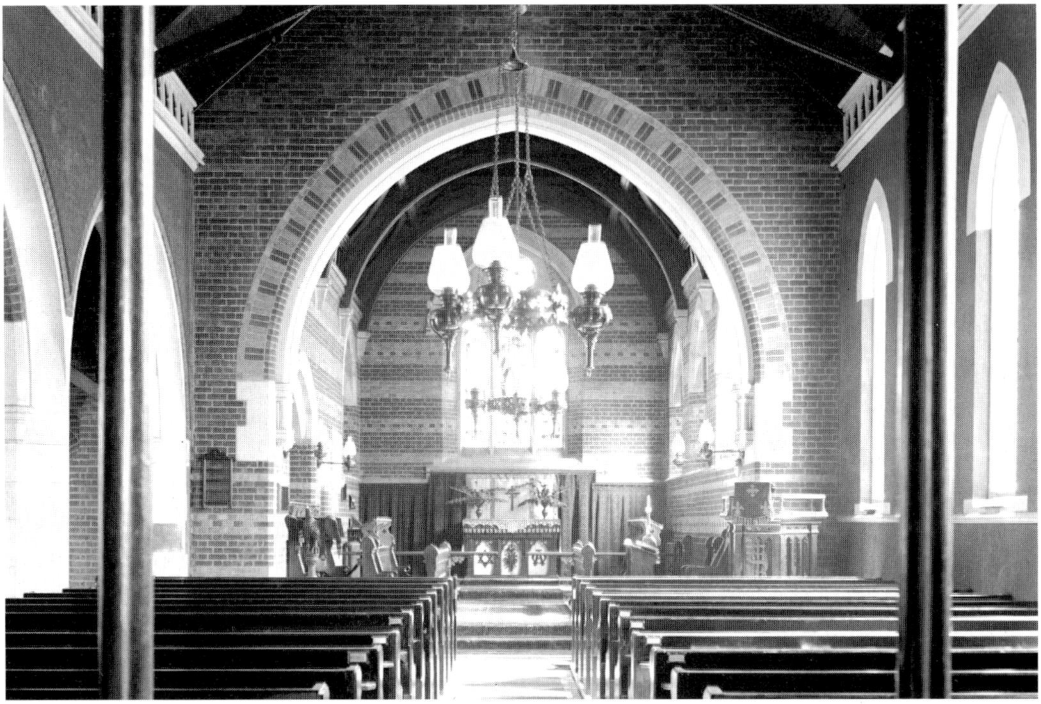

St Luke's Church, Sway has often been adorned with a wealth of wild flowers, which abound in the Forest borderlands.

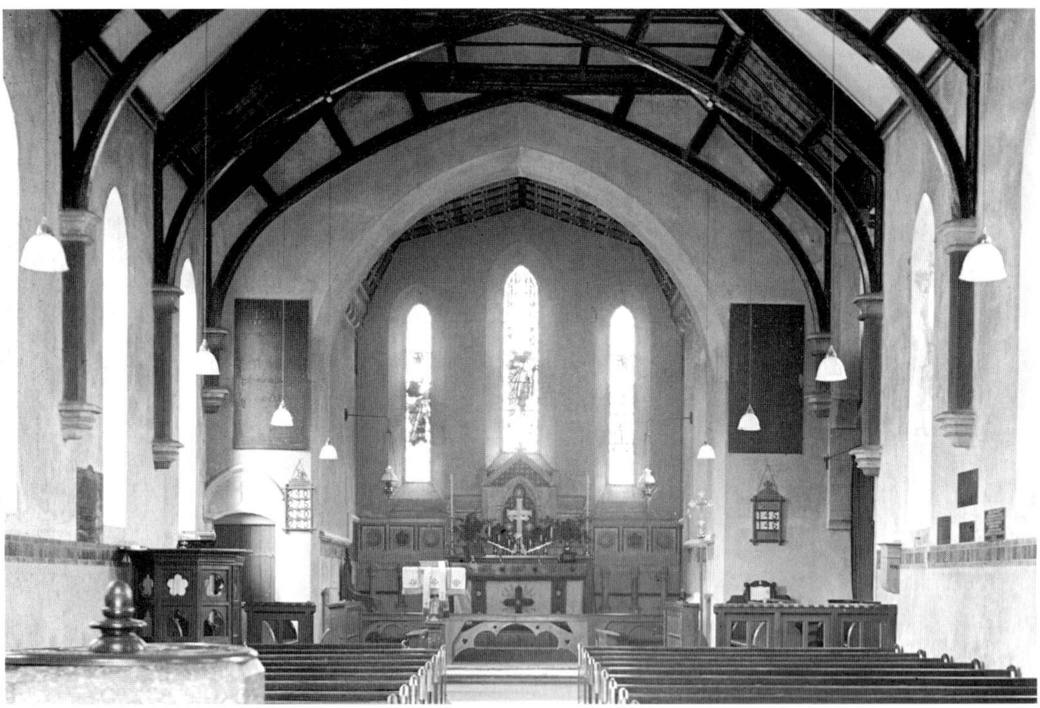

The church of St John the Baptist, Burley has changed considerably since it was consecrated in 1839. The earliest stained glass dates from the restoration of 1886.

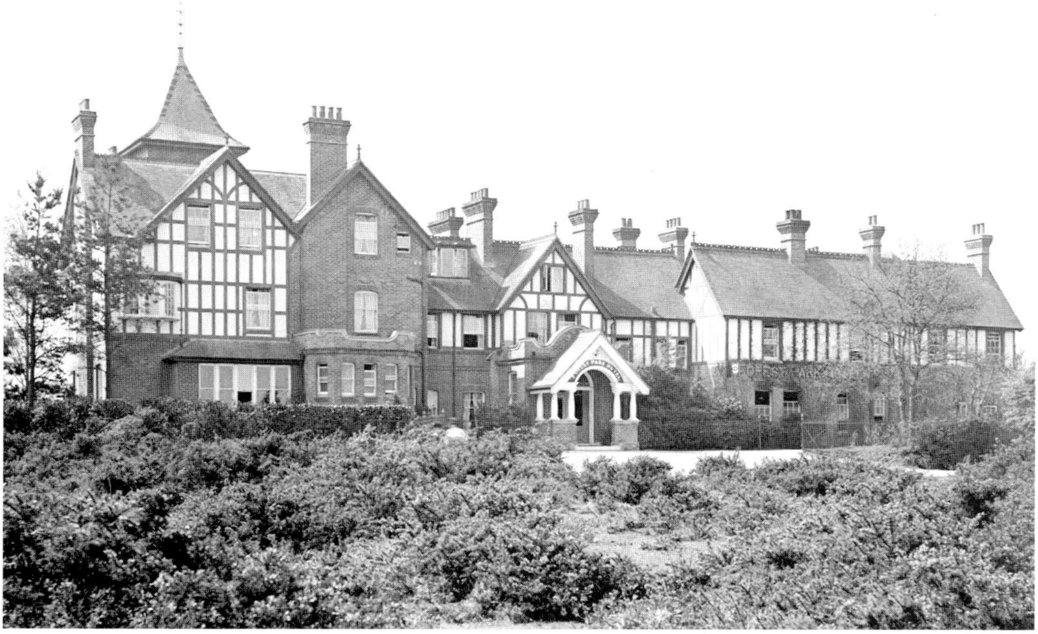

Built as a vicarage in 1879, Brockenhurst's Forest Park Hotel opened to the public in 1902 and was temporarily a hospital during World War I.

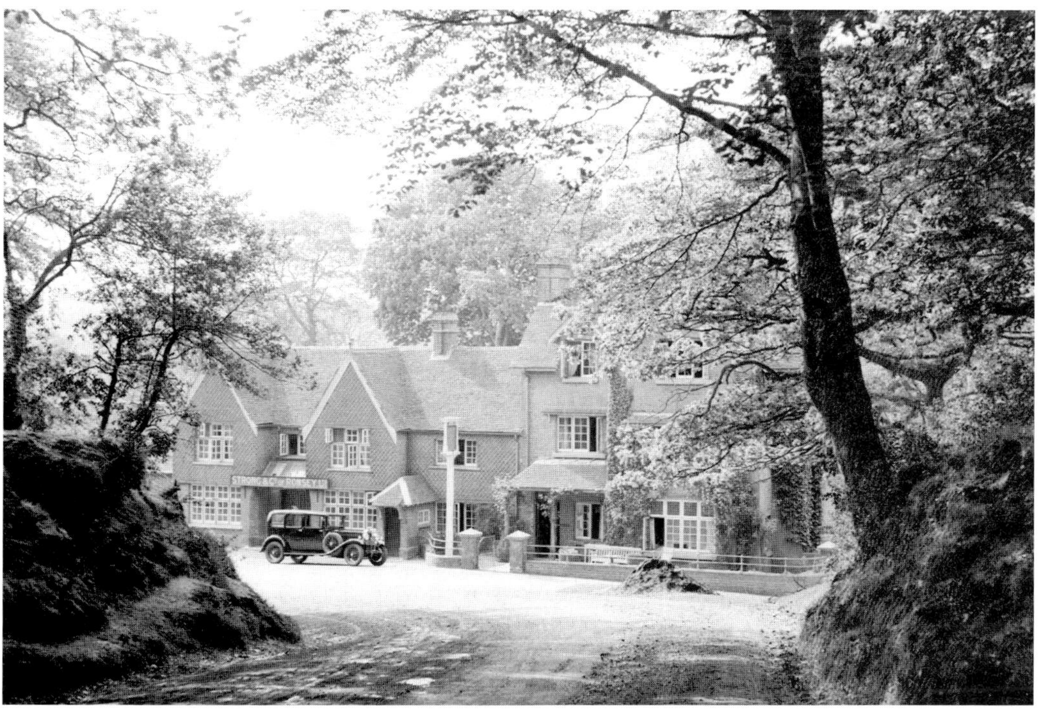

The delightfully situated Queen's Head, Burley dates from 1633 and is the oldest surviving building in the village.

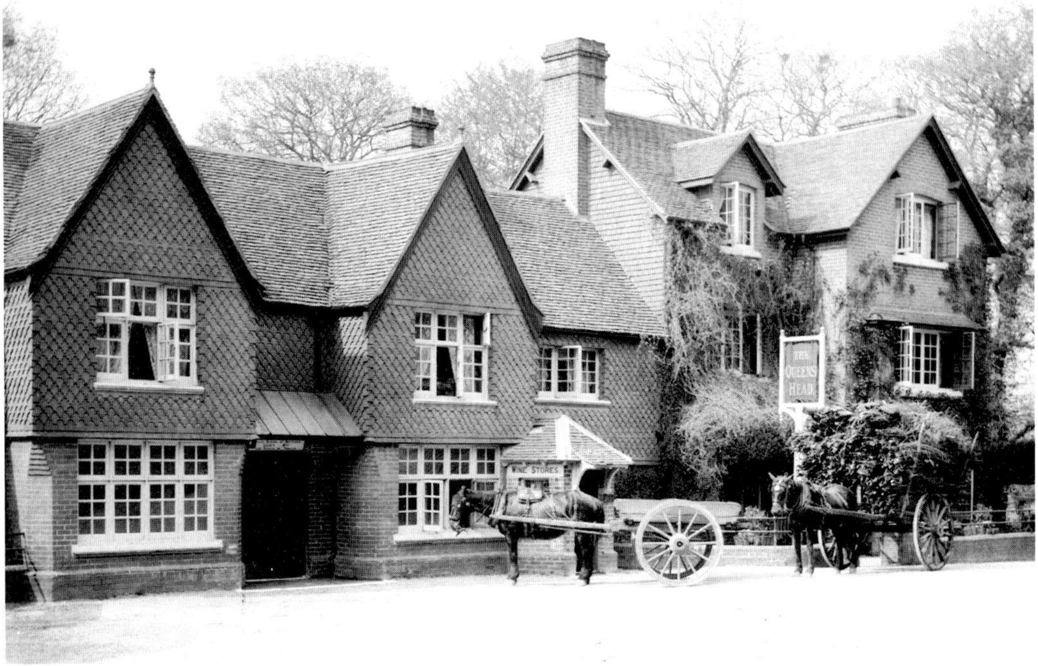

Two horses wait patiently while their owners slake their thirst at the Queen's Head Burley, or are the faggots being delivered there?

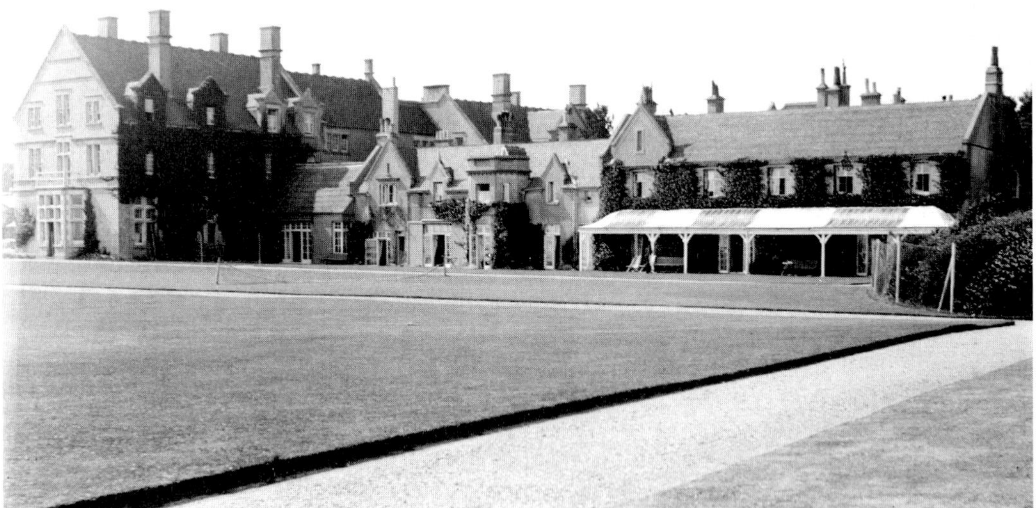

Barton Court, Barton-on-Sea.

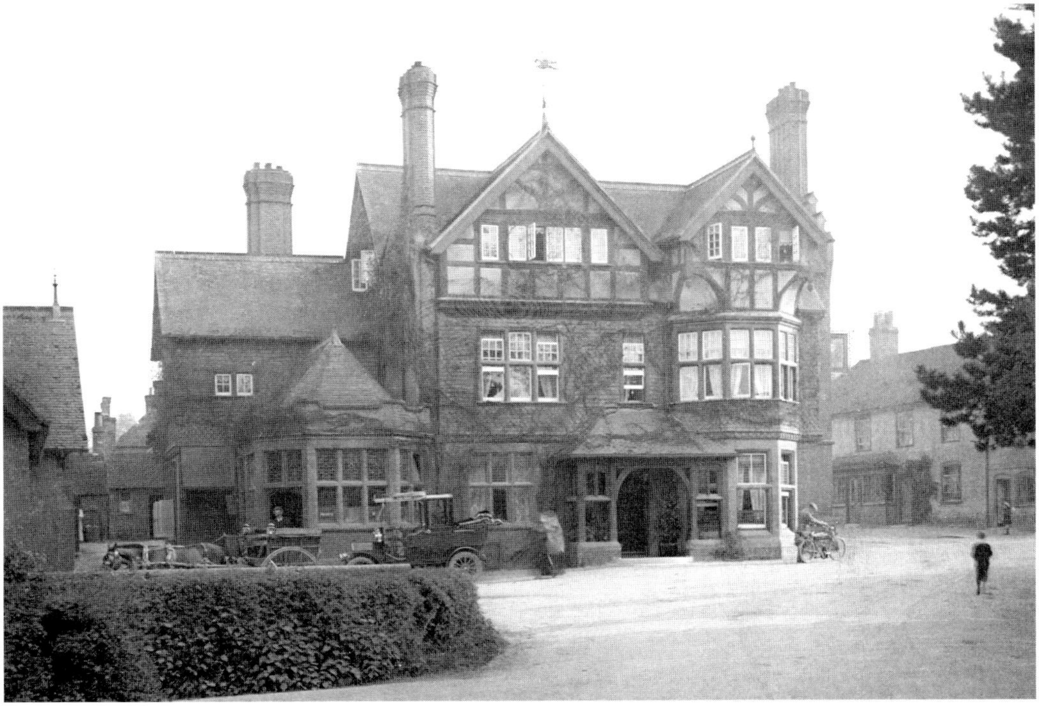

Dating from the 16th Century, the picturesque, creeper-clad Montagu Arms, Beaulieu, was substantially enlarged in the 19th Century.

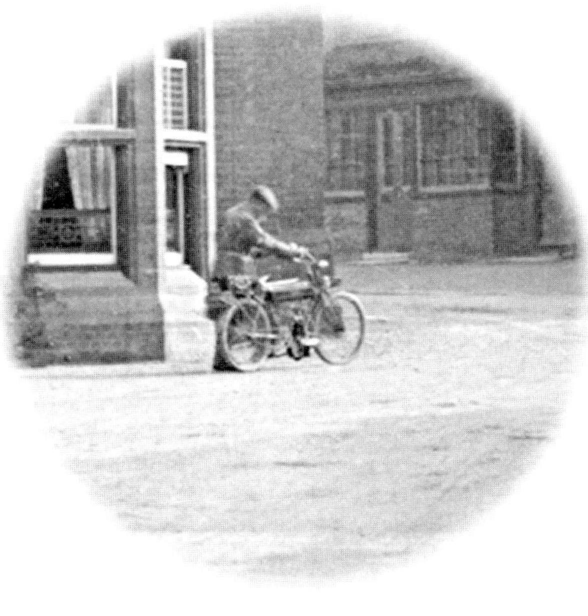

We hope the motor cyclist wasn't drinking and driving.

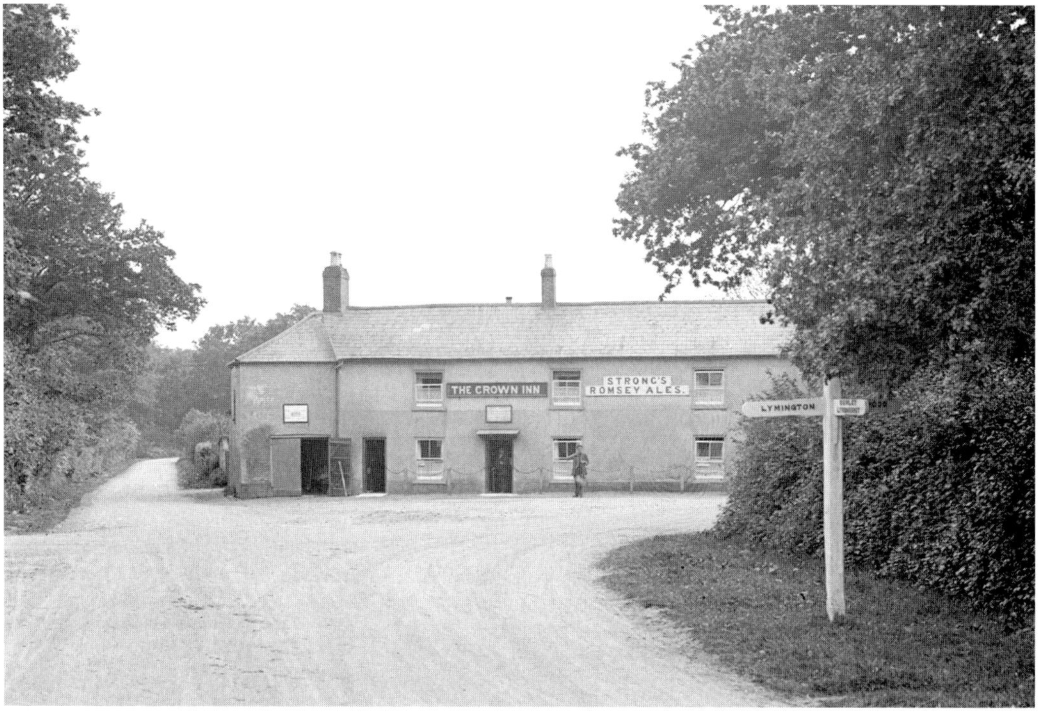

The front of the Crown Inn, Bransgore, was built in 1802 and in the early 1900s the pub was owned by Romsey brewery Strong & Co.

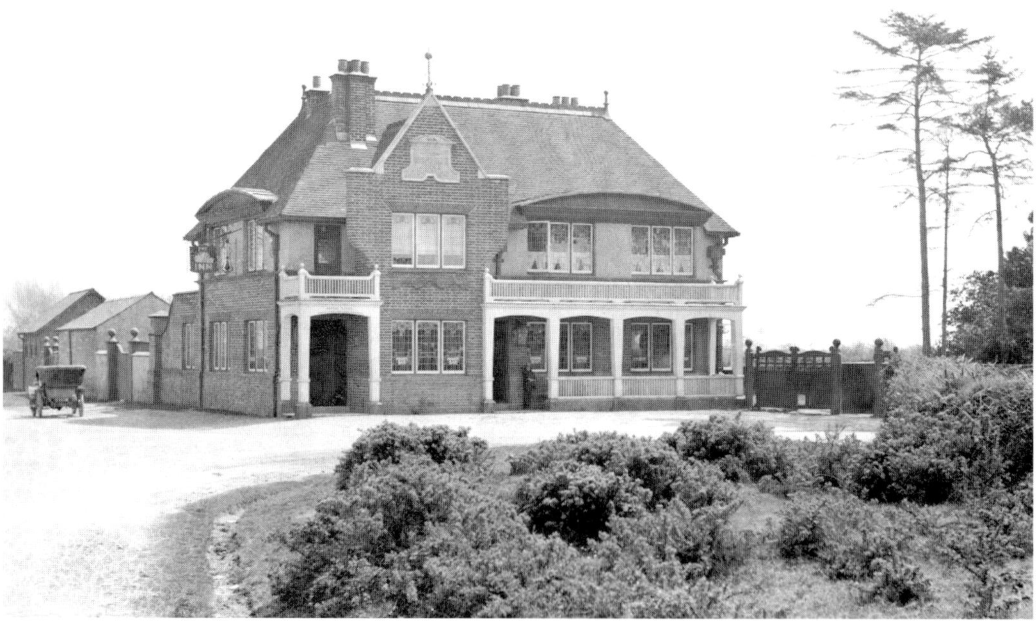

Re-built in 1904, the Rising Sun Inn, at Bashley, is said to have been the haunt of smugglers.

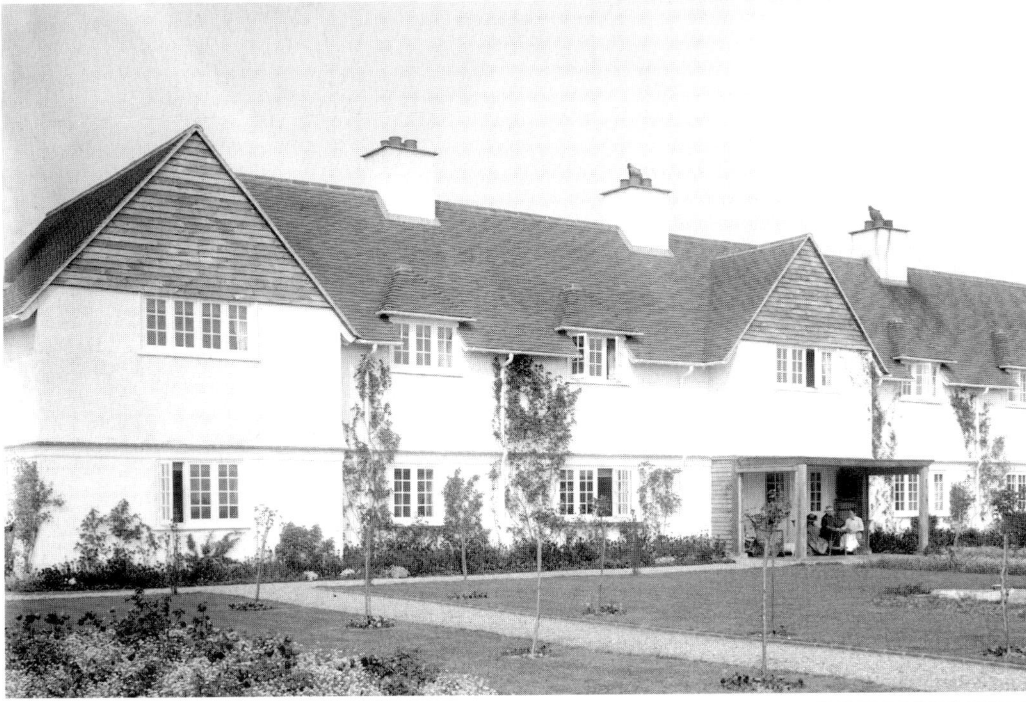

Old ladies watch the world go by from the porch of their relatively new retirement home at Bransgore.

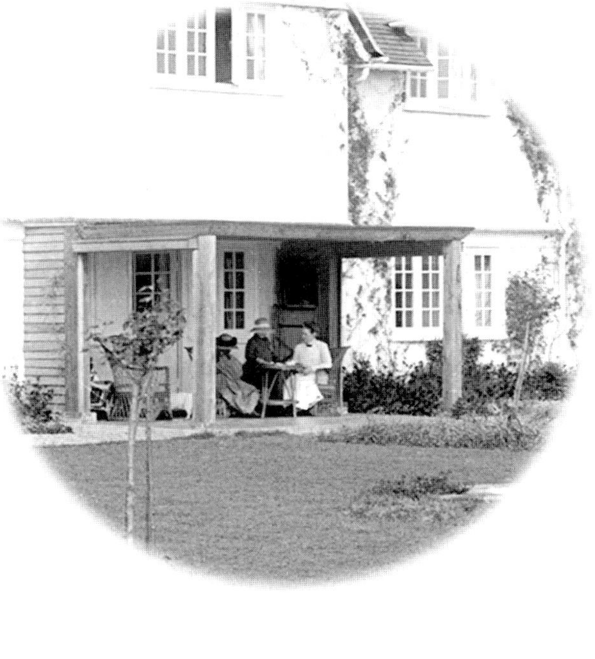

A comfortable place to reflect on the hardships of yesteryear.

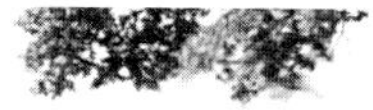

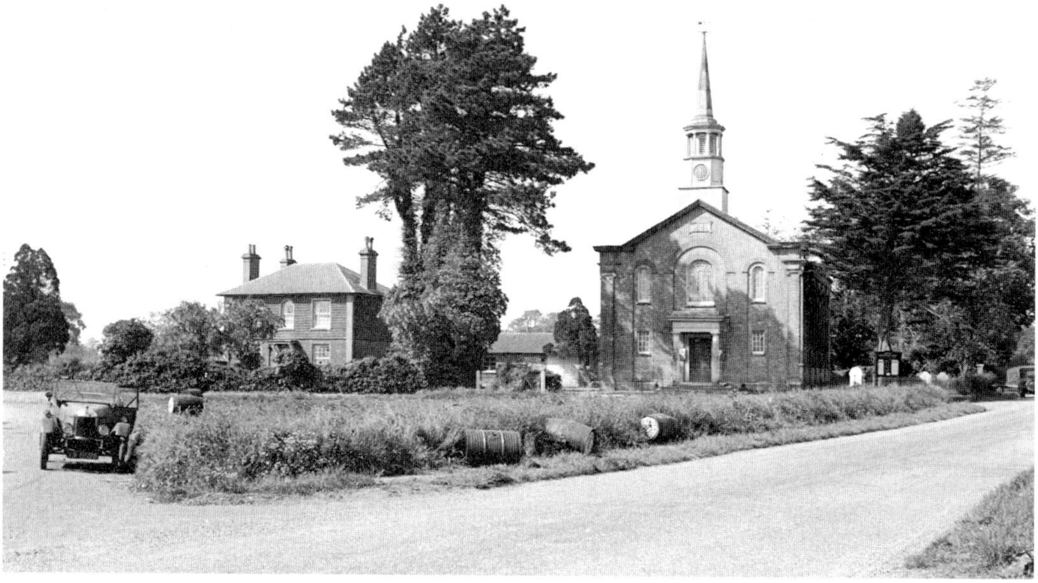

Longham's United Reformed Church, built in 1841, before the junction of main roads shattered its peace. Did the barrels fall off the back of a lorry?

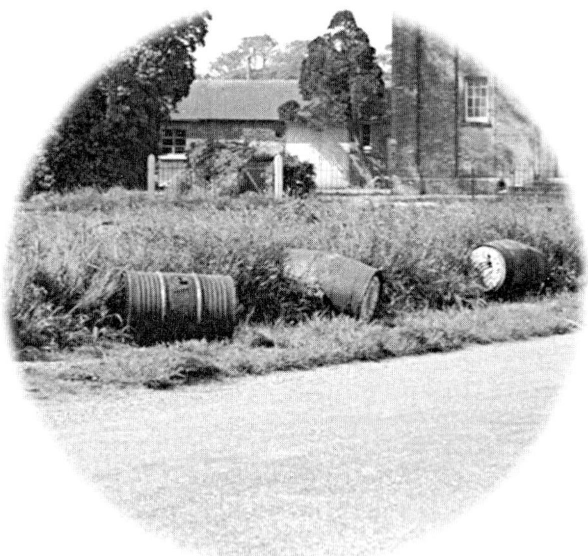

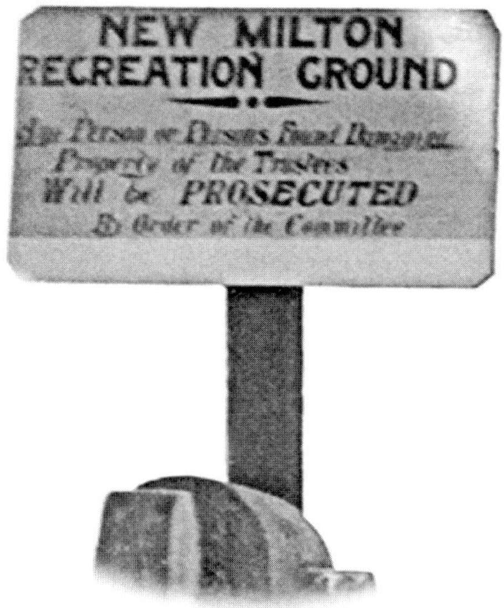

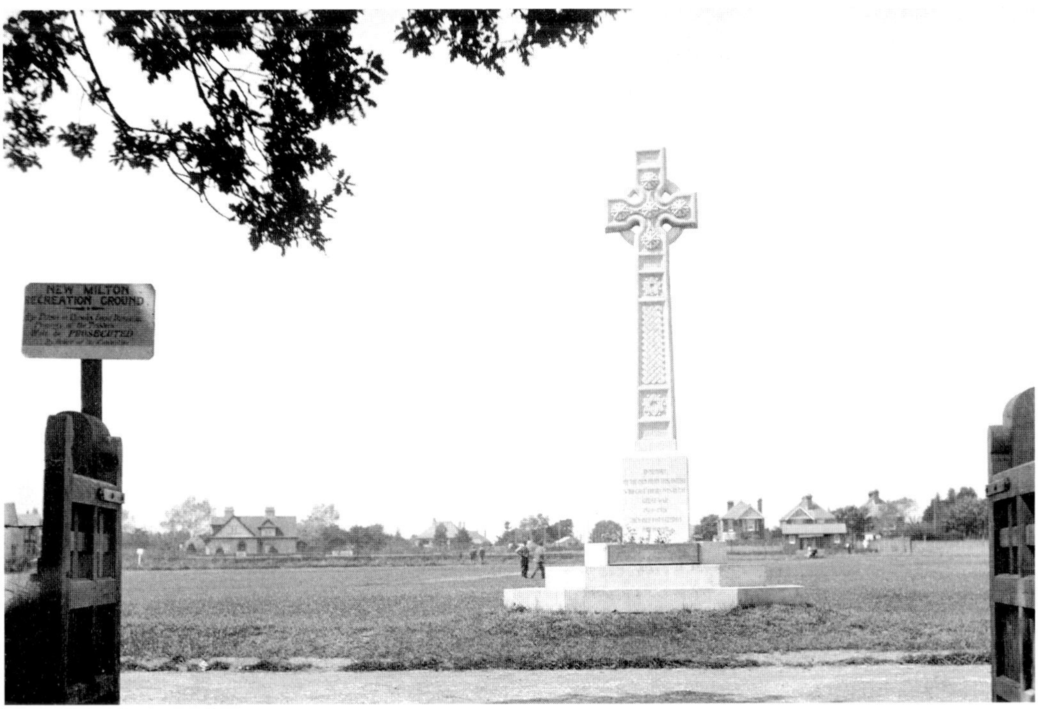

New Milton's recreation ground and recently erected war memorial in memory of men of the parish killed in the Great War.

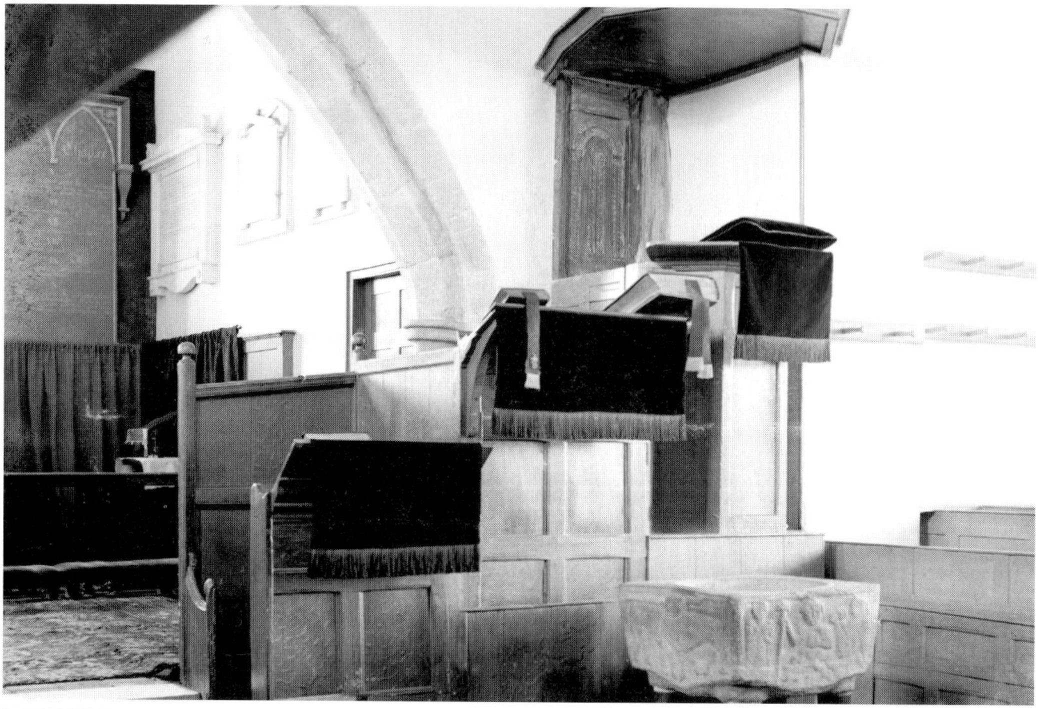

The ancient basin of the font, at All Saints Church, Minstead, was dug up in the garden of the old rectory in 1893 and is considered to be Saxon.

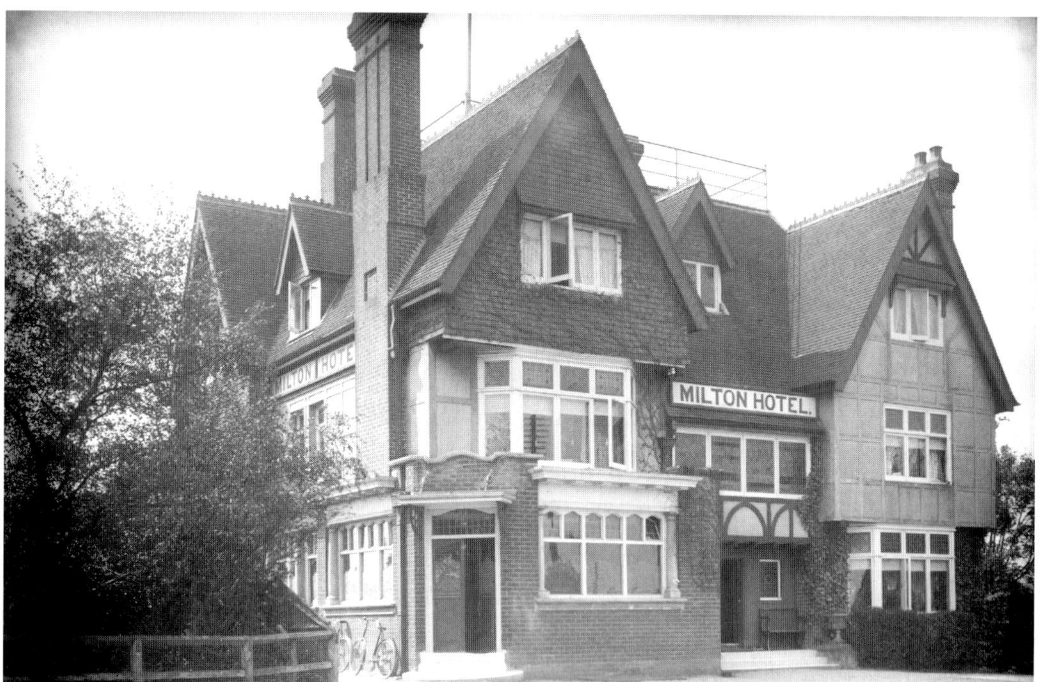

The Milton Hotel became the Speckled Trout before it was demolished.

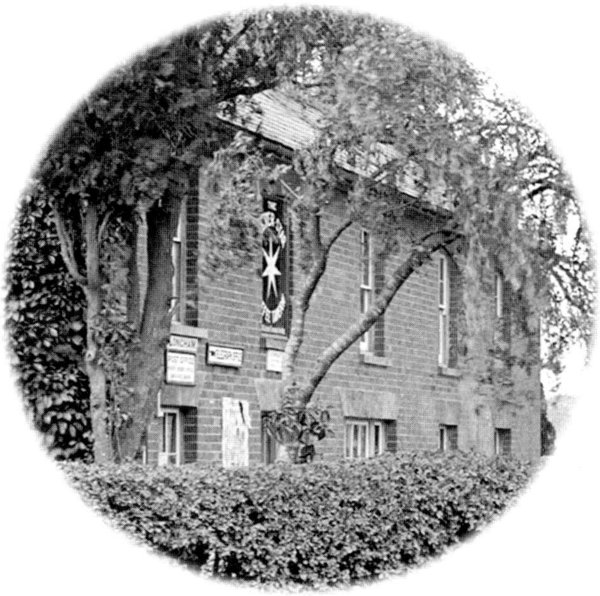

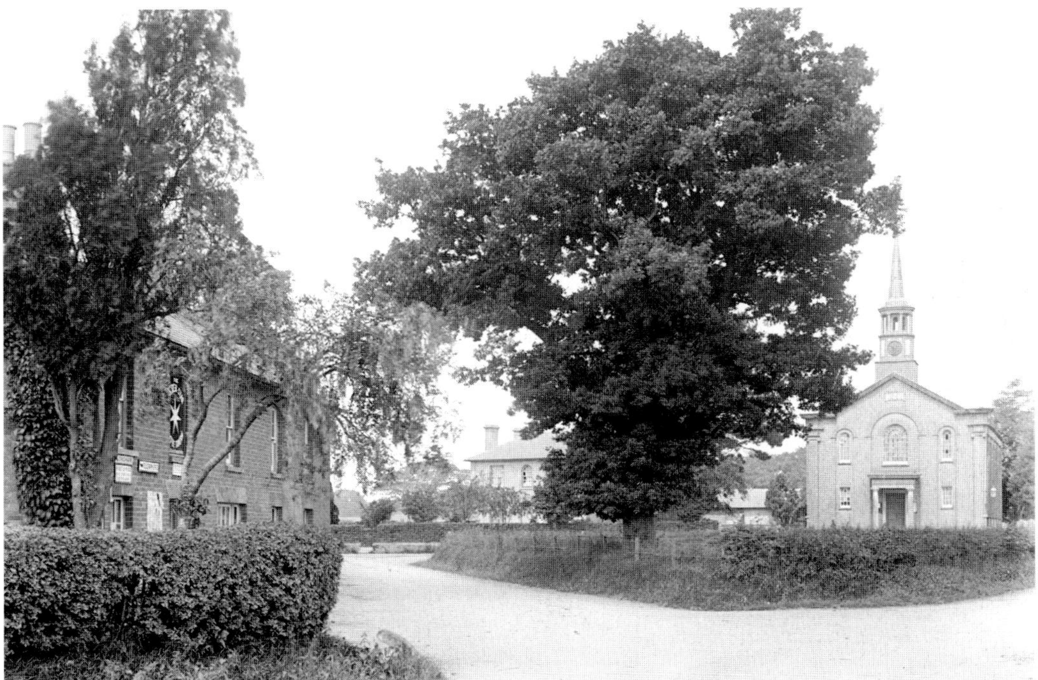

Longham, with the old post office. Sadly, the fine tree in front of the church has long since disappeared.

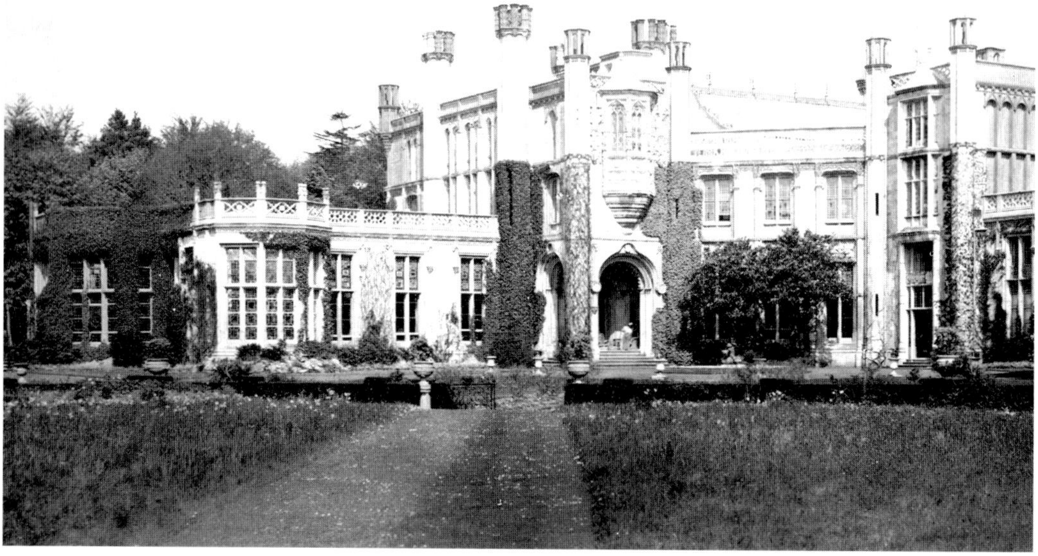

The Gothic-style Highcliffe Castle was built in the 1830s for Lord Stuart.

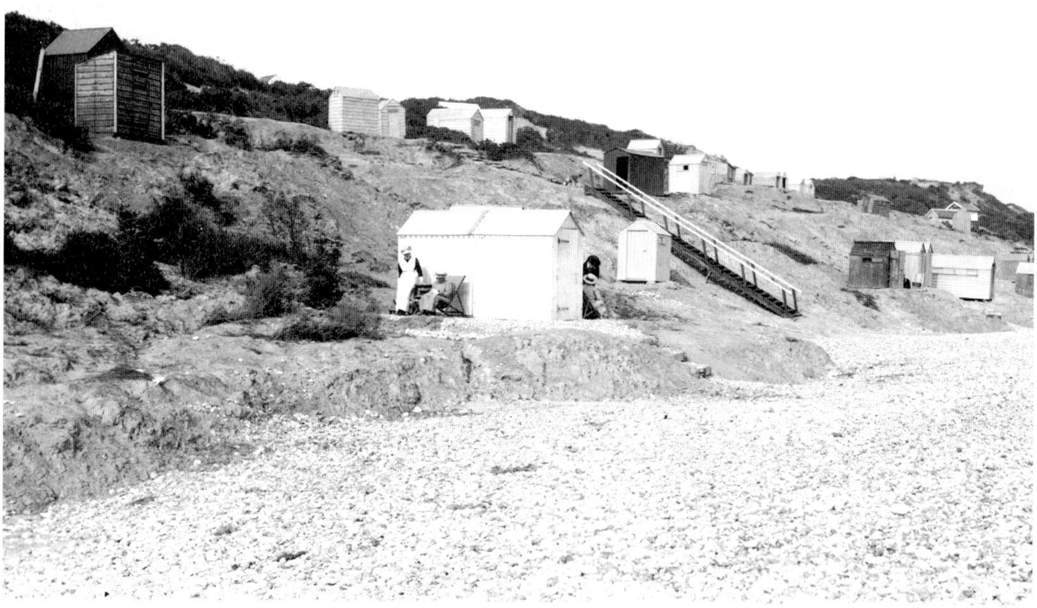

More simple housing at Highcliffe.

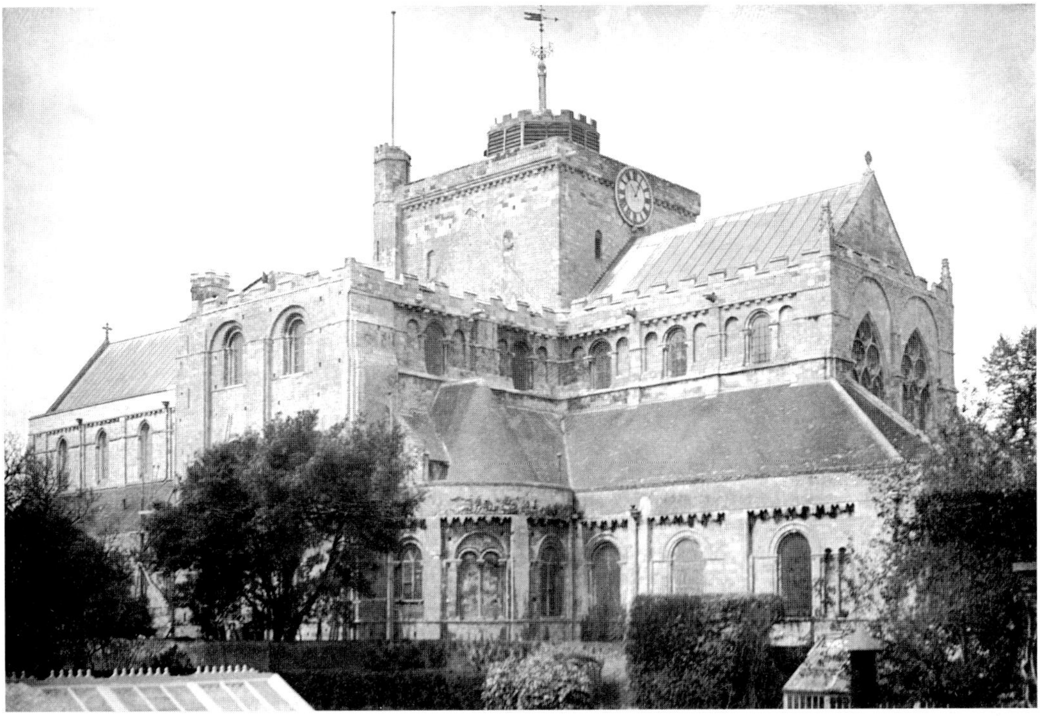

The fine 12th Century church is all that remains of Romsey's great abbey, which was sold for £100 at the Dissolution.

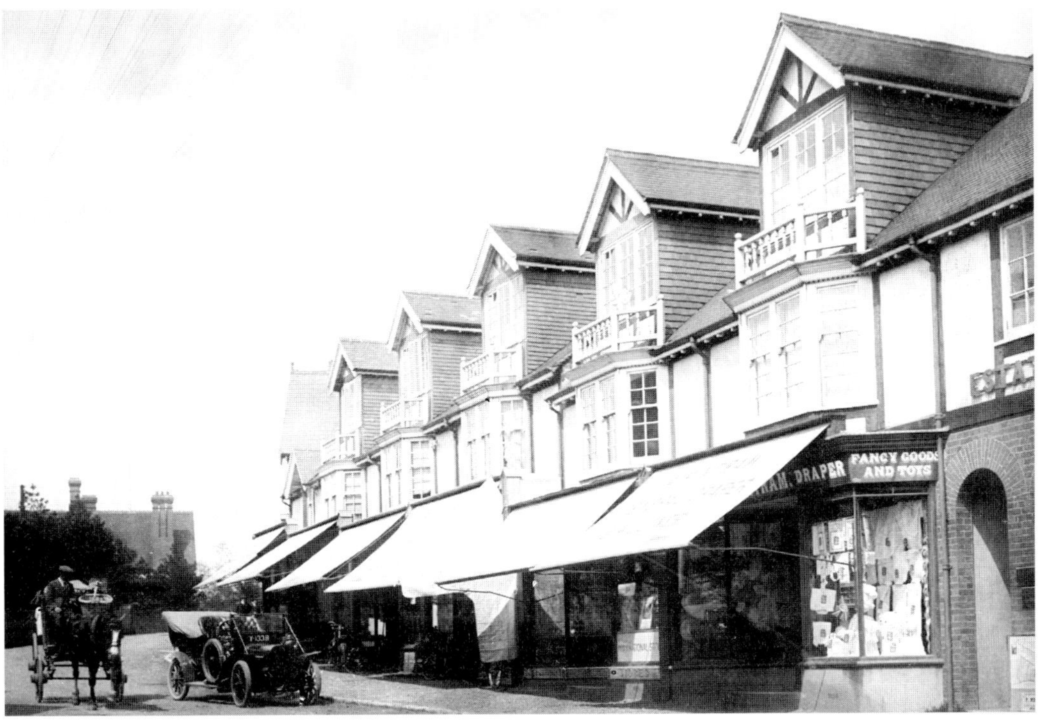

No supermarkets at New Milton!

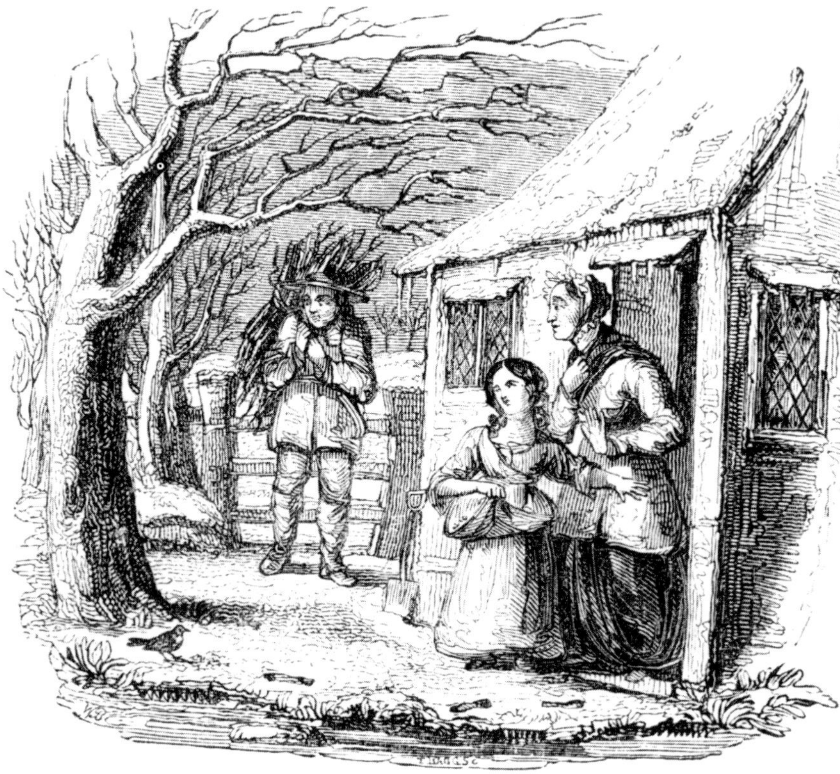

'A Winter such as when birds die
In the deep forests, and the fishes lie
Stiffened in the translucent ice, which makes
Even the mud and slime of the warm lakes
A wrinkled clod, as hard as brick; and when
Among their children, comfortable men
Gather about great fires, and yet feel cold;
Alas! then, for the homeless beggar old!'

Shelley

AT WORK, REST & PLAY

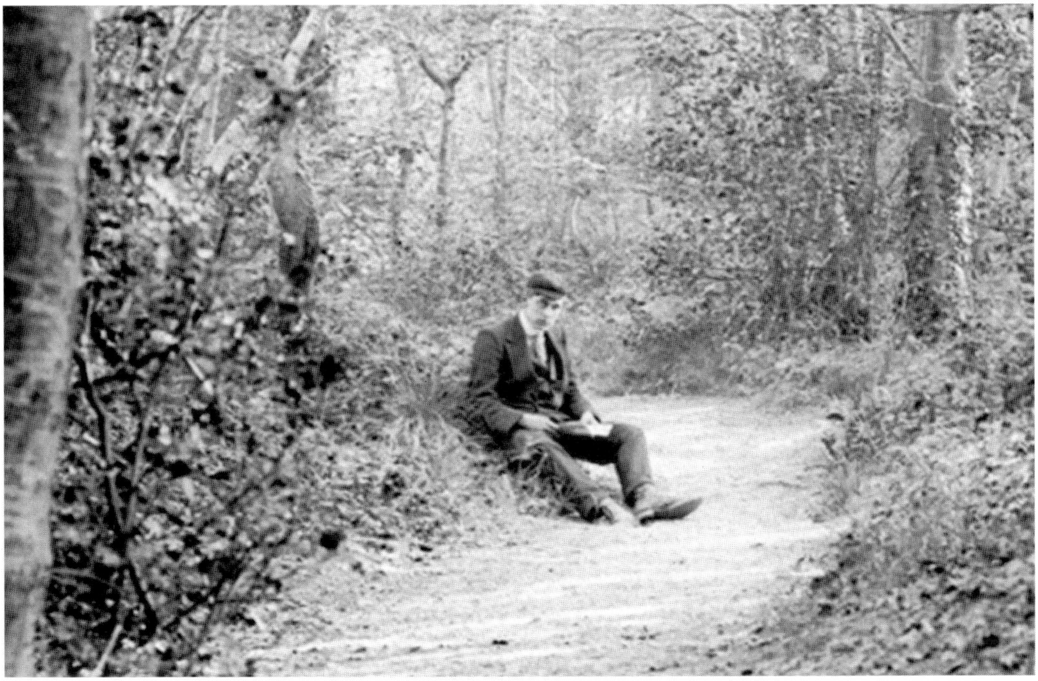

Above When people walked much more frequently even the strongest needed a rest.
Next page Ringwood market, once a great social as well as commercial gathering.

It is hardly surprising that early Foresters were described as a wild bunch, when struggling to exist on such poor land was hard enough without the worry of dire penalties such as being blinded simply for disturbing the King's deer. Ironically, many locals managed to escape deep poverty through becoming part of the entourage required to support royal sport, in serving as watchmen, keepers, harbourers, farriers and so on. When timber production became important many men took full-time work in forestry, and charcoal-burners continued their ancient craft into the 20th Century. Unfortunately, as more sophisticated machines came in, fewer and fewer men were required to work on farms and in the woods, while the arrival of cars and tractors brought redundancy for many horsemen and carters. Luckily, the period coincided with the great rise in tourism and development, so many turned their hand to providing accommodation and sport, working in hotels, constructing buildings and roads, working on the railways or in garages, and so on. Now, of course, when so many locals do not even work in the area and Forest blood is well mixed through the constant comings and goings of incomers, it is increasingly hard to spot characteristic Forest features. In his 1903 book 'Hampshire Days', WH Hudson wrote: 'Visitors to the New Forest district often express astonishment at the darkness and 'foreign' appearance of the people, and they sometimes form the mistaken idea that it is due to a strong element of gipsy blood. The darkest Hampshire peasant is always in shape of head and face the farthest removed from the gipsy type.'

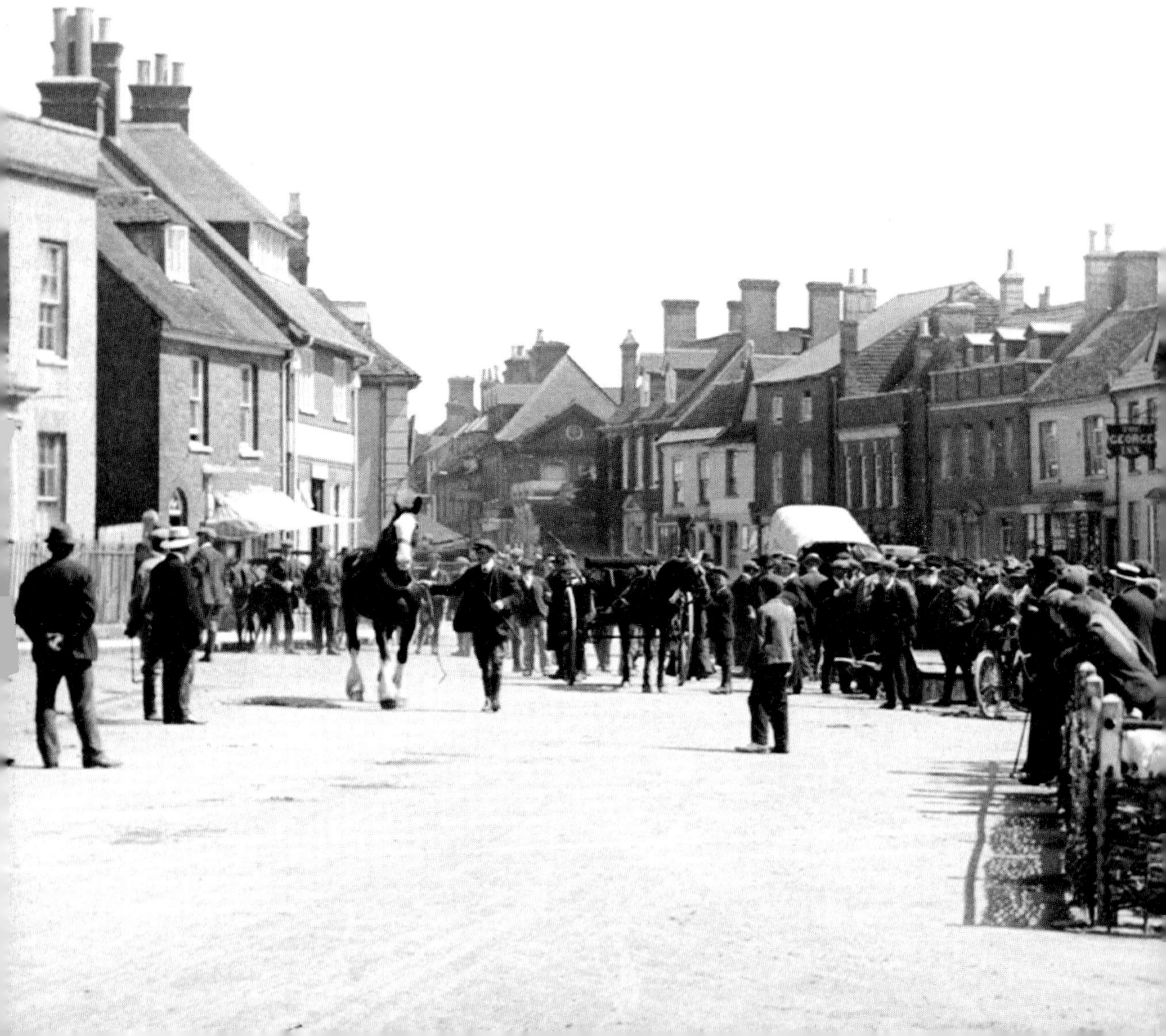

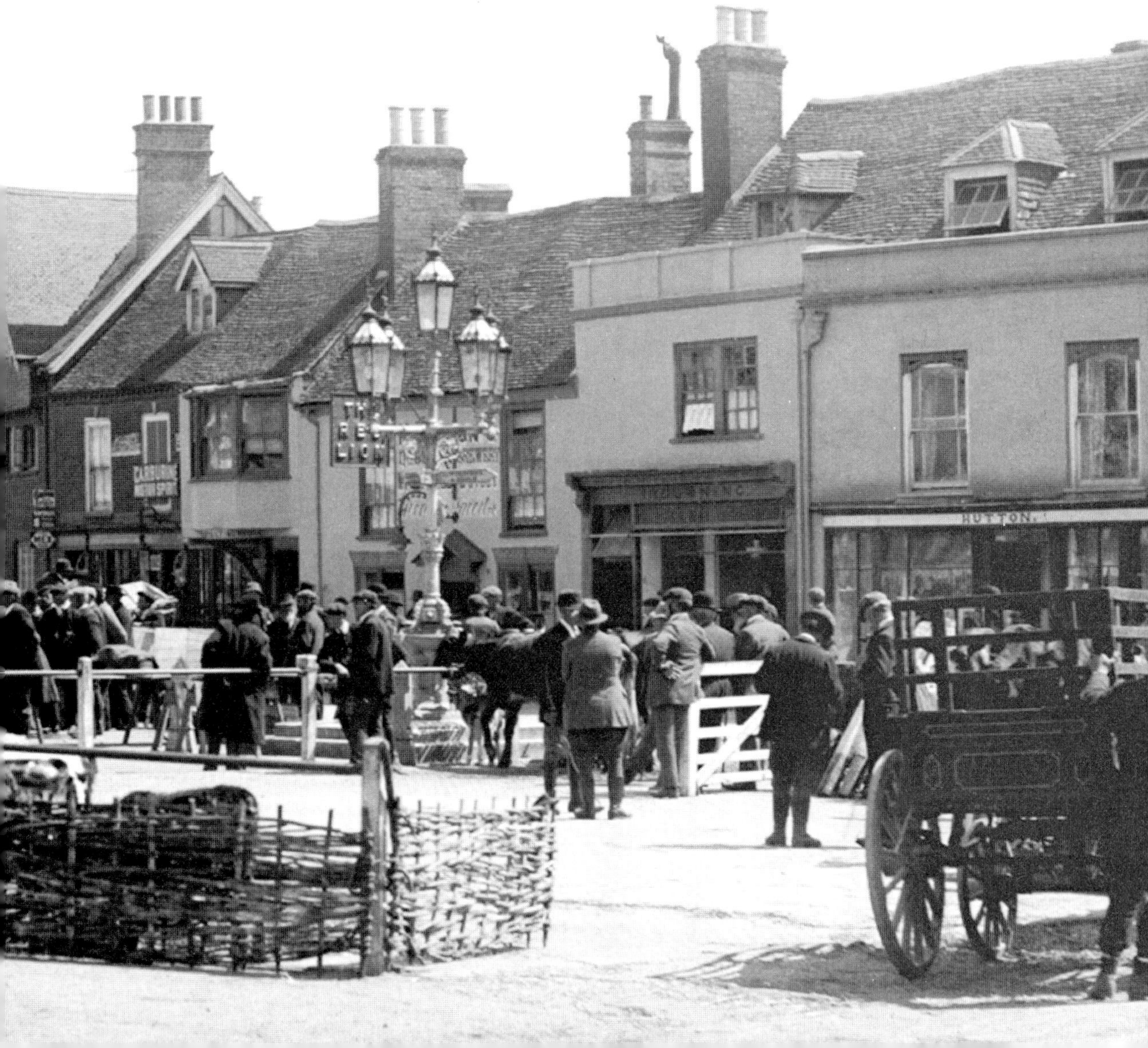
CARBURINE
HUTTON.

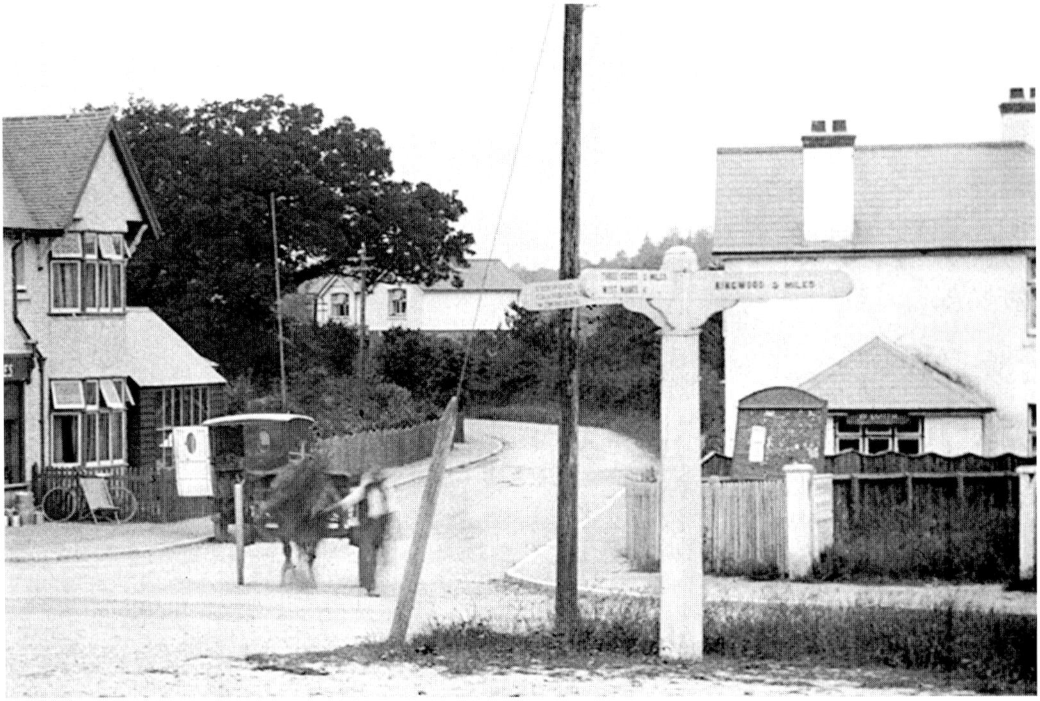

Above The carter plods home through Verwood.

Bringing back the groceries at Ringwood.

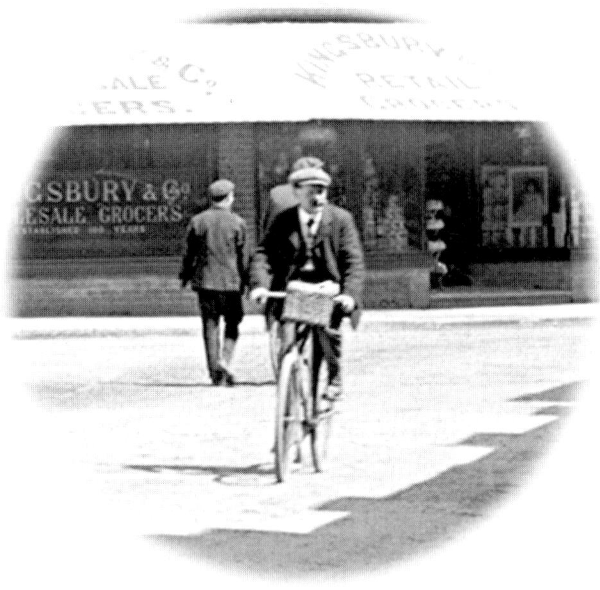

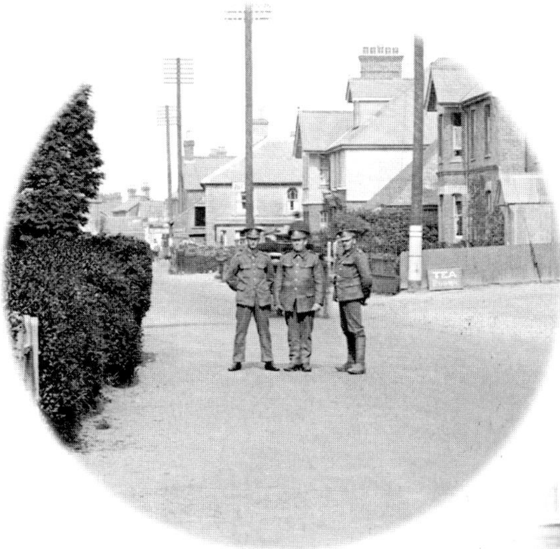

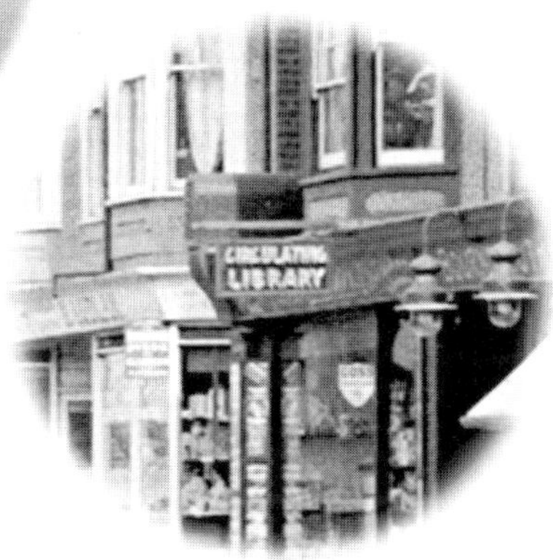

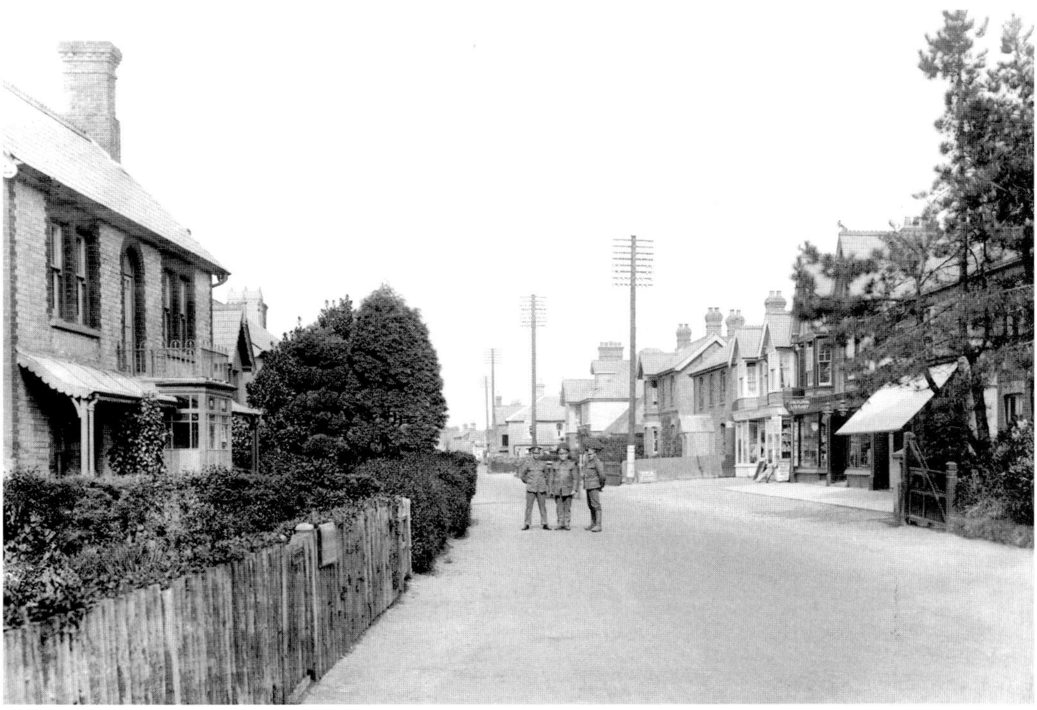

On parade at Highcliffe. Note the old circulating library sign above one of the shops.

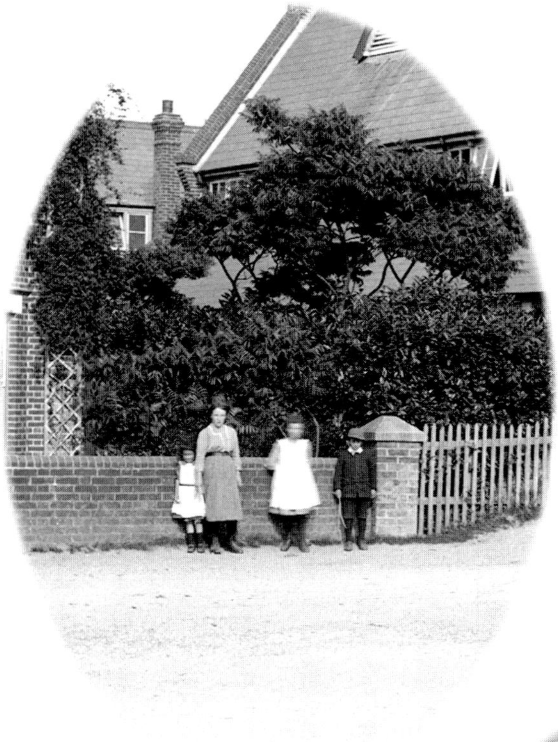

One happy family
at Ashley.

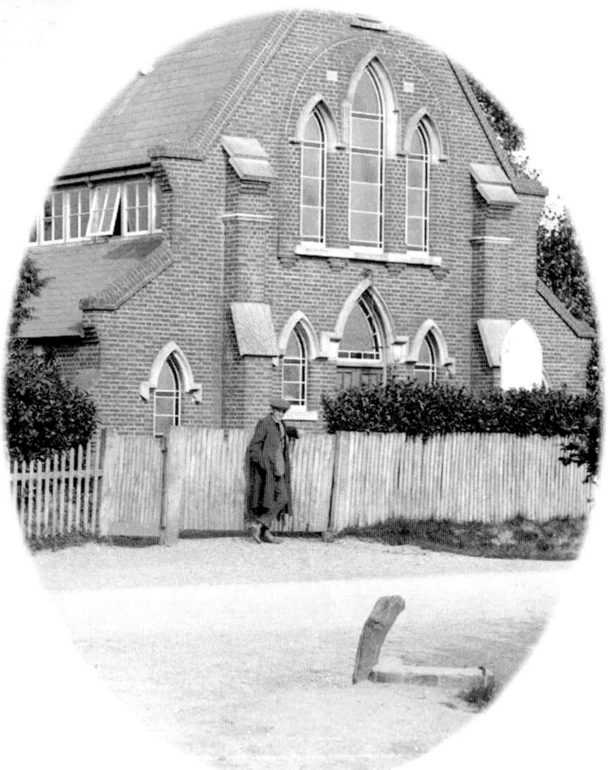

A 'fence leaner',
also at Ashley.

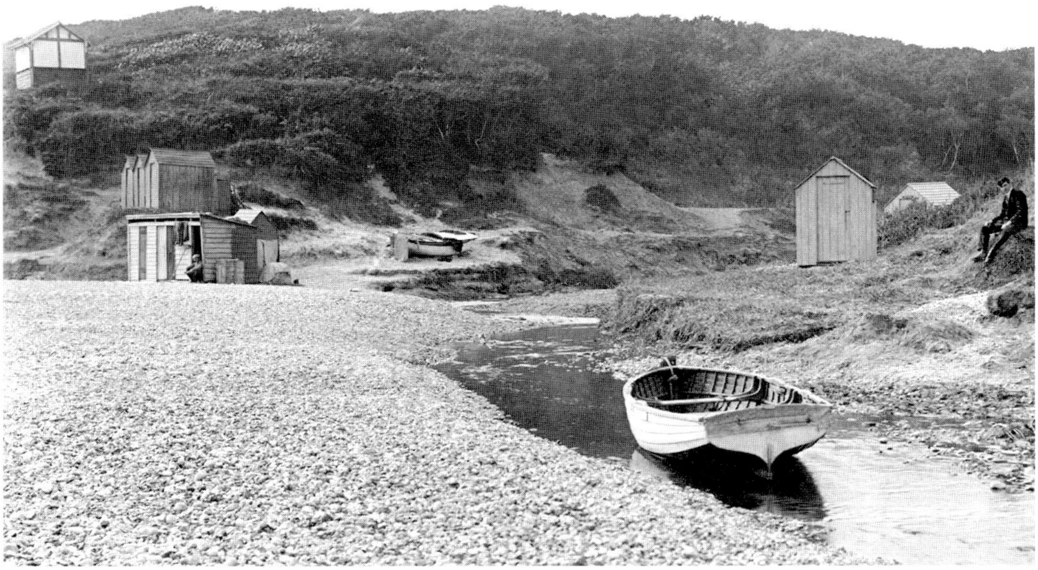

A quiet corner for the boatmen at Highcliffe, where rowing and fishing provided diversion for tourists.

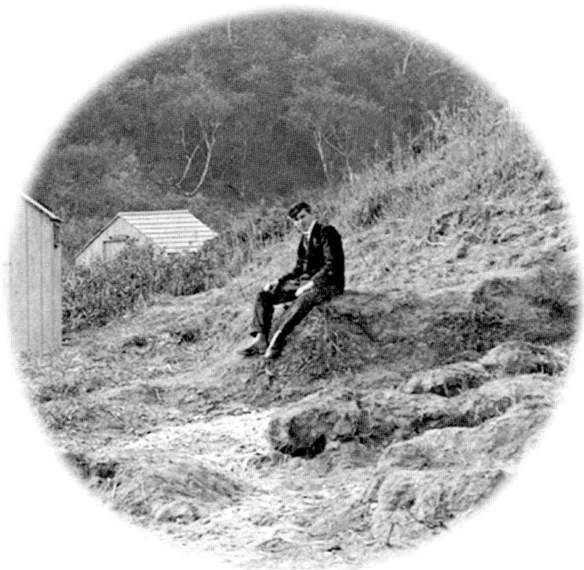

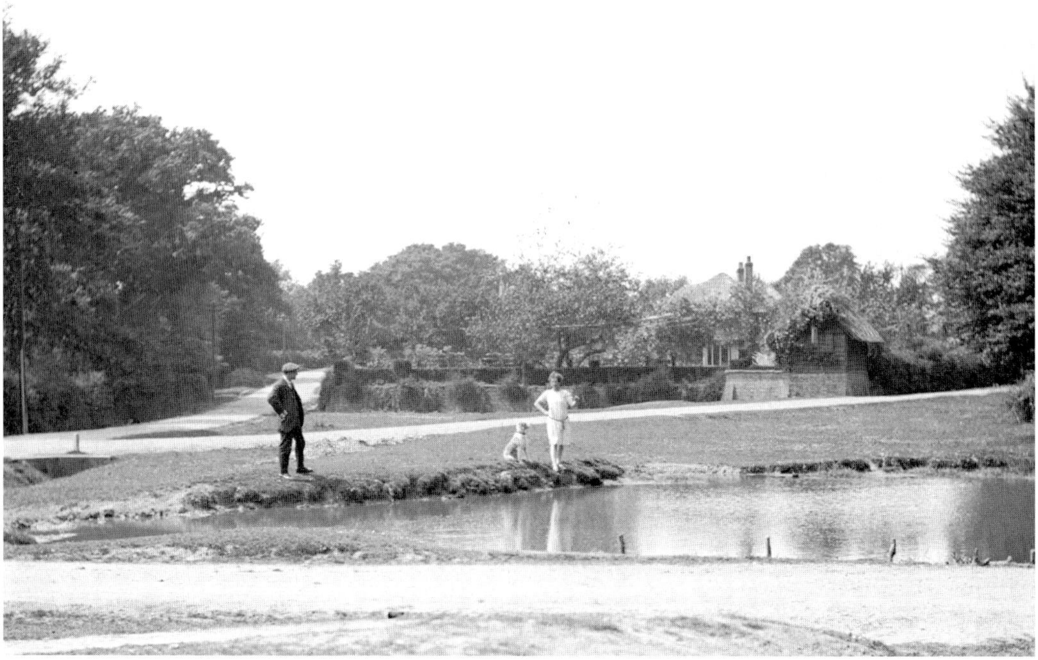

The first person to identify the location of this 'pond' wins a free framed print of his/her choice, from this book.

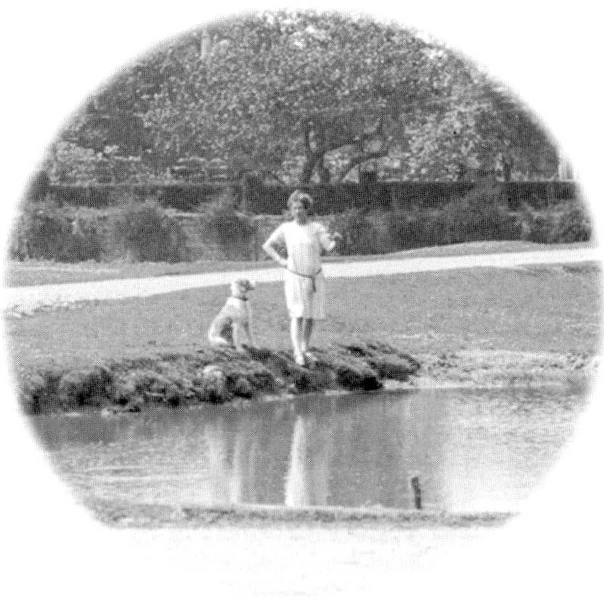

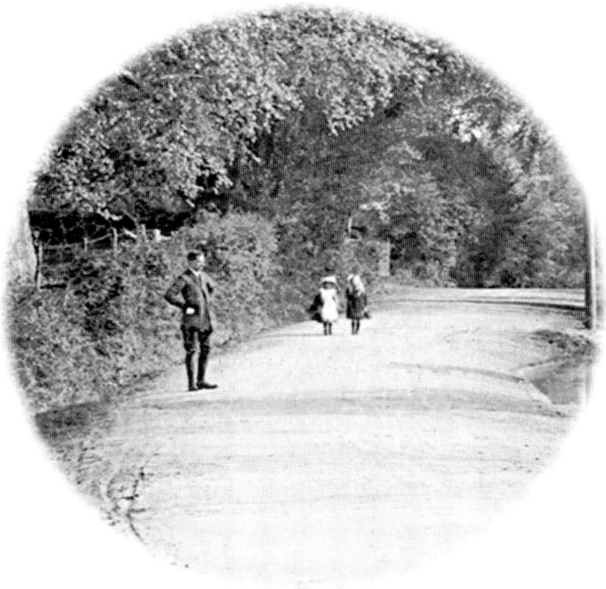

Now come along girls!

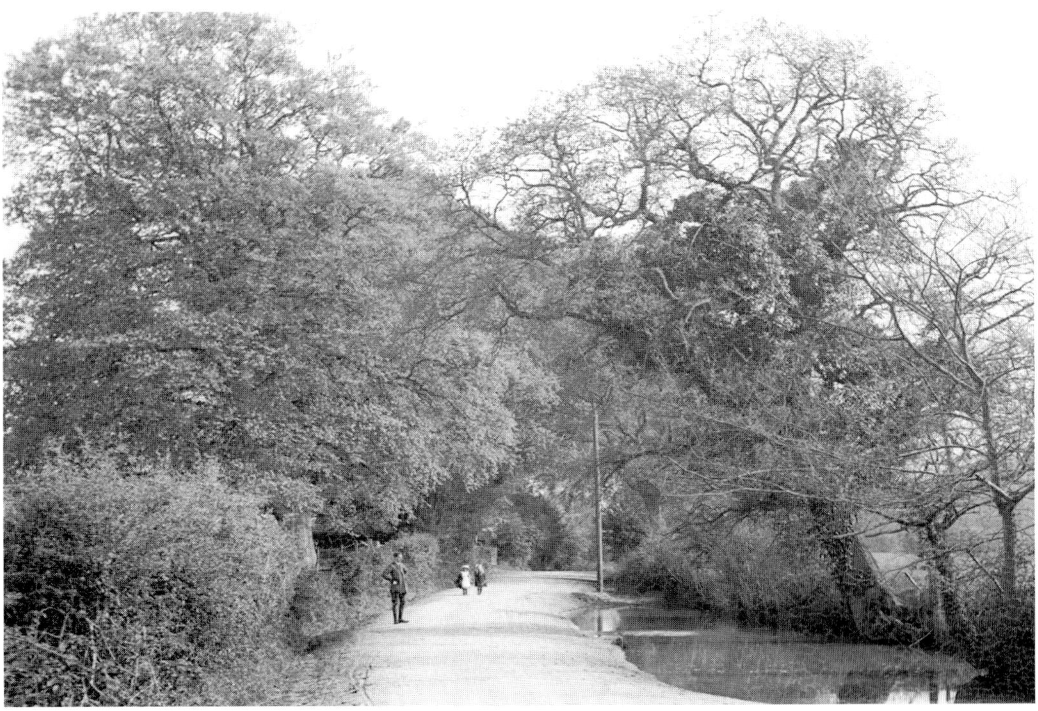

The beauty of a country lane.

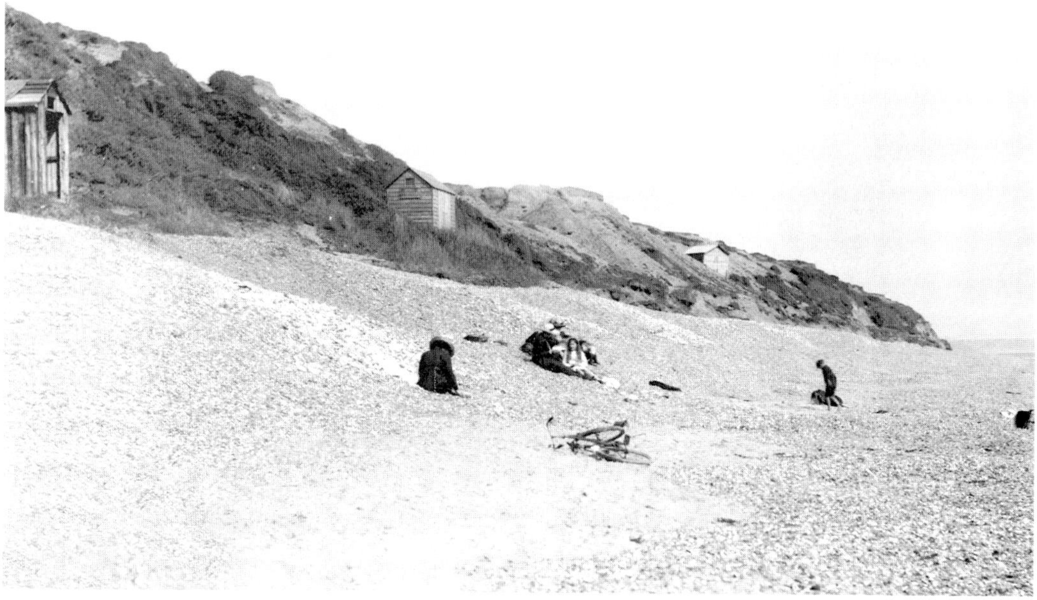

Beaches are more crowded now.

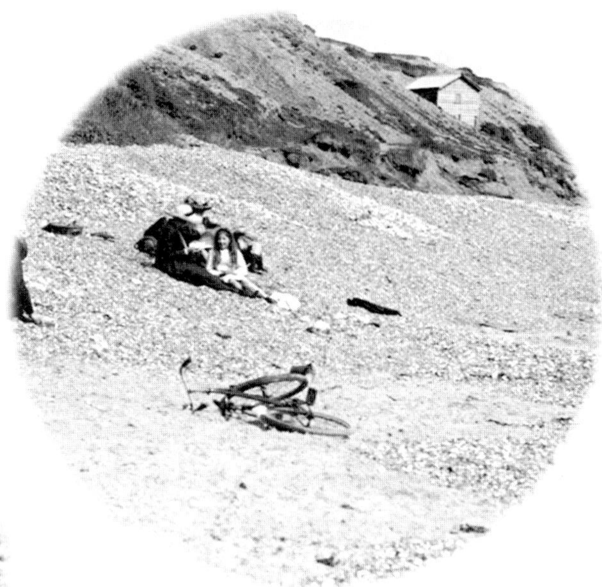

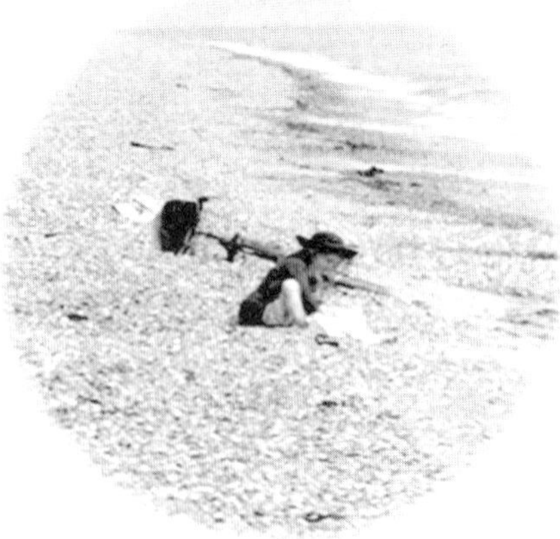

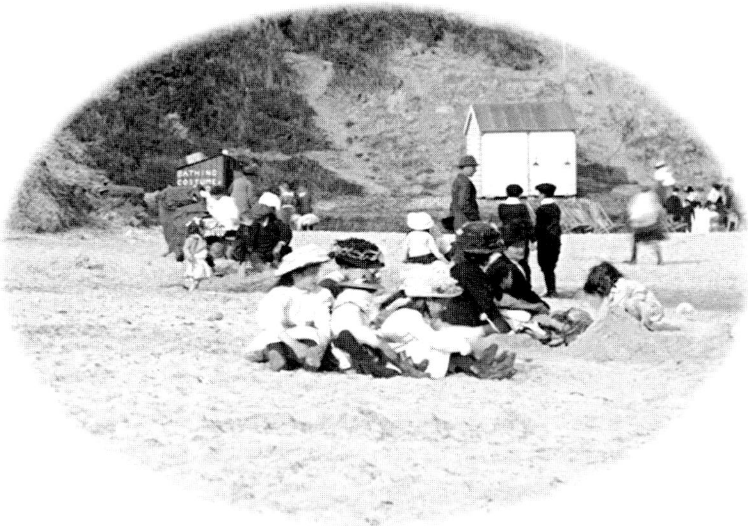

Sandcastles have been fun through the ages.

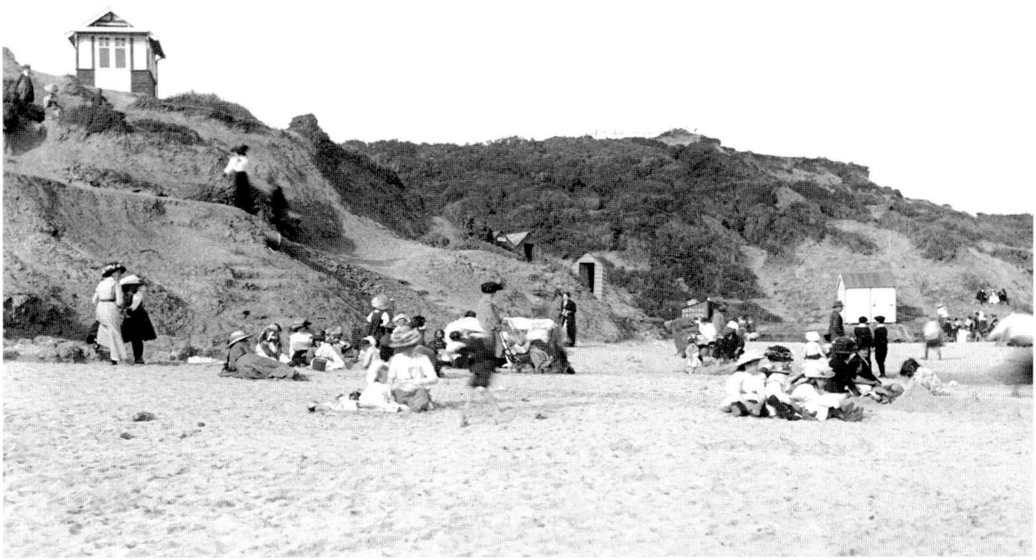

The perfect Sunday afternoon.

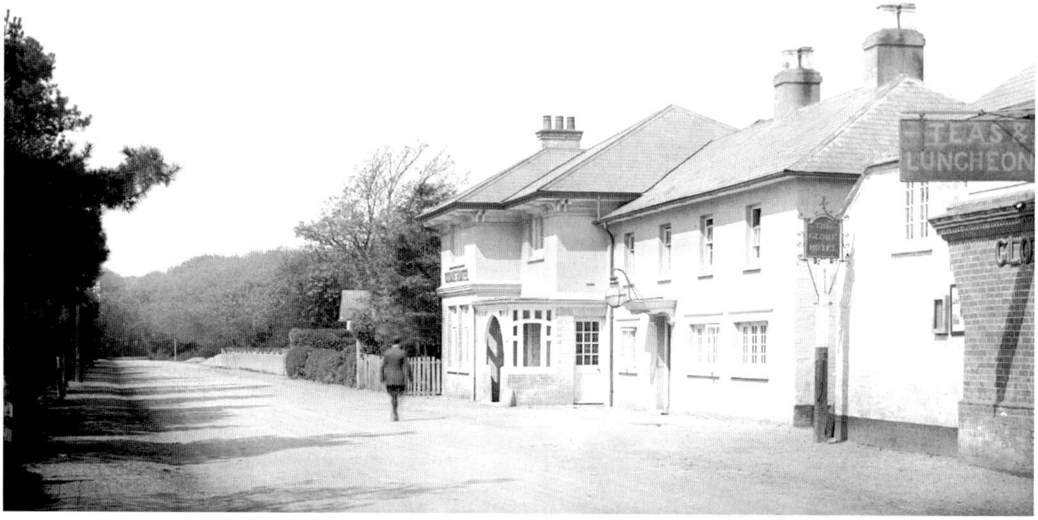

Globe Hotel at Highcliffe.

Where did I
leave that car?

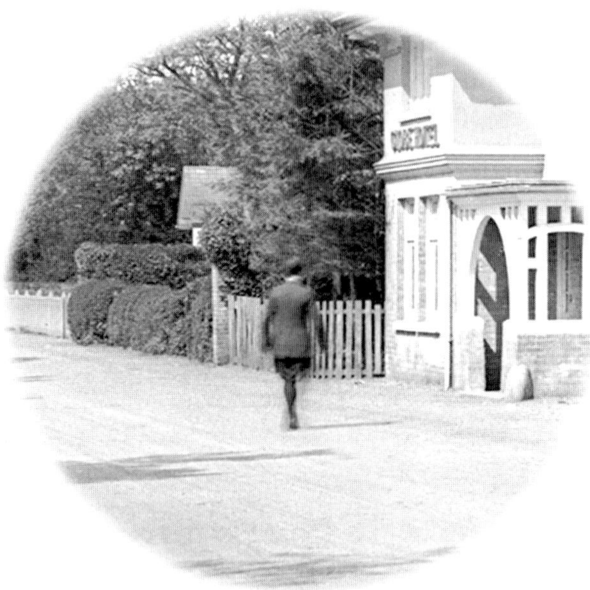

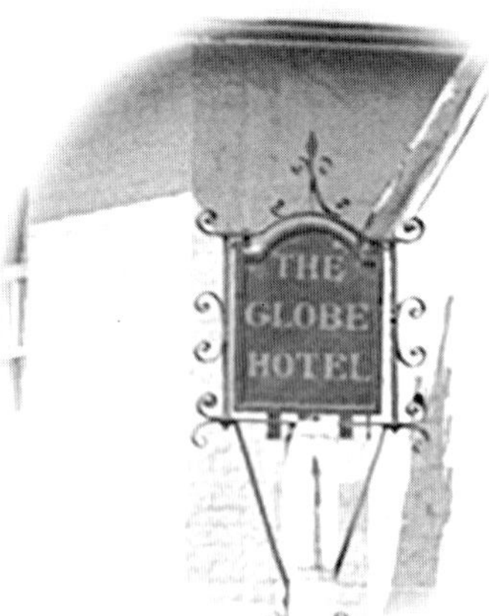

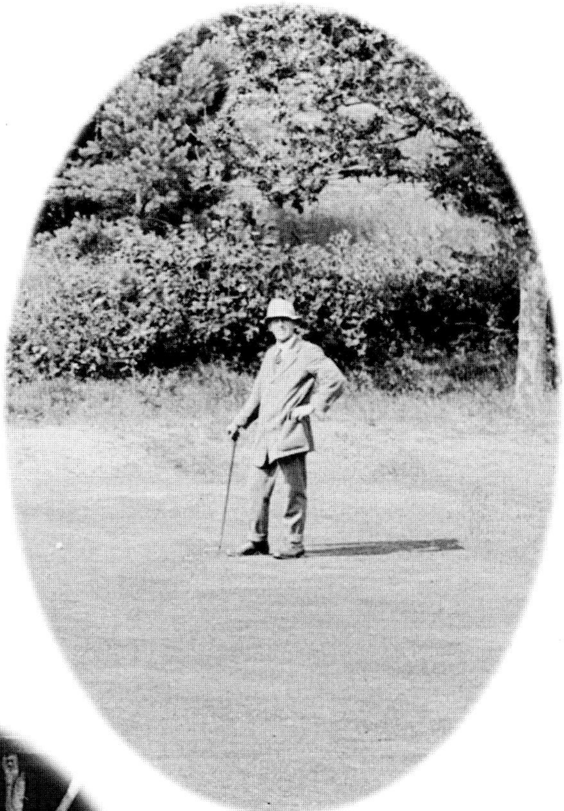

'Has anyone seen my caddy?'

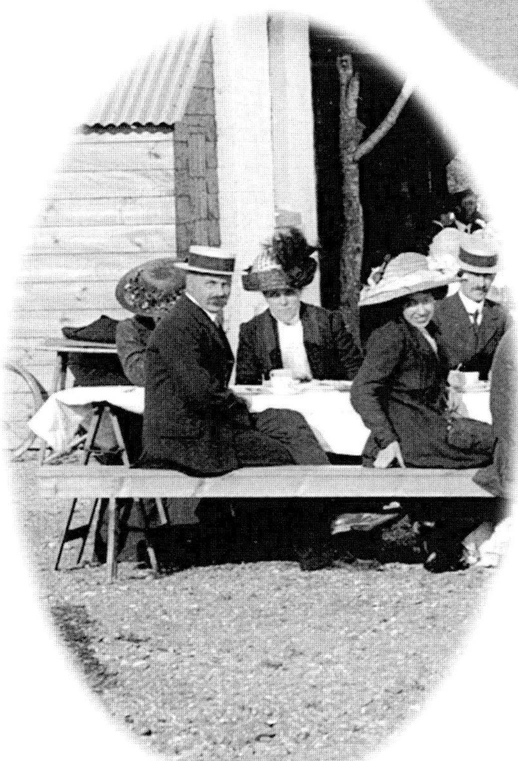

Taking tea - British through and through

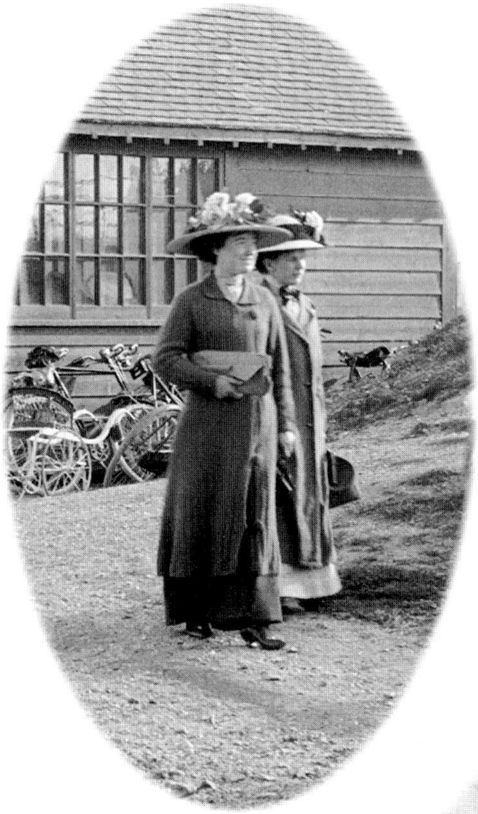

Don't look back
'Mildred' - I think
he's still looking.

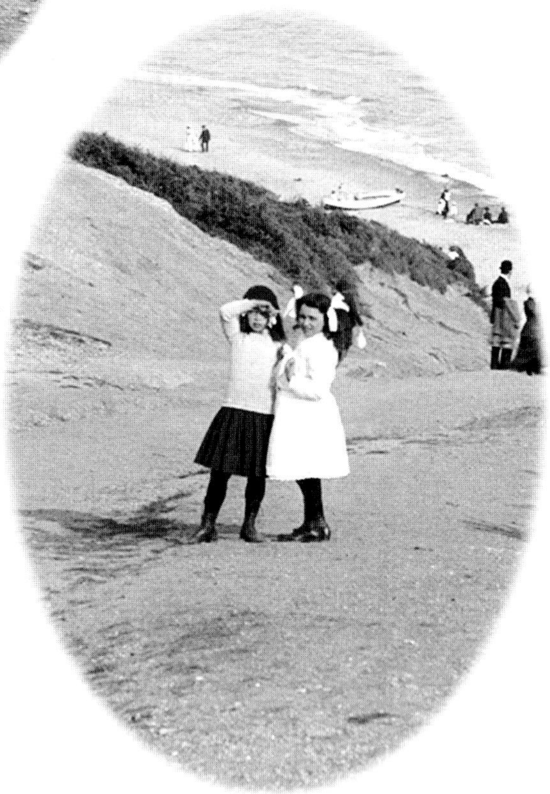

'If he doesn't hurry
up that ice-cream
will have melted!'

'I bet you wish your bike was as big as this!'

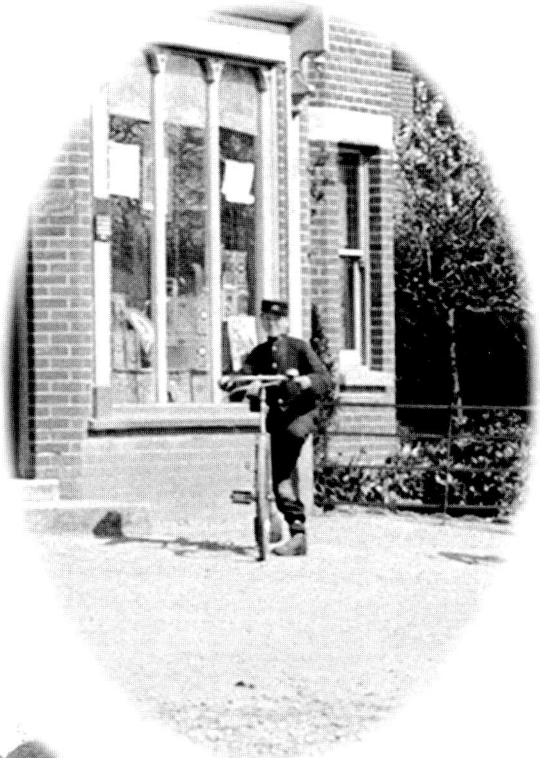

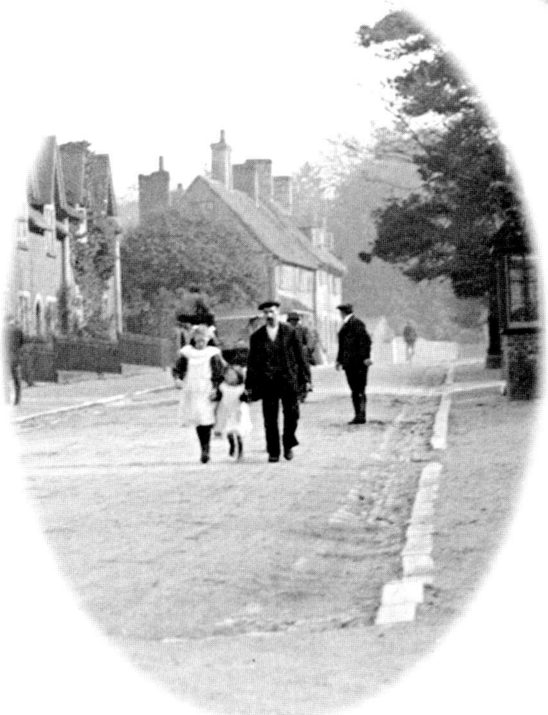

'Are we nearly there yet?'

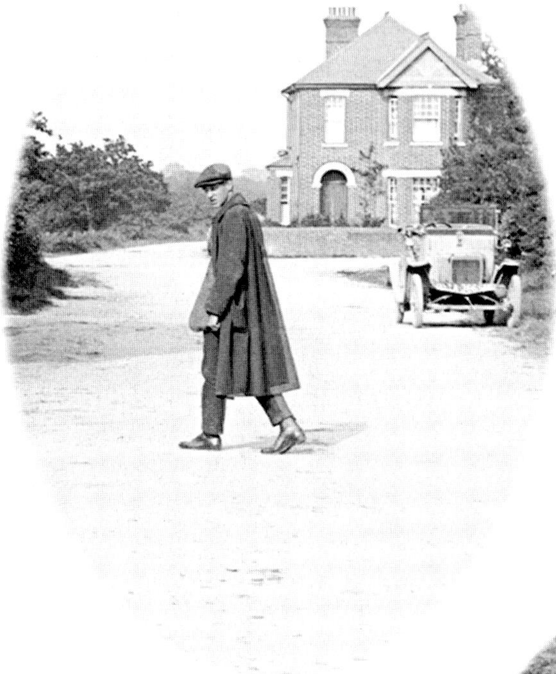

'I thought I put
an X in the box
for no publicity!'

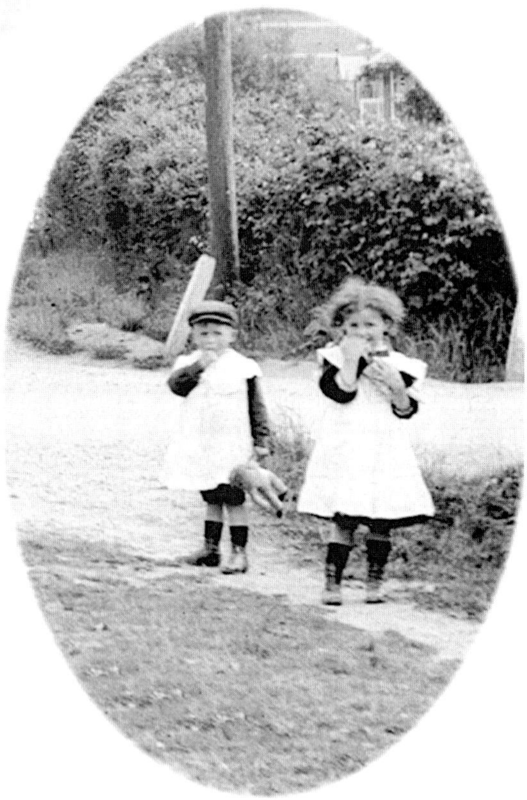

Butter wouldn't melt
in their mouths.

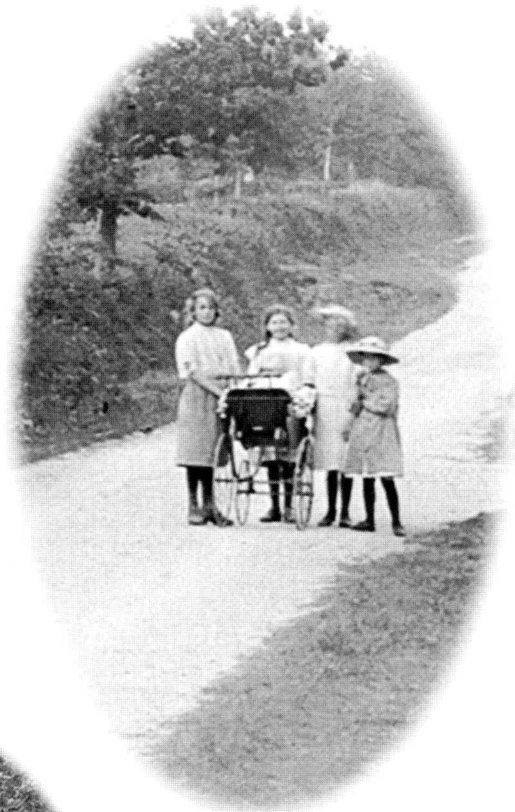

Practising for the day when they'll all be mothers.

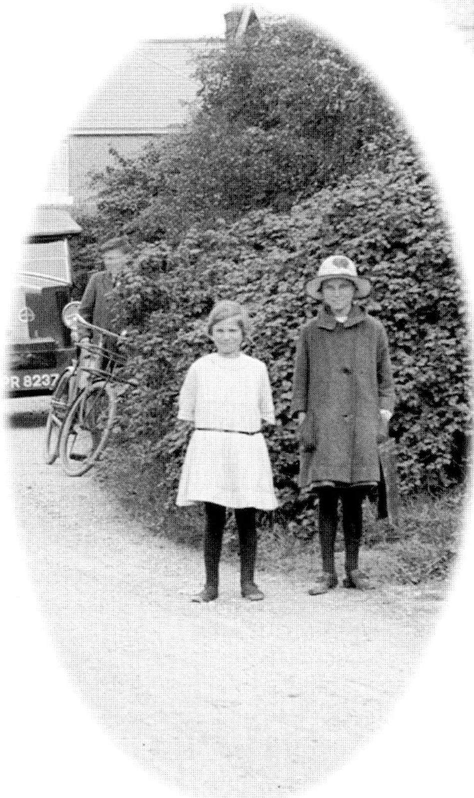

'Hurry up with that photo or we'll be late for school.'

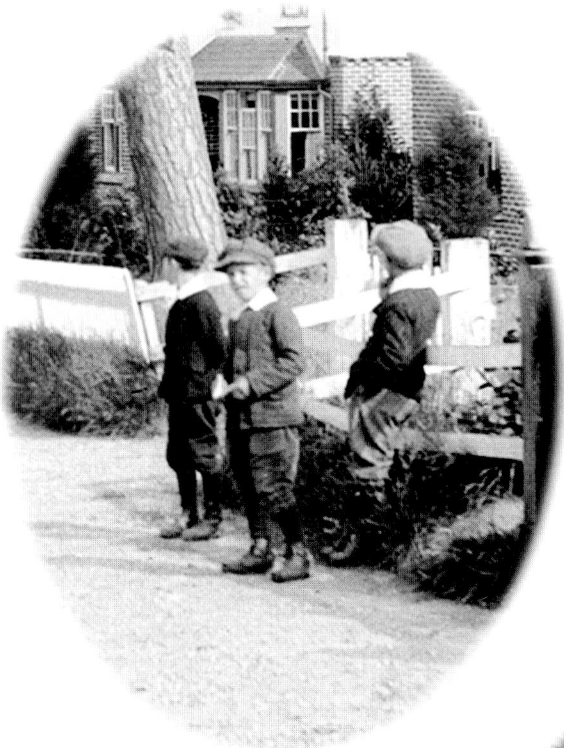

'You watch that way and I'll let you know when the man with the camera has gone.'

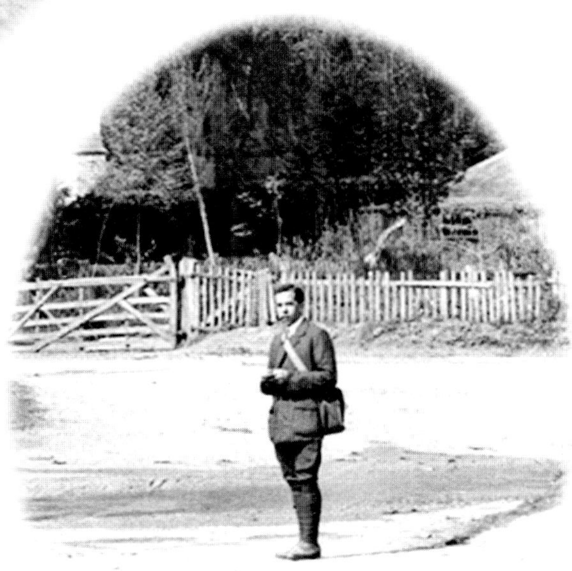

'Which way to the Forest Park Hotel?'

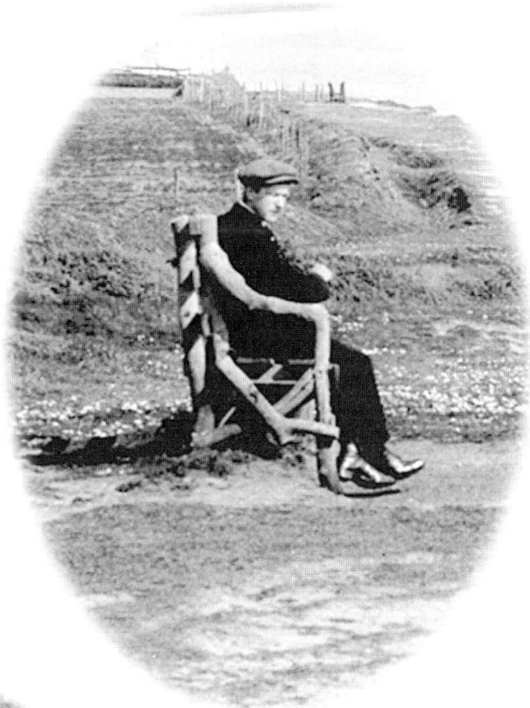

'Nice view but the seat's a bit on the lumpy side.'

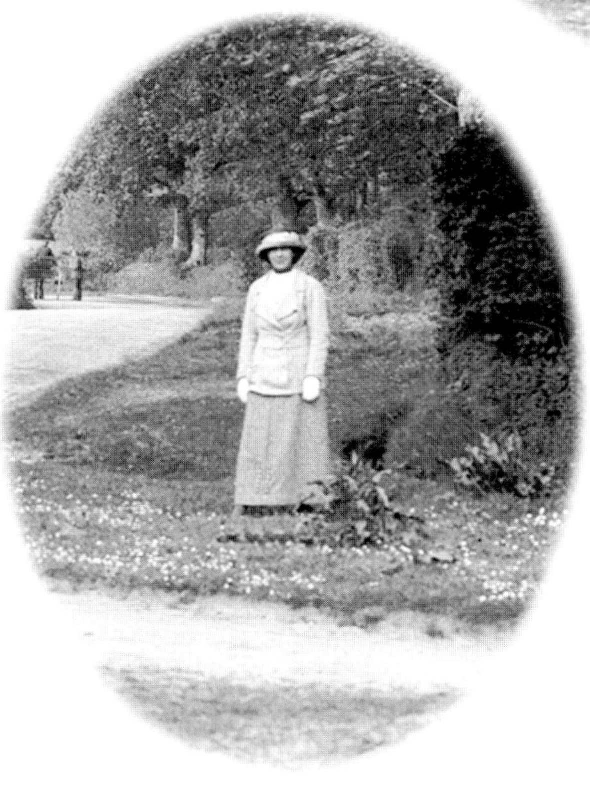

'Oh, not another photo PW!'

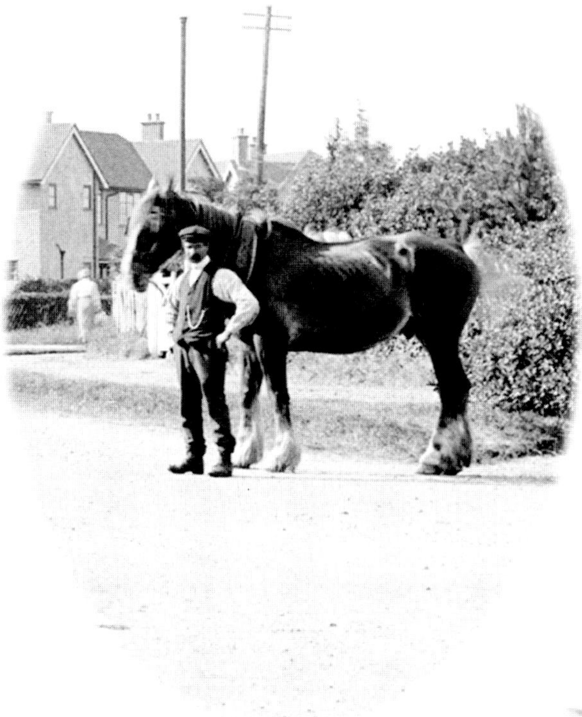

'Now don't you go fright'nin' my old 'orse with that thing!'

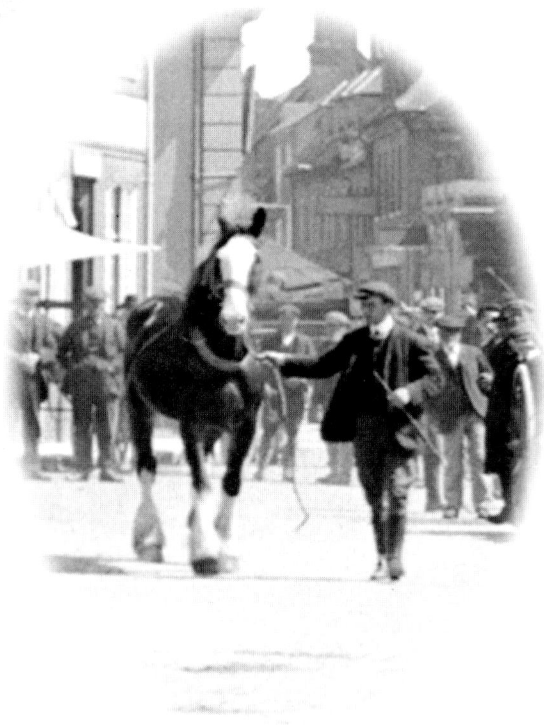

Proud of his horse at Ringwood Market.

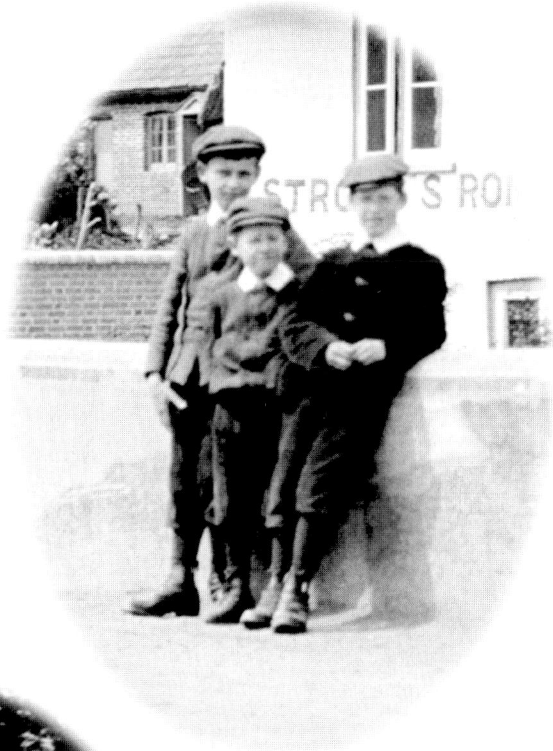

Waiting outside the pub for Dad to bring a bottle of ginger beer.

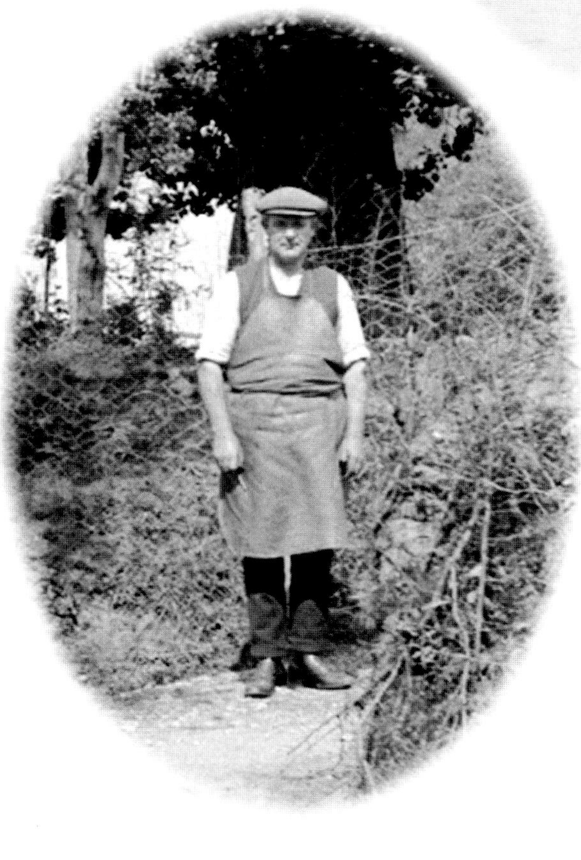

A strong apron for farriery and other heavy work.

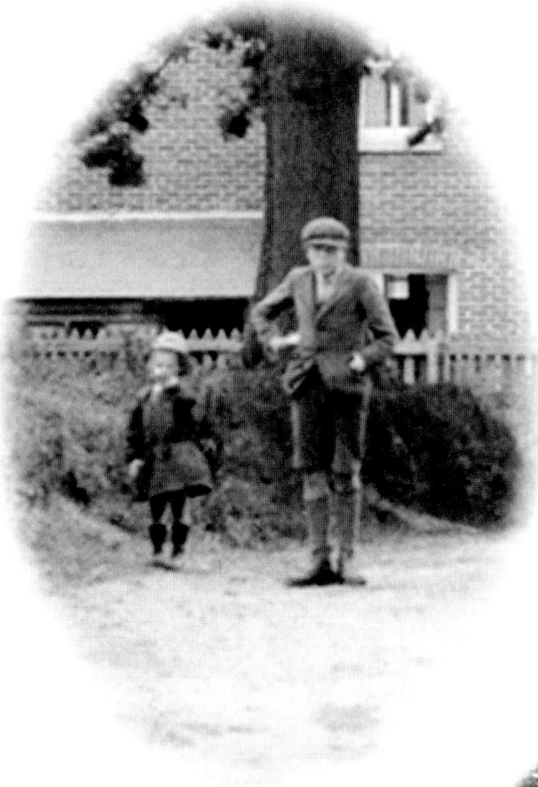

'Even my little sister thinks I'm too big for short trousers.'

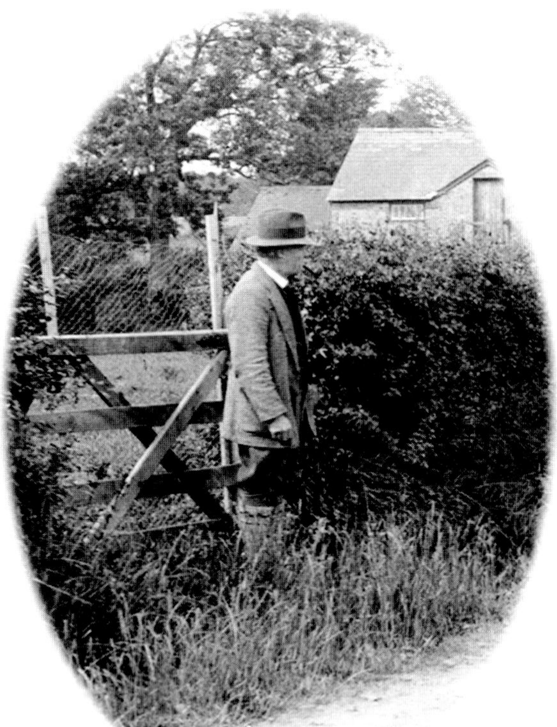

Possibly a rare photo of the late PW Hobbs.

FROM CENTURIES PAST

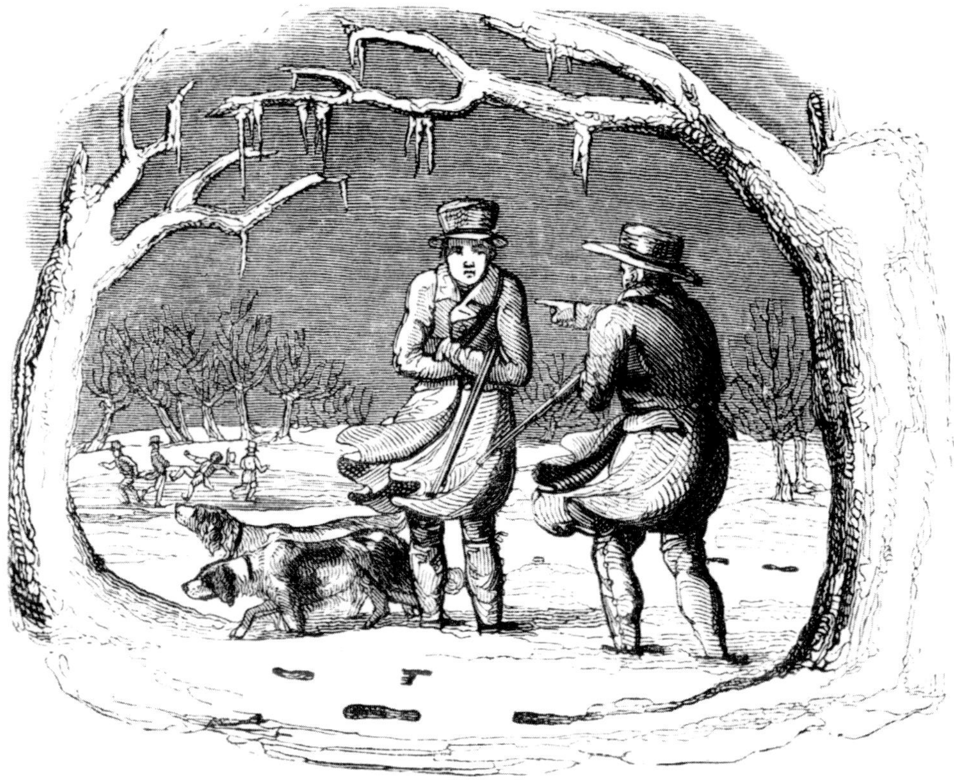

Although photography was invented in early Victorian times it was considerably later that widespread use of reliable, more portable cameras started to record the olde England which was disappearing so rapidly. Furthermore, in rural districts the photographic record is particularly sparse. Thus there is a great period of Forest history for which we must rely on engravings - for so long the main type of illustration in books and newspapers - to reveal how it once was. Here is a selection to show typical Forest scenes mostly before the late PW Hobbs started his unique Forest focus, and to accompany them are some intriguing contemporary quotations.

CRUEL FOREST LAWS

'Constant encroachments upon private property, cruel punishments - such as tearing out the offendor's eyes, or mutilating his limbs - inflicted for the infraction of Forest law; extravagant payments in the shape of heavy tolls levied by the rangers on all merchandise passing within the purlieus of a royal chase; frequent and arbitrary changes of boundary, in order to bring offences within the Forest jurisdiction were only a portion of the evils submitted to by the victims of feudal tyranny. No dogs, however valuable or dear to their owners - except mastiffs for household defence - were allowed to exist within miles of the outskirts, and even the poor watch-dog, by a 'Court of Regard' held for that special purpose every three years, was crippled by the amputation of three claws of the forefeet close to the skin - an operation, in woodland parlance, termed expeditation, intended to render impossible the chasing or otherwise incommoding the deer in their coverts.'

Chambers, Book of Days, 1866

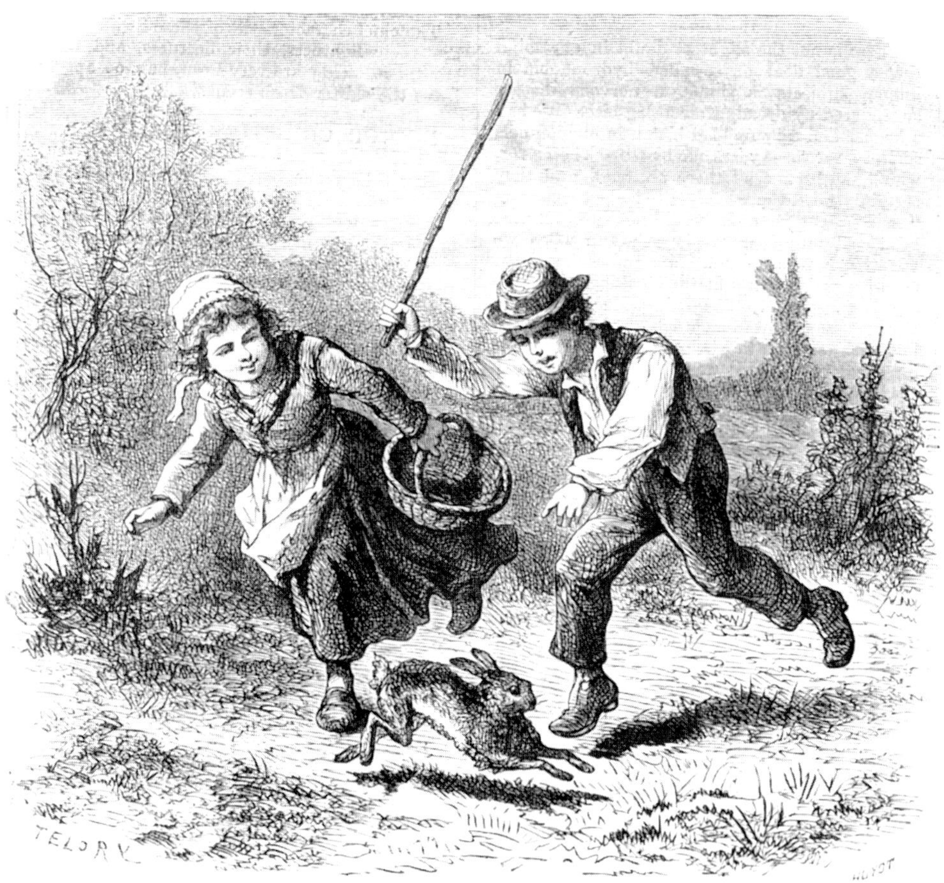

AMATEUR POACHING.

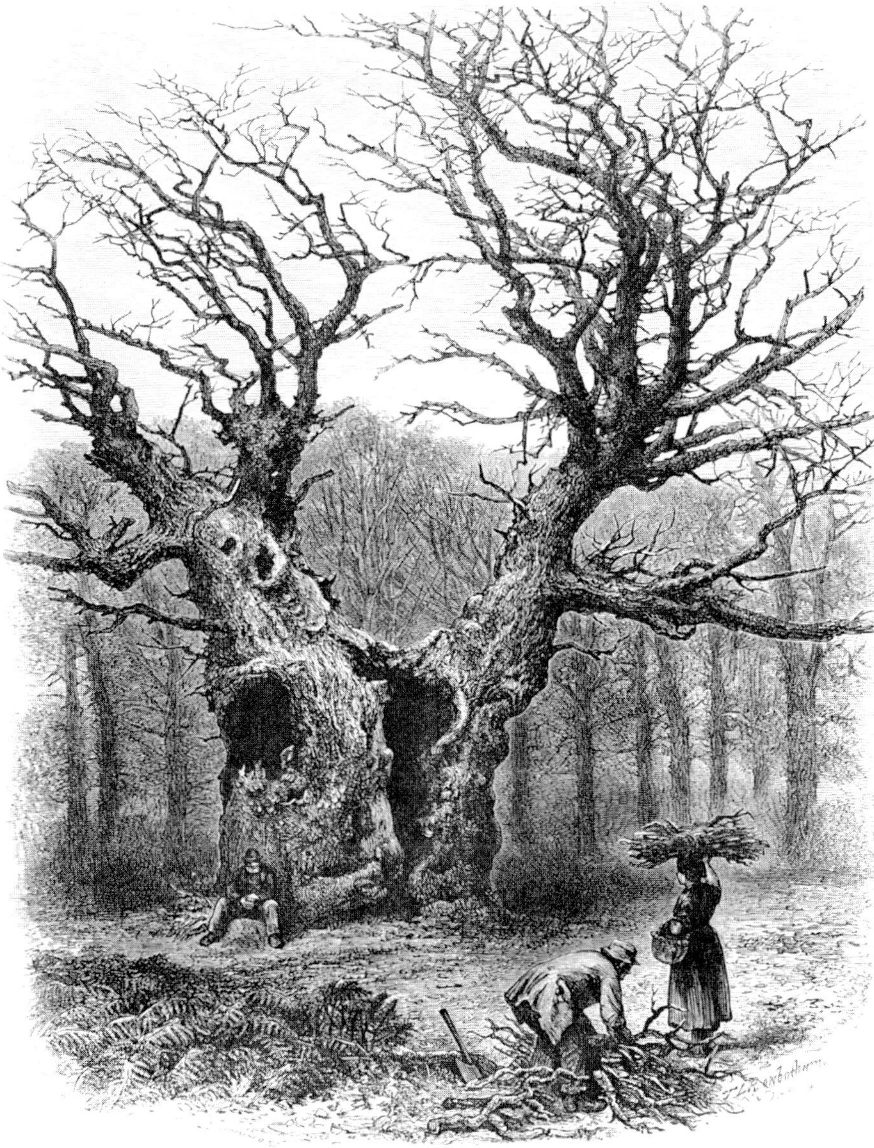

WILD PEOPLE

' "Foresters and Borderers", says John Evelyn, "are not generally so civil and reasonable as might be wished". And that seems to be exactly the character of those in the New Forest. Many of them, like those in the woods of America, are mere squatters, but the attempt to disturb them is much the same as to disturb a hornet's nest... In severe winters the distress and destitution of these wild people have sometimes been found to be beyond description, both in intensity and extent.'

William Howitt, The Rural Life of England, 1844

FOREST ARMY

'The New Forest had an establishment of verderers and keepers, paid by the Crown, amounting to some forty or fifty men. At the commencement of the Civil War they remained at their posts, but soon found, in the disorganised state of the country, that their wages were no longer to be obtained; and then, when the King had decided upon raising an army, Beverley, who held a superior office in the Forest, enrolled all the young and athletic men who were employed in the Forest, and marched them away with him to join the King's army. Some few remained, their age not rendering their service of value... Those who remained in the Forest lived in cottages many miles asunder, and indemnified themselves for the non-payment of their salaries by killing the deer for sale and for their own subsistence.'

Captain Frederick Marryat (1792-1848), Children of the New Forest

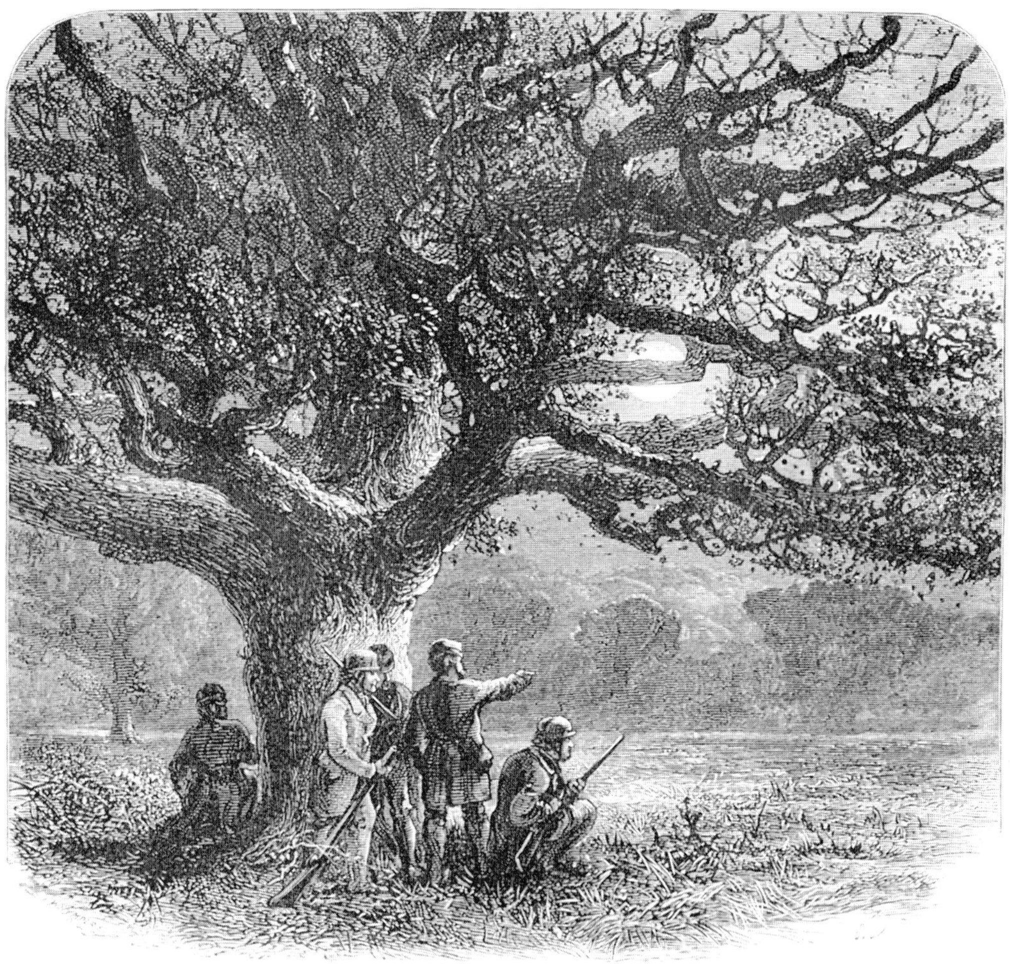

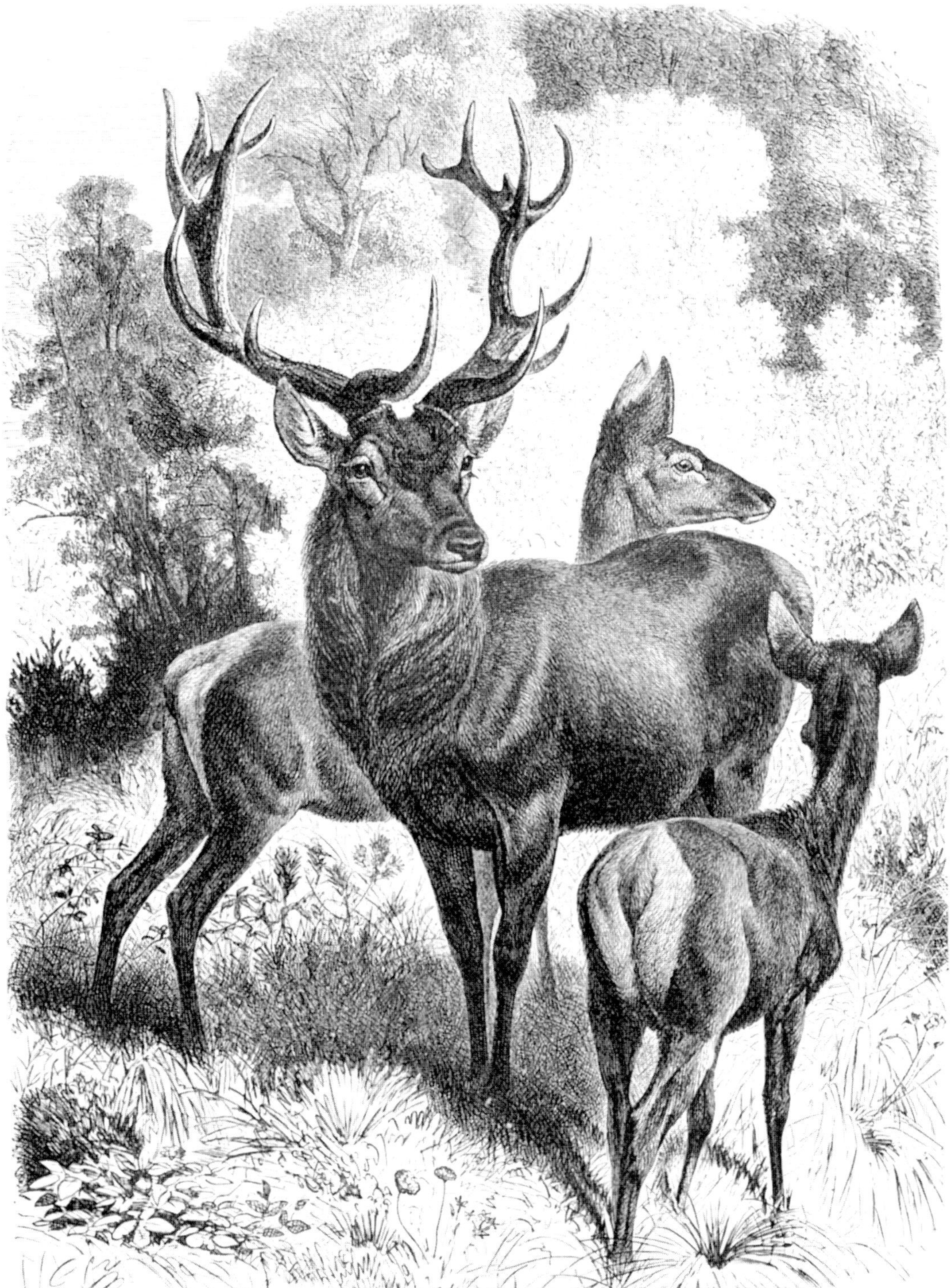

Red deer: a noble quarry, long at the centre of controversy.

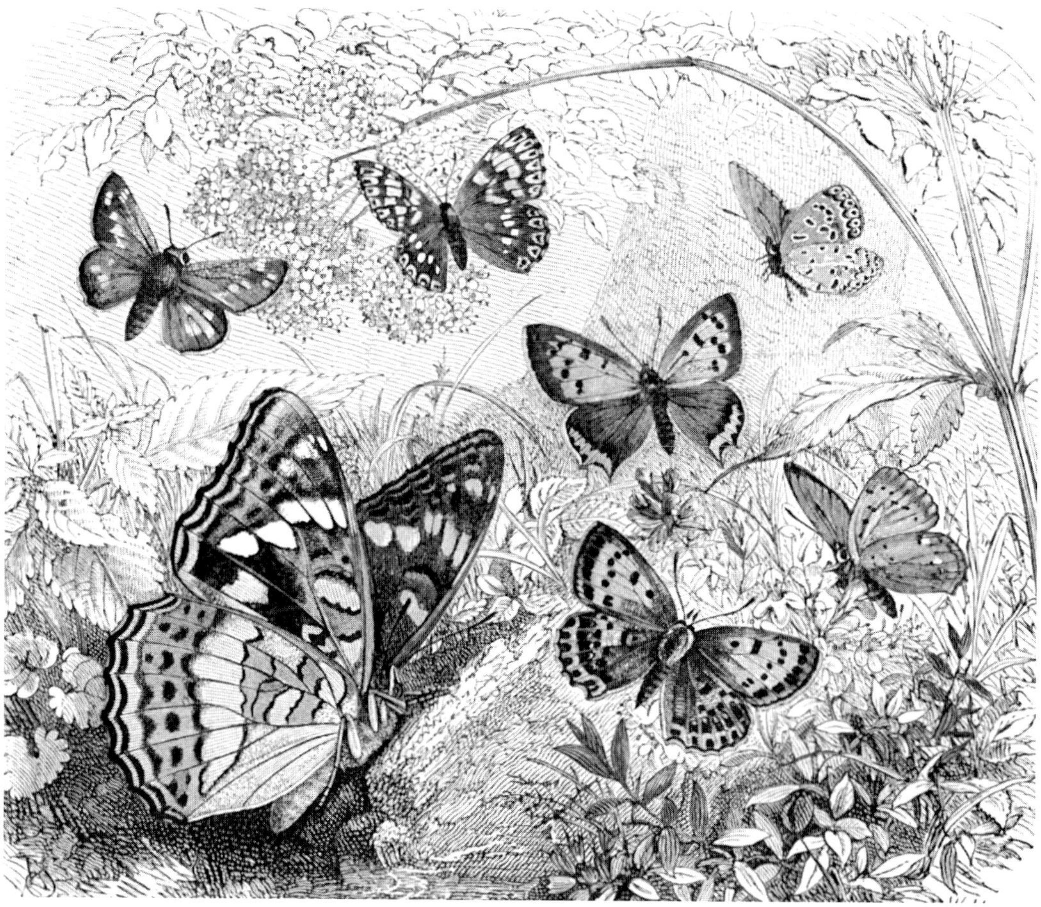

COLLECTORS

'Lyndhurst is the spot on which London vomits out its annual crowd of collectors, those hated beings with white, spectacled town faces and green butterfly nets.'

WH Hudson, Hampshire Days, 1903

FEUDAL CHARACTER

'This forest seems to retain not only more of the forest character than all our other forests, but to have maintained more exactly its ancient boundaries. William of Malmsbury says, the Conqueror laid waste thirty miles of country for this forest. The perambulation of the 22nd of Charles II, extending from Milton south along the Avon west, to Bramshire north, and within Southampton Water east, by Fawley and Boldre back to Milton, includes about thirty miles square, and this is the extent that is now attributed to it by the inhabitants of the neighbourhood. In the present hundred of New Forest, we have the parishes of Minstead, Fawley and Boldre; the chapels or curacies of Lyndhurst, Beaulieu, Exbury and Brockenhurst. It is indeed the only one of our forests which can now give us a perfect idea of what an English forest was in the feudal ages.

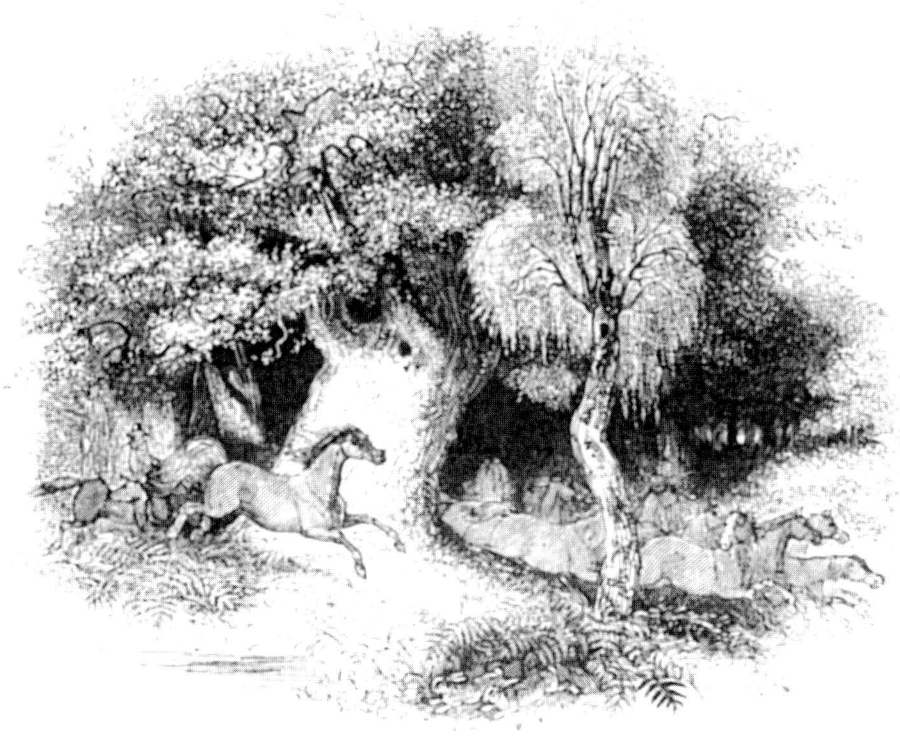

It has not acquired, like Windsor, too much of a park-like character by containing a royal residence; nor has it been enclosed, and shaped into quadrangular fields: but there it is, in its original extent, - vast, wild, stocked with deer; with its alternations of woods and heaths, morasses and thickets; interspersed with hamlets and farms, and forest-huts, as were the forests of old.'

William Howitt, The Rural Life of England, 1844

DEEP BEAUTY

'There, in the long aisles, settles that depth of shade which no pencil can give.'

John Wise, The New Forest: Its History and Scenery, 1862

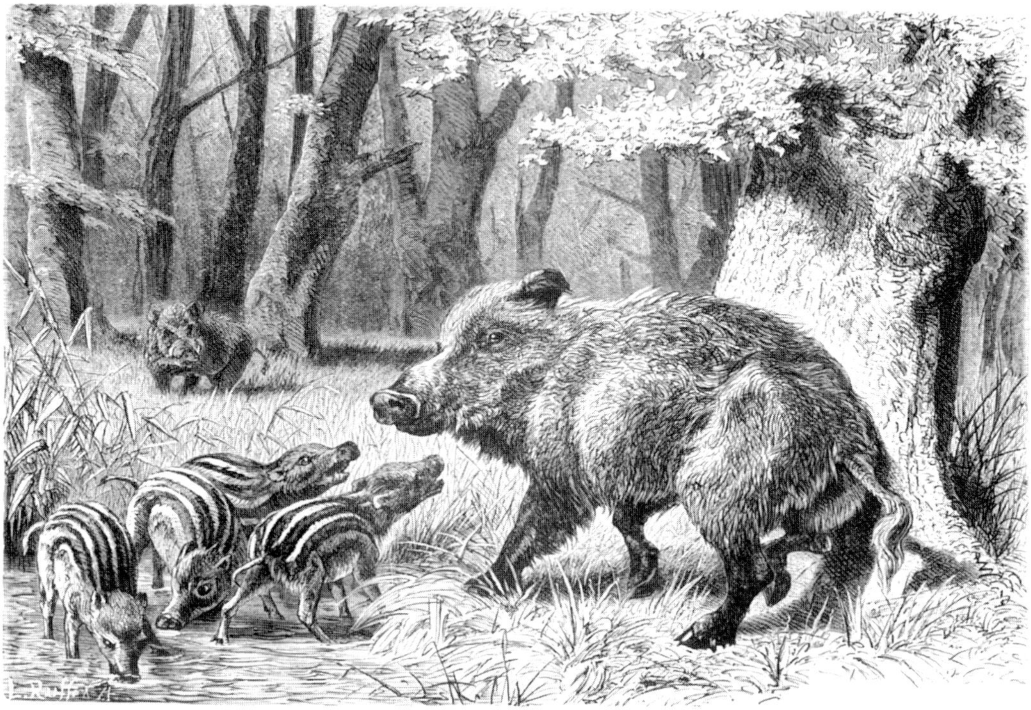

The wild boar lingered on in the Forest into the 17th Century.

OVERWHELMING SILENCE

'There are times when the silence of the great Forest is overwhelming. Pushing my way one still autumn day through Perry Wood to the great moor beyond, over a springy carpet of moss and leaves that deadened every sound, the silence seemed prophetic and almost unbearable in its intensity. It was silence that contrasted grimly in one's mind with the ear-splitting chorus of Hell, amid which less than a day's journey away many a son of this quiet forest land was:

> ... facing fearful odds
> For the ashes of his fathers
> And the temples of his Gods.

George Tweedie, Hampshire's Glorious Wilderness, 1925

EAST OF THE SUN AND WEST OF THE MOON

'But the worst enemy of the Forest is its admirer. He comes, falls in love with it, craves a house within its borders, praises it to his friends, and invites them down. So the fashion comes, and the fashion creates a demand. Land rises to a fancy value, and when times are so hard for the landowners, what can they do but relinquish their fairest sites to the speculative builder? If this goes on, our descendants may wonder why we cared so much for the endless firwood, diversified with "artistic" villas - or perhaps they will like it. In the country that lies East of the Sun and West of the Moon they would doubtless pass a law that all manors within the Forest, coming into the market, should be resumed by the Crown and enclosed as wood or waste for ever.'

Elizabeth Godfrey, The New Forest (Blackie), circa 1910

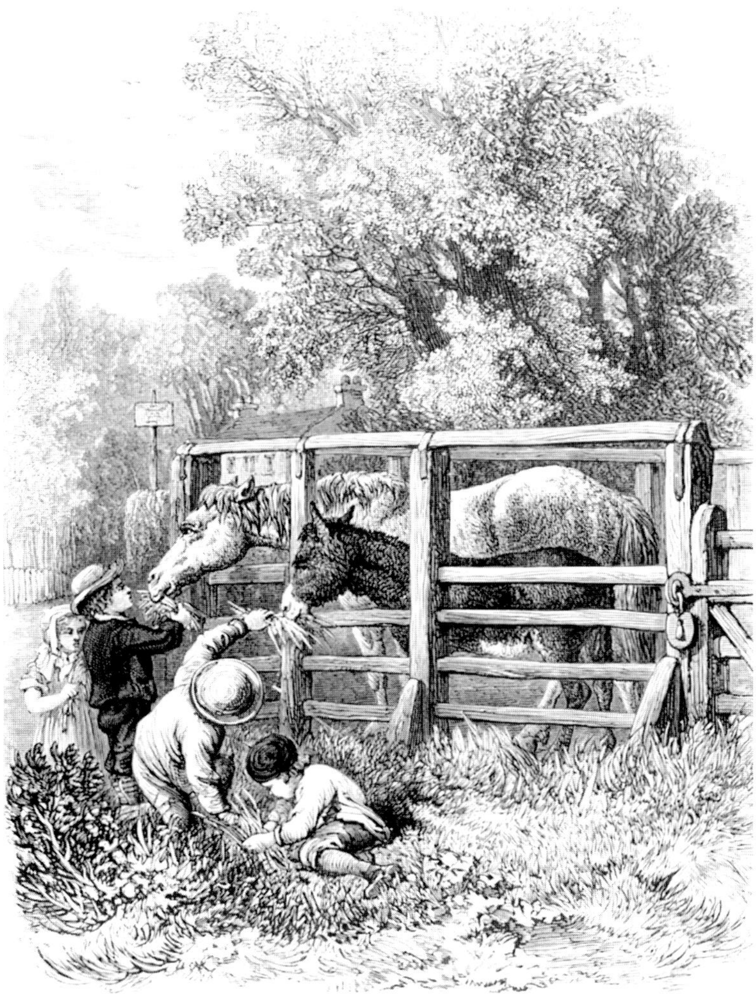

FOREST RIGHTS

'There are many Forest rights and laws which in every case are attached to certain chimneys and hearthstones. These cannot be rebuilt or the right is forfeited. Comparatively few houses have these rights. They include cords of Forest wood free, and the right to turn cows, pigs and horses into the Forest, on paying a small fee. These rights never go to the individual or family, but to the chimney. "Pannage", for instance, meant the allowing of pigs to browse on the acorns and beechmast of the Forest, and "lawing" or "expeditation" of dogs, was a Forest custom whereby a dog that belonged to a dweller had to have his three front claws cut off with an axe, if the said dog was too large to pass through a certain sized stirrup. It was to disable them to chase a deer. Taxation afterwards took the place of "lawing". The branding of ponies, to show their ownership, and the "notching" of their tails, was also enforced.'

Winifred Beddington and Elsa Christy, It Happened In Hampshire (WI), 1937

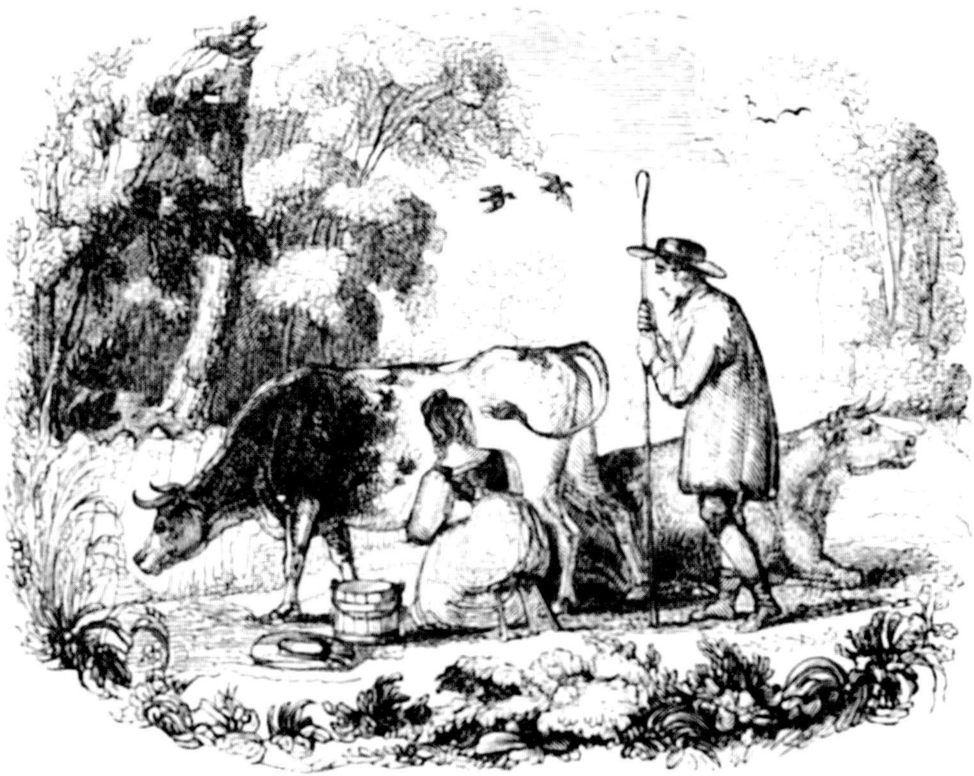

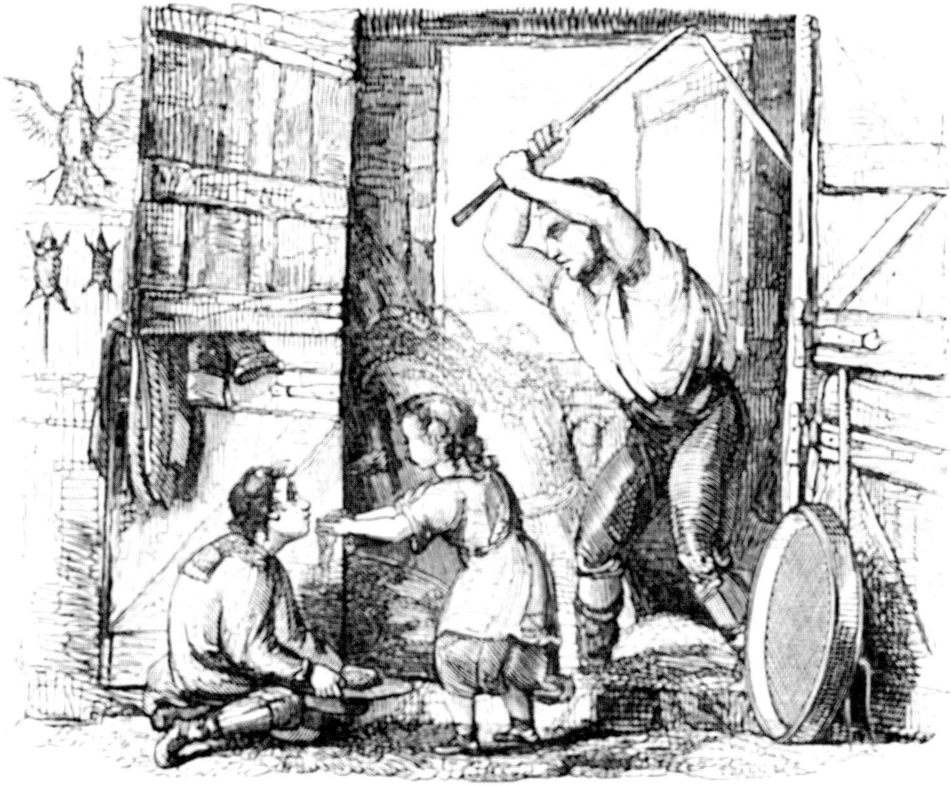

THE OLDEST FAMILY

On 2 August 1100, William II - Rufus the 'Red King' - was hit by an arrow released by French knight Sir Walter Tyrrel, while the two hunted together in the New Forest. The arrow is said to have glanced off a tree but some say the shot was intentional. Whatever the truth, terrified Tyrrel fled to France and joined the Crusade.

'About Sundown, one Purkiss, a charcoal burner, driving homewards with his cart, discovered a gentleman lying weltering in blood, with an arrow driven deep into his breast. The peasant knew him not, but conjecturing him to be one of the royal train, he lifted the body into his vehicle, and proceeded towards Winchester Palace, the blood all the way oozing out between the boards, and leaving its traces upon the road. There is a tradition that for this service he had some rods of land, to the amount of an acre or two, given to him; and it is very remarkable that a lineal descendant of this charcoal-burner, bearing the same name, does now live in the hut, and in possession of the land, and is himself a charcoal-man; that all the family, from the first, have been family, therefore is rightly esteemed the most ancient in the county of Hants.'

Chambers, Book of Days, 1866

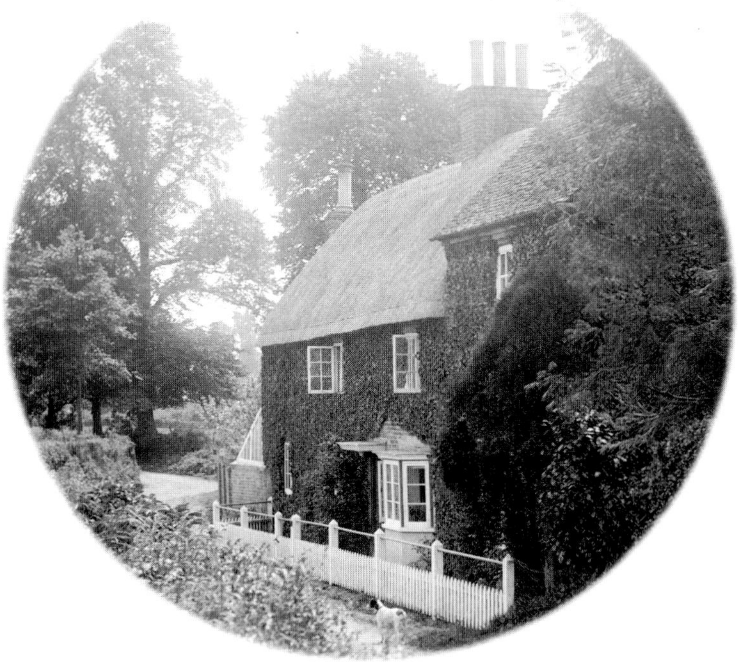

Quintessential Forest Cottage.